Also by Norman Van Aken

Norman Van Aken's Feast of Sunlight

The Great Exotic Fruit Book

NORMAN'S NEW WORLD CUISINE

NORMAN'S

NEW WORLD

CUISINE

Norman Van Aken

with John Harrisson

Photographs by Tim Turner

Random House New York

For Janet and Justin, the light and love of my world

"Can we ever have too much of a good thing?"

—Miguel de Cervantes, preface to

Don Quixote de la Mancha

Photograph on page 293 by Hope Frazier

Library of Congress Cataloging-in-Publication Data

Van Aken, Norman
Norman's new world cuisine/Norman Van Aken with John Harrisson.
p.   cm.
Includes index.
ISBN 0-679-43202-7
1. Cookery, American—Southeastern style.   2. Cookery,
International.   I. Harrisson, John.   II. Title.
TX715.2.S69V26   1997   641.5919—dc21   96-39675

Random House website address: http://www.randomhouse.com/

Printed in the United States of America on acid-free paper

24689753

First Edition

Designed by Georgiana Goodwin

FRAGMENTS FROM THE DIARY OF A GENOESE SAILOR

Today I landed on the enchanted beach. It was hot and the sun rose at an early hour. The radiance of the water was brighter than the light in the sky. No sea is more translucent, as green as the lemon juice my sailors craved, ravaged as they were by scurvy during the long voyage from Palos. You can see all the way to the bottom, as if the surface of the water were a sheet of glass. The bottom is white sand, crisscrossed by fish of every color.

The storms shredded my sails. There were three caravels, but all that remains is the ship's boat I managed to save after the mutiny and massacre. I am the only survivor.

Only my eyes see this shore, only my feet walk it. I do what habit orders me to do. I get down on my knees and give thanks to God who is certainly too busy with more important matters than to think about me. I cross two old branches and invoke the sacrifice and the benediction. I claim this land in the name of the Catholic Kings who will never set foot in it and understand why they showed such magnaminity when they granted me possession of everything I might discover. They knew very well that without resources, I couldn't dominate anything. I've reached these shores naked and poor, but what will they or I possess? What land is this? Where the hell am I?

—Carlos Fuentes, *The Two Americas*

"The circus men knew no other earth but this; the earth came to them with the smell of the canvas and the lion's roar. They saw the world behind the lights of the carnival and everything beyond these lights was phantasmal and unreal to them...their life was filled with the strong joy of food, with the love of traveling."

.Thomas Wolfe, "His Father's Earth".

I worked as a carny one summer and came to know the games like the 'wheel' and the 'pool ball-silver dollar game'. We traveled from town to town and I did feel that the real world became a phantom to the charming, glittery, greasy carnival world. The 'snow cones' that were sold at the concession stands were the first 'ices' I ever remember eating. ----Norman, July 12, 1995

FOREWORD:
THE NEW WORLD CUISINE

If the map of the world were a tablecloth and I could choose any place at that table, I would sit at the southern tip of Florida, at the nexus of North America and the Caribbean. My plate would touch Cuba, the Florida Keys, the Yucatán, the West Indies, the Bahamas, and South America.

And, if time could tell, I would listen to the tales of voyagers, discoverers, traders, and mystics who, in searching for "the Indies," the Great Khan, and the riches of China, discovered something much more valuable and enduring: a New World of culinary treasures.

Almost instantly, the cuisines of the Old World began to merge with foods of this New World. This evolutionary and inexorable fusion lies at the heart of New World Cuisine.

Norman

CONTENTS

INTRODUCTION: MY SHIP'S RULES

All ingredients should be fresh.

Herbs should always be fresh, unless otherwise indicated.

Always peel garlic, shallots, and onions just before they are needed.

Always remove the stems, seeds, and internal ribs of bell peppers and chiles. Likewise, dried chiles should be stemmed and seeded.

Wash leeks thoroughly and use the white part only, unless otherwise indicated.

Avoid washing mushrooms; if necessary, quickly clean them with a mushroom brush or a slightly damp towel. Black trumpets and morels need a brief dip in the drink, but quickly spin them dry.

Potatoes should always be scrubbed clean.

Carrots should always be peeled.

Fruit juices should be freshly squeezed.

All butter should be sweet (unsalted).

All cream should be pasteurized, not ultrapasteurized.

"Grated cheese" means freshly grated.

Eggs should be extra-large.

Whenever possible, spices should be bought whole, and then freshly toasted and ground as required.

Pepper should be freshly cracked or ground from a peppermill. Use black pepper, unless otherwise indicated.

Salt refers to sea salt or kosher salt.

Add salt to beans only once they are cooked. Adding it before will make them tough.

Dried beans should be picked through for stones, twigs, and foreign objects, and rinsed before soaking.

Sugar refers to granulated white sugar, unless otherwise indicated.

Flour refers to unbleached all-purpose, unless otherwise indicated.

✸ CAPTAIN'S MAIN COMPASS POINTS

Or...some helpful techniques, pointers, markers, tricks, and favorite ports of call to help you to avoid those shark-infested waters!

Long, long ago, before mariners had compasses to steer by, they sailed by looking up at the heavens and steering from star to star. A cloudy night and you could end up in Jersey! I don't want you to ever feel lost in my recipes, so I have included various "compass points" along the way to guide you, reassure you, and pilot you safely to the exciting and mouth-watering harbor of New World Cuisine. Here are a few points of reference.

So, to the decks, mates! We're off on a wondrous discovery together. For me it has already been a most soul-satisfying voyage; for you, well, just know that you can always send me a message in a bottle. Sails up!

FLAVORS

Our desire to find flavor has assumed epic proportions in the culinary history of man. In my first book, *Norman Van Aken's Feast of Sunlight,* I talked about the "North, South, East, and West" of flavors: sweet, sour, salt, and bitter. The seeming complexity of some of my dishes results from the fact that the flavors are designed to travel in several directions at once. They provide the dishes with a balanced worldview.

INFUSION CONFUSION
What the heck is an infusion? This is a question that many people are too shy to ask. A good example of an infusion is a cup of tea. We heat water and put a bag of tea or a tea ball into it, let the flavors exchange, and then remove the tea bag. Also popular these days are infused or flavored oils and vinegars (see Chapter 12). We add a flavoring ingredient and let it pervade the oil or vinegar. Because we don't want to chew on the flavoring, we strain it out. The flavor is there, but in another useful medium.

LEFTOVERS
Leftovers is a word that needs reimaging. "Visually challenged but potentially flavor-enhanced food materials" might work. You can shake leftovers from their sleep with renewed seasoning.

Some expensive leftovers such as foie gras, truffles, smoked salmon, or caviar can be used in "compound butters." Just whip them into fresh sweet (unsalted) butter and freeze.

Then, when you are looking for a simple alternative to making a sauce you can use the flavored butter to jazz up an impromptu grilled fish, pasta, or rice dish.

ICING DOWN

Cooling things down as rapidly as possible after finishing—a sauce or soup, for example—is crucial for sanitary as well as aesthetic reasons (it preserves good texture). Bacteria love food when it is close to 100 degrees, so don't let things cool on their own. Surround them with very icy water and change the water if need be.

PREPARING VEGETABLES

When preparing vegetables for sautéeing or stirfrying, it's okay to cut them up a few hours ahead of time, but store them in the refrigerator on paper toweling to absorb any "weeping" and to help keep the maximum crispness alive.

BLANCHING AND SHOCKING VEGETABLES

This technique is often called on to preserve color and texture. When shocking in ice water, lay a strainer or perforated pan in the water. Then, when the vegetables are cool, you can just pull the strainer up and avoid having to dig your vegetables out of the ice water.

CARAMELIZING VEGETABLES

Many of the recipes that follow call for caramelizing vegetables to allow their natural sugars to be released. Well, let me say this plainly: caramelization is to food what foreplay is to sex. It makes the final dish that much better. Take the time. Marinades, rubs, paints, cures, pastes, and blends are similar to caramelization in this respect (see Chapter 12).

COOKING AROMATICS: GARLIC, ONION, CHILES, GINGER, AND SO FORTH

To get more flavor when sautéeing these ingredients as well as various aromatic spices, I add them to the heated oil or butter *first* before going on to add other ingredients. This gives them a chance to lay down their power, and that makes for a more pronounced flavor. More flavor and nourishment, rather than bigger portions, is what satisfies us in eating well.

FIXING A BROKEN SAUCE

A broken emulsified sauce such as Hollandaise is one that didn't stay within the necessary ratio of air to weight, and very simply crashed. It will look irredeemable, but faith! To put a broken emulsified sauce back together, just take one egg yolk and beat it well in a clean bowl. Add a couple drops of olive oil and then very slowly begin adding the broken sauce. It will reincorporate and be ready once again to fly.

MEAT: PULLING OR SHREDDING

Sometimes you take the time to braise what would otherwise be a very tough cut of meat. The parts of an animal that do a lot of hard work, like the shanks, have some of the best flavors that braising unlocks. They tend to lock back up when chilled. So when braising meat to make a filling for ravioli or tamales or won tons, I always take the meat and pull it apart while it's still quite warm. That way it pulls apart along its natural seams and makes the meat really tender.

COOKING FISH

Like land-based meat, fish should be cooked according to the properties and qualities specific to each variety. Cooking shrimp rare is undercooking it. When restaurant guests say, "I like my tuna (or swordfish or salmon) undercooked," they are delicately asking the chef not to ruin it. Fish such as snapper or grouper need to be cooked just through or it will feel rubbery and resistant.

EGGPLANT

Salting, weighting down, rinsing, and then draining eggplant rids it of bitter juices. The elongated Japanese varieties don't require this technique.

EXOTIC FRUITS

Many fruits have more than one name. For example, the soursop is also known as the guanábana, the star fruit sometimes live under the alias of carambola, and the egg fruit doubles as canistel. I can recommend a wonderful field guide that unshrouds these and many other mysteries: *The Great Exotic Fruit Book* by one Norman Van Aken (Ten Speed Press).

FRUIT JUICES

Some fruit juices can be scarce when you need them, especially some of the more exotic ones that I like to use. I stock up on the fruit when they are in season, juice them, and freeze the juice in airtight containers. It's nice to be able to make a passion fruit recipe in the dead of winter when you want a little sunshine in your day.

CHILES

Everyone has a different tolerance and attitude when it comes to spicy chiles. I find it fascinating that many people who were not chile enthusiasts in the past are becoming converts now—and in a big way. But still, if you're not convinced yet, I am not here to force my love for heat upon you. Follow the recipes, I would advise, but if you make the dish once and it seems too hot for you, make a note right on the pages of the book. It's okay; you're probably not in high school anymore and you won't get into trouble! Let me make another suggestion: If you make an adjustment, do it in pencil, because every year I think you'll be ready to push the thermostat up one more notch! Finally, a word of warning: When handling chiles, especially the incendiary Scotch bonnets and habaneros, avoid touching your eyes with your hands, and be sure to wash your hands thoroughly afterward.

ROASTING FRESH BELL PEPPERS AND CHILES

I use different techniques for roasting bell peppers and chiles, which facilitates removing the thick, bitter-tasting skin and adds intriguing smoky, sweet flavor tones. I like to roast bell peppers on a fiery grill; their thick, meaty walls don't break down like the very thin walls of most chiles. Alternatively, you can roast them on a wire rack over a gas flame on the top of a stove.

For poblanos and other chiles, which have a thinner skin than bell peppers, I shock them out of their skins another way. Heat plenty of vegetable oil in a deep-fryer or deep heavy saucepan to 365 degrees. Carefully add the chiles so they are submerged in the hot oil. You can get the job done in less oil if you turn the chiles on all sides from time to time. Keep them submerged or turn them occasionally until evenly blistered all over. Then remove them and put them in a large bowl with absorbent toweling in the bottom of it; cover the bowl tightly with plastic wrap. Allow the chiles to "steam" for about 5 minutes. Now, protecting your hands with rubber gloves, remove the chiles and delicately pull off the skins, using your fingers or a knife. You can also use this technique for bell peppers, if you prefer.

SEEDING CHILES

To seed or not to seed . . . that is the burning question. I almost always seed chiles. The range of heat in the seeds is inconsistent, and there's the rub, for in those seeds what screams may come?

TOASTING DRIED CHILES

Dried chiles are something only a shaman could fully appreciate. That's because of the vastness of their powers—flavor as well as "fire" power! To help realize their potential you generally want to toast them in a dry skillet (or on a comal) until they become aromatic. Do not overtoast and burn. Then soften them in water, vinegar, or stock (depending on their application).

ROASTING GARLIC

Roasting eliminates the sharpness of garlic and brings out its full mellow tones. The method is described in the Roasted Garlic Power recipe on page 281

TOASTING DRIED HERBS AND SPICES

Toasting heightens the intensity of herbs and spices. Place them in a dry, heavy-bottomed skillet and toast over low heat for about 1 minute or until fragrant, stirring frequently. Do not scorch or they will taste bitter.

TOASTING SEEDS AND NUTS

Like roasting coffee beans, this process brings out the natural richness and full flavors of seeds and nuts. Place seeds in a dry, heavy-bottomed skillet over medium-high heat for 2 to 3 minutes until lightly browned, stirring occasionally. Toast nuts the same way; they will take about 5 to 7 minutes.

ROASTING CORN

Roasting corn gives it a smokiness and an appealing complexity of flavor. Cut the kernels from the cob with a sharp knife. Heat a large heavy-bottomed sauté pan or skillet over high heat until almost smoking. Place no more than two layers of the corn kernels at a time in the pan, and dry-roast them for about 5 minutes, tossing continuously, until smoky and dark.

0 40B COTE ROTIE
10 SPEC PIZZA
9 QUESADILLA
8 STEAMED CLAMS
8 DUCK PANCAKE
10 SCALLOP APP
12 SPRING ROLLS
15 PAELLA
15 HANDKERCHIEFS
7 WHOLE TAIL
11 CHICKEN
14 PORK TENDERLOIN
7 SEA BASS
21 SCALLOP
19 TUNA
14 TEA SALMON
10 CATFISH
23 BEEF MEDALION
19 LAMB LOIN
14 VEAL CHOP
0 CRAB SALAD
10 BLOND BROWNIE
10 CREME BRULEE
16 CHOC CAKE
13 BANANA SPLIT
3 NATILLA
5 LOVE TRIANGLE
10 PROFITEROLL
6 RHUM FLAN
5 STRUDEL

A DAY IN THE LIFE

"Work is alone noble. . . . A life of ease is not for any man, nor for any god."

—Thomas Carlyle, *Past and Present*

NORMAN'S NEW WORLD CUISINE

CHAPTER 1
COCKTAILS, GROGS, BATIDOS, AND SUNSET SNACKS

Norman's Wake-Up Call (Iced Con Leches)

Kampong Batido

A Hot Lolita

Cayo Hueso Catnap

A Peroxide Blonde

Miami Mojito

Machete Colada

Norman's Last Call

Norman's Hot 'n' Nasty Nuts

New World Chips and Bajan Guacamole

Hawaiian Plantain Tostones with Jamaican Pigeon Peas

Voodoo Beer-Steamed Shrimp with a West Indian Cocktail Salsa

Hot Bacalaítos with a Cool Cilantro Sabayon

Cornmeal-Crusted Oysters with Roasted Garlic Allioli

Spanish Cava Fondue with Torn Pepper-Cheese Bread

Hot-Fried "Caribbasian" Chicken Wings with Sesame, Sriracha, Honey, and Mustard Drizzle

Calypso Calamari with Pickled Scotch Bonnet Tartar Salsa

Bread with Everything (Pa Amb Recapte)

A good rum punch was the wiliest of cocktails. It was the drink to which all teetotalers relented because of its healthy tropical image, all the ingredients of a vitamin-laden breakfast juice therein, the uncommon flavors of passion fruit and nutmeg, bitters and lime that imbued enough natural ping to disguise the devilish proportion of alcohol in the glass. A superb rum punch had all the characteristics of merciful execution. It assumed no virtue in going slow so that the victim might pause to lament what was being lost, and it valued stealth, the surreptitious wham: the victims of a superb rum punch never knew what hit them. They were swept from one shore of reality to another more liberated coast, a new world where they had temporary license to do absolutely anything that entered their heads.

—Bob Shacochis, *Swimming in the Volcano*

Some of the tasty foods that are served at the cocktail hour are presented in this chapter. Cocktail- and wine-friendly foods are not served enough in this country. All too often, a bowl of goldfish-shaped crackers are offered that spoil the taste of cocktails and ruin wine. In Spain, on the other hand, the tradition of imbibing a glass or two is intelligently coupled with an array of little bites called *tapas*.

The easy but brassy dishes that accompany the drinks in the following pages will stimulate the appetite while providing the nourishment to make it through to dinnertime.

Norman's Wake-Up Call (Iced Con Leches)

Yield: 1 serving.

I first drank *café con leche* in 1971. I was 19 years old and breakfasting at the original Pepe's in Key West. At that age, I was hardly used to American coffee, let alone Pepe's "con leche." Pepe's was a real shrimper joint near the docks back then and not a place to spring an early-morning quiz, so I drank the café con leche and made mental notes.

It's sweet—and I mean *sweet*—because that's the way Cubans drink their coffee. When I asked Pepe later on why it's *so* sweet, he said "because the sugar is sweeter in Cuba than it is here." The coffee is *strong* too! One day I decided to mess around with a cold version that would keep our energy up and ourselves cool.

 Adding a scoop or two of your favorite coffee ice cream makes this drink almost dangerous! You may use decaf espresso if you like. You can scale this recipe up; just maintain the proportions.

¹/₂ tablespoon honey or sugar

*¹/₃ cup fresh-brewed espresso coffee. cooled to
room temperature*

¹/₂ cup milk

5 ice cubes

Put all the ingredients in a blender and blend together. Pour into a chilled tall glass.

Kampong Batido

Yield: 6 servings.

The Kampong Estate, in Coconut Grove near Miami, was the home and botanical garden of plant explorer Dr. David Fairchild during the first half of this century. Fairchild wanted to teach people to appreciate tropical plants and trees. He sailed the globe to find seeds and bring them to his home where he could nurture the tamarind, pomelo, sugar apple, and many, many other growing things. As you walk down the winding path toward the house, and then past the house and through the grounds overlooking a bright blue inlet and the open sea beyond, you will be enchanted with this heavenly place. Leaving is, of course, the hardest part.

Batidos are fruit shakes popular in many parts of the Caribbean.

1 cup peeled, seeded, and roughly chopped papaya

1 cup peeled, pitted, and roughly chopped mango

2 cups peeled, cored, and roughly chopped pineapple

2 small, ripe, sweet bananas, peeled and roughly chopped

3 tablespoons fresh lime juice

1 1/2 cups fresh Coconut Milk (see recipe), or canned, or cow's milk

2 tablespoons sugar

10 to 12 ice cubes

Place the papaya, mango, pineapple, and bananas in a blender. Add the lime juice and blend until smooth. Add the coconut milk, sugar, and ice cubes. Blend again.

Pour into chilled tall glasses. If desired, garnish with the tropical fruit of your choice.

COCONUT MILK

Yield: about 2¼ cups.

For roughly one-third of the world's population, coconut milk is more important than cow's milk. Typically, it is used in recipes in the same way. However, canned coconut milk can actually be fresher if the "fresh" variety has been overly aged.

1 coconut

2 cups cow's milk

Pierce the coconut's "eyes" to drain the water; set the water aside. Crack the coconut open and remove the meat. In a saucepan, boil the milk. Place the coconut meat in a blender or food processor and purée. Add half of the milk and the reserved coconut water to the puréed coconut and pulse. Let rest for 30 minutes.

Strain the mixture through cheesecloth into a bowl. Remove the coconut from the cheesecloth and return it to the blender or food processor. Heat the remaining cup of milk in a saucepan and add to the blender or food processor. Pulse again and let rest for 30 minutes.

Strain the mixture through cheesecloth into the same bowl containing the first straining. Discard the coconut meat. Keep the milk chilled and use within 2 to 3 days, or freeze.

A Hot Lolita

Yield: 4 servings.

I called this Lolita because it's a hot little number.

 For a hot-hot garnish, sprinkle a few crushed red chile flakes on the top and watch them swirl!

*2 1/2 ounces (5 tablespoons) Hot-Hot Honey
(see recipe), or regular honey*

3 ounces (6 tablespoons) gold tequila

1 ounce (2 tablespoons) Grand Marnier liqueur

5 teaspoons sugar

1 1/4 cups fresh lime juice

3 ice cubes

Crushed ice

4 lime wedges, for garnish

Prepare the honey.

Salt the rim of 4 "old-fashioned" glasses by gently squeezing a lime wedge along the rims and then dipping into bar salt.

Place the tequila, Grand Marnier, sugar, lime juice, honey, and ice cubes in a cocktail shaker and shake vigorously. Fill the glasses almost to the top with crushed ice. Strain the contents of the shaker into the glasses over the crushed ice. Garnish with a wedge of lime.

HOT-HOT HONEY

Yield: about 1/2 cup.

1/2 cup honey

1 teaspoon crushed red pepper flakes

Bring the honey almost to a boil in a small saucepan. Stir in the crushed red pepper and remove from the heat. Let steep for 1 hour. Strain and reserve.

Cayo Hueso Catnap

Yield: 1 nap.

After a full morning and afternoon in the tropical heat, sunning, swimming, snorkeling, and windsurfing, nothing sounds as refreshing as a cold drink, a good snack, and an afternoon nap before a night on the town. This drink, named for the feline creatures that abound in Key West, makes it easy to doze off and dream lazily, drifting in the Gulfstream of the mind.

 Cayo Hueso ("bone key") was the name given by the first Spanish explorers to Key West. They called it this because of the old Indian bones they found there.

1 ounce (2 tablespoons) kahlua

1 ounce coconut-flavored rhum

1 ounce spiced rhum, such as Captain Morgan's

1 ounce half-and-half

Fill an "old-fashioned" glass with ice. Add the kahlua and rhums. Slowly float the half and half on top, and serve.

A Peroxide Blonde

Yield: 4 tall blondes!

Here's a drink *everyone* prefers.

 Lemon or lime, that is the question. A squeeze of lime juice makes it a little more sour, so it depends whether you want your drink sour or only mildly sour.

1 cup champagne

1 cup Absolut Citron vodka

8 melonball scoops of lemon sorbet, preferably Häagen-Dazs

4 teaspoons heavy cream

4 to 6 ice cubes

Squeeze of fresh lemon or lime juice

4 lemon or lime slices, for garnish

Put the Champagne, Absolut, lemon sorbet, cream, and ice cubes in a blender, and blend until smooth. Pour into tall Champagne flutes. Squeeze a little lemon or lime juice on top and serve with a slice of lemon or lime.

Miami Mojito

Yield: 1 serving.

With hot weather in Miami a given for most of the year, I advise chilling the rhum and glasses in the freezer for the best mojitos of all.

 Garnish with more mint leaves or a lime slice, as desired.

Juice of 1 lime

2 teaspoons superfine sugar

1 mint sprig

Crushed ice

2 ounces (1/4 cup) white rhum

Cold sparkling mineral water

Place the lime juice, sugar, and mint in a bowl. Press the mint with the back of a spoon until it is crushed. Stir until the sugar dissolves.

Fill a tall glass almost to the top with the crushed ice. Add the lime mixture, pour in the rhum, stir, and top with mineral water.

Machete Colada

Yield: 1 serving.

It may seem a touch *turista,* but in the marketplaces here and down in the Caribbean, it's fun to watch an experienced man wield the hard, dark steel of a machete across the smooth, tough sphere of an unripened water coconut. With a sudden blow, we see the snow-white perfection of the previously sun-ignorant coconut. Its sweet, sticky, clear juice awaits only a straw. But to fill the coconut with a perfectly blended piña colada takes nature's recipe one better. This recipe will work in the more common confines of a glass, but if you can arrange the water coconut and machete, you're doing it "island style."

4 large ice cubes

1 1/2 tablespoons heavy cream

1 1/2 tablespoons cream of coconut

1/4 cup fresh pineapple juice

1/4 cup white rhum

Place all the ingredients in a blender and blend until smooth. Pour into a hollowed-out coconut or a glass, and serve.

Norman's Last Call

Yield: 1 serving.

We started the day with hot *cafés con leche,* and as the day got hot we had these with ice. By midnight the bartender yelled, as usual, "You don't have to go home, you *just have to go!*" We would take this drink in little "go cups" and ride our rickety bicycles, our tiny flashlights bouncing weakly in the dark curtain of late evening, over to the old dock area called Mallory Square. Eight or nine hours earlier, hundreds of people had celebrated the sunset on this dock. Most of us were working "on the line" at that time, getting ready for the dinner rush; we could hear the shouts go up as the final ray of the sun yielded to the horizon. Now, in the darkness, just three or four hours before dawn, we smoked and talked about work, life, or nothing at all, and we watched heat lightning over Christmas Tree Island. When it was over, we said goodnight and hauled our bikes up and walked them slowly, down the little lanes, to home to sleep, at last.

 By all means use either caffeinated or decaffeinated espresso. In sweetening the drink to taste, bear in mind that the rhum and Tia Maria will already taste sweet.

1 orange slice

*1 tablespoon sugar and cinnamon mixed
together*

1 ounce (2 tablespoons) golden rhum

3/4 ounce (1 1/2 tablespoons) Tia Maria

1/4 cup espresso coffee (Cuban or Italian)

1/4 cup warm milk

Honey, or sugar, optional

Rub the orange slice around the rim of a glass or mug to moisten. Place the sugar and cinnamon mixture on a small plate and dip the rim into it so it sticks.

Pour the rhum and Tia Maria into the glass or mug. Heat the espresso and milk together in a pan. When hot, transfer to a blender, add honey or sugar to taste, and blend for 10 seconds. Pour into the glass or cup. Ahhhh!

Norman's Hot 'n' Nasty Nuts

Yield: 1 pound of *hot* nuts.

A great place to watch the mesmerizing, rocking motion of the ocean is the Pier House Havana Docks Bar in Key West. Day or night, rough or calm. And what better partner for cocktails there than these hot little peanuts. Cheers!

 Spanish peanuts are available at most health food stores. These hot nuts are just the thing to put on the bar with cold beer or any of my cocktail recipes. Or you can use them in any recipe calling for spicy peanuts.

1 pound raw, unsalted Spanish red-skinned peanuts

1 teaspoon cayenne

1 teaspoon crushed red pepper

1 teaspoon hot paprika

1 teaspoon chile molido, or pure red chile powder

1 1/4 teaspoons salt

2 tablespoons plus 1 teaspoon Hot Chile Oil (page 277), or olive oil

Preheat the oven to 375 degrees. Lay the peanuts on a sheet pan, and roast in the oven until crunchy and toasted, about 15 to 20 minutes.

In a bowl, combine the cayenne, crushed red pepper, paprika, chile molido, and salt. Transfer the nuts to a large mixing bowl and add the mixed spices. Stir in the chile oil and coat the nuts thoroughly.

Line an airtight container with a couple of paper towels. Transfer the nuts to the container and keep refrigerated.

New World Chips and Bajan Guacamole

Yield: 8 to 10 servings.

Bajans (pronounced "bay-szhans") are the natives of Barbados—the name of the island is derived from the Spanish word meaning "bearded," because of the "bearded" fig trees that the first discoverers encountered as they waded ashore. You can use leftover paste for the recipe on page 146.

You can make chips from yuca, boniato, malanga, lotus root, breadfruit, sweet potato, Peruvian purple potatoes, and, of course, plantain. These fruits and vegetables aren't all indigenous to these shores, but they're here now and they contribute to our new culinary diversity. Choose one, or any combination.

 The different sugar content of different vegetables or fruit means that cooking times will vary. No problem! Just fry each different chip by type and then mix them all up.

Bajan Spice Paste (see recipe)

GUACAMOLE

2 large ripe Haas avocadoes, or 1 ripe Florida avocado, peeled and pitted

1 large ripe tomato, peeled, seeded, and diced

3 cloves garlic, minced

1/2 cup diced red onion

1 tablespoon cilantro leaves

Juice of 1 lime

Salt to taste

1 Scotch bonnet chile, seeded and minced

CHIPS

Peanut oil, for deep-frying

3 Peruvian purple potatoes, unpeeled and sliced paper thin

1 boniato, peeled and sliced paper thin

1 yuca, peeled and sliced paper thin

1 malanga, peeled and sliced paper thin

1 green plantain, peeled and sliced paper thin

Salt and freshly ground black pepper to taste

New World Spice Blend (page 287), optional

Prepare the spice paste.

To prepare the guacamole: lightly mash the avocadoes in a mixing bowl. Combine all the remaining guacamole ingredients together in a separate bowl, mix in 2 tablespoons of the spice paste, and then add to the avocado. Mix gently and adjust the seasoning to taste. Keep refrigerated.

To prepare the chips: heat the peanut oil in a deep-fryer to 360 degrees. Carefully drop each batch of chips into the oil and deep-fry for about 2 minutes, or until nicely brown and crisp. Scoop out with a skimmer or slotted spoon and drain on paper towels. Keep warm. Season with salt, pepper, and the New World Spice Blend to taste.

BAJAN SPICE PASTE

Yield: About ¾ cup.

Most grocery stores stock hot paprika.

¼ cup virgin olive oil

Juice of 1 lime

2 tablespoons packed thyme leaves, roughly chopped

2 tablespoons packed sage leaves, roughly chopped

2 tablespoons packed basil leaves, roughly chopped

2 cloves garlic, peeled and roughly chopped

1 Scotch bonnet chile, seeded and minced

3 scallions, minced

2 small inner stalks celery, minced

½ teaspoon hot paprika

¼ teaspoon ground cloves

¼ teaspoon ground mace

¼ teaspoon salt

Freshly ground black pepper to taste

Place the oil, lime juice, herbs, and garlic in a blender or food processor, and blend until fairly smooth. Transfer to a mixing bowl and add the chile, scallions, and celery. Stir in the paprika, cloves, mace, salt, and pepper. Keep refrigerated until needed.

Hawaiian Plantain Tostones with Jamaican Pigeon Peas

Yield: 8 to 10 servings.

Peas? Beans? Either way, nice.
But bellies will rest with peas and rice.

Or is it beans and rice? Or is it *gandules* and rice, or *congo, gunga,* or *gungoo,* or any of the different names these peas (beans!) go by. Rice is the traditional partner, but the starchy, slightly sweet and colorful cooked plantain *tostones* make a new twist to this Caribbean classic.

The tradition-loving Cuban-American population of Miami would not be quick to change the type of cooking banana for making *tostones,* or refried plantain cakes—a custom so near and dear to them—unless it was for a *very* good reason. The reason occurred when Mr. William O. Lessard, a major fruit grower and authority in South Florida, introduced the squatly rounded Hawaiian *hua moa* plantain variety to the markets down here in the early 1970s. "Banana Bill" christened them "Hawaiian plantains" for the American market, although they actually originated in Tahiti. The *hua moa* offers a creamier texture, which is the key to a great *tostone.* They're eaten as a snack, with salsa, or as an accompaniment to meat, fish, or chicken.

 You can buy pigeon peas fresh, but they are most often sold dried in the United States. Cooked this way to make a dip, they are also perfect with tortilla chips, toasted pita bread, or grilled corn bread. For a spicier version, add some of your favorite hot sauce, or some minced Scotch bonnet chiles. Cooling and then reheating the peas gives them a better texture, rather like refried beans.

PIGEON PEAS

¹/₂ *Bean Kit recipe (page 280)*

1 teaspoon cayenne

1 cup dried pigeon peas, soaked overnight

1 cup tomato concassé

5 cups Light or Dark Chicken Stock
(pages 270, 271)

Salt and pepper to taste

HAWAIIAN PLANTAIN TOSTONES

Vegetable oil, for frying

3 Hawaiian hua moa *or regular green plantains, ends cut off and cut in half across*

Salt and freshly cracked black pepper to taste

Prepare the bean kit to the "ready point." Stir in the cayenne and add the drained pigeon peas, concassé, and stock. Bring to a boil over high heat and skim off any impurities with a spoon. Reduce the heat to medium-low and cook the beans until they are just tender, stirring occasionally, about 2 hours.

Season to taste and transfer to a bowl. Mash with a potato masher while they are still warm. Let cool, and reheat when ready to serve.

To prepare the tostones: Heat 1 inch of vegetable oil in a large heavy skillet to 375 degrees. Alternatively, use an electric French fryer. Make a slash lengthwise through the tough skin of the plantains and peel the skin away, using a knife if necessary. Cut the plantains into ¾-inch-thick slices. Place as many slices as will comfortably fit without crowding into the hot oil and fry over medium-high heat until golden, about 2 minutes on the first side, and 1 minute on the other. Remove from the oil with a slotted spoon and drain on paper towels.

Place all of the cooked plantains between 2 pieces of wax paper and mash them with the heel of your hand, a meat pounder, or the back of a wooden spoon until they are ¼ inch thick. Place the mashed plantains back into the hot oil and refry in batches until golden brown and crispy, about 2 to 3 minutes. Drain on paper towels and keep warm.

Season the tostones with salt and pepper, spoon about 1 tablespoon of the peas on each tostone, and serve.

Voodoo Beer-Steamed Shrimp with a West Indian Cocktail Salsa

Yield: 4 to 6 servings.

Here's my take on a simple dish of "peel 'n' eats" that's perfect for an informal gathering of pals. Put a little salsa music on too—with Tito Puente or Celia Cruz playin' on in the background, you might think the perspiration gathering on your brow is coming from the energy of the music as much as it will (in fact) be from the Scotch bonnet chiles in the dipping salsa. It's New World *hot, hot, hot!*

 For a less spicy salsa, use 1 jalapeño and leave out the Scotch bonnets. The salsa makes about 1¾ cups and can be refrigerated for a couple of days in an airtight container. You can use any beer you enjoy for steaming the shrimp; if you need to steam more shrimp than called for in this recipe, factor up the beer and the other ingredients accordingly. This dish can be turned into a summertime dinner with the addition of some simple boiled potatoes and corn on the cob.

West Indian Cocktail Salsa (page 225),
or 1 ³/₄ cups of your favorite sauce

SHRIMP

1 tablespoon fennel seeds

1 teaspoon mustard seeds

1 tablespoon black peppercorns

1 tablespoon allspice berries

1 teaspoon whole cloves

2 tablespoons olive oil

1 red onion, roughly chopped

1 head garlic, cut in half crosswise

2 or 3 jalapeño chiles, with seeds, chopped

2 bay leaves

Zest of 1 orange

3 bottles (12 ounces each) Blackened Voodoo Beer, or the beer of your choice (light or dark)

32 large shrimp (about 1 ¹/₂ to 2 pounds), heads removed and shells intact

Prepare the salsa and chill until needed.

For the shrimp, heat a large saucepan. Add the fennel and mustard seeds, peppercorns, allspice, and cloves. Toast over medium-high heat for about 30 seconds, or until they become fragrant. Add the olive oil and when warm, add the onion, garlic, chiles, bay leaves, and orange zest. Stir well and reduce the heat to medium.

When the vegetables are translucent (about 10 minutes), add the beer and bring to a boil. Add the shrimp to the pan and return to a boil. Remove the shrimp as soon as they are done and shock briefly in ice water to stop them cooking (do not leave them in the water long enough to wash away the flavors). Chill the shrimp until cold.

Place some crushed ice in a serving bowl and put the cold shrimp on top of the ice. Serve with the salsa on the side. Have an extra bowl so your guests can toss in their shrimp shells (not to mention the beer bottlecaps or wine corks).

Hot Bacalaítos with a Cool Cilantro Sabayon

Yield: 5 to 8 servings (about 25 fritters).

Bacalaítos is the diminutive word for bacalao (salt cod) fritters. My mother taught me how to make and love these fritters.

 These fritters can be made ahead of time and frozen, well wrapped, for up to 3 months. Defrost them in the refrigerator overnight, or for 6 hours before you need them. If you like, you can serve the fritters with lemon and lime wedges and your favorite Caribbean salsas or hot sauces. instead of the sabayon.

8 ounces bacalao (salt cod)

1 quart water

1 cup Garlicky Mashed Potatoes (page 196), or leftover mashed potatoes

2 cloves garlic. minced

2 egg yolks. beaten

2 jalapeño chiles. or 1 Scotch bonnet chile. seeded and finely minced

1/2 tablespoon black pepper

1/2 cup flour

1 egg

1 teaspoon water

1 cup fresh breadcrumbs

2 tablespoons chopped cilantro leaves

Cilantro Sabayon (see recipe)

Canola oil. for deep-frying

Soak the bacalao in enough water to cover it overnight. The next day, change the water several times over the course of the day. Drain. Bring the water to a boil in a saucepan and add the bacalao. Reduce the heat immediately and cook for about 20 minutes. Lift the cod out of the water with a slotted spoon and let cool.

When cool enough to handle, crumble the bacalao into a mixing bowl. Stir in the potatoes, garlic, egg yolks, chiles, and pepper. Mix well and allow to cool.

Pour the flour onto a plate. Whisk together the egg and water in a small bowl. Form the bacalao mixture into small round balls, about 1 inch across. Roll the balls in the flour and then in the egg wash. Combine the breadcrumbs with the cilantro and roll the balls in this mixture to coat. Cover and refrigerate until ready to cook.

Prepare the sabayon.

Heat the canola oil in a deep skillet to 365 degrees. Fry the bacalao balls for about 1½ minutes, until golden brown. Remove with a slotted spoon and drain on paper towels. Transfer the fritters to a platter or serving plates and serve with the sabayon.

CILANTRO SABAYON

Yield: About 1 cup.

⅓ cup heavy cream

¼ cup cilantro leaves, washed, dried, and chopped

2 egg yolks

½ tablespoon fresh orange juice

⅓ cup olive oil

1 tablespoon truffle oil, optional

½ tablespoon Spanish sherry vinegar

Salt and cayenne to taste

Bring a saucepan of water to a simmer. Whip the cream in a cold mixing bowl until soft peaks form. Add the cilantro. Cover and chill.

In a separate mixing bowl, whisk the egg yolks with a drop or two of water. Place the bowl over the pan of water and whisk like hell! When the egg yolks are thick enough, you can draw a stripe across the bottom of the bowl with the whisk. Remove the bowl from the heat. Whisk in a little of the orange juice. Then slowly whisk in the olive oil and truffle oil. Add the remaining orange juice and the vinegar. Season with salt and cayenne, and let cool.

Fold in the reserved cilantro cream. Cover and reserve the sabayon in the refrigerator until needed.

Cornmeal-Crusted Oysters, with Roasted Garlic Allioli

Yield: 4 to 6 servings.

Bold flavors go with the cocktail hour, and finger foods contribute to a feeling of relaxation that's an important part of this time. Here they are together. Be bold! Drink up! Eat a hot oyster! Don't burn your fingers!

 This recipe also works well with shucked hard-shell clams. Wasabi is a root that's grown commercially in Japan and Hawaii and invariably accompanies sushi.

¹/₂ cup Roasted Garlic Allioli (page 45)

4 cups peanut or vegetable oil

1 egg, beaten

¹/₂ cup milk

1 cup yellow cornmeal

1 cup flour

¹/₂ tablespoon salt

1 tablespoon black pepper

24 shucked oysters

2 lemons, cut into wedges

Prepare the allioli.

Heat the peanut or vegetable oil in a deep-fryer to 360 degrees. Whisk the egg and milk together in a bowl. In a separate bowl, mix together the cornmeal, flour, salt, and pepper. Dip the oysters first in the egg-milk mixture and then in the seasoned flour mixture. Repeat the dipping process and lay the oysters on a dry plate.

Deep-fry the oysters, in batches of six, for about 2 minutes, or until golden brown. Remove the oysters with a slotted spoon and drain on paper towels.

Serve on a platter and drizzle with the allioli. Serve with lemon wedges.

Spanish Cava Fondue with Torn Pepper-Cheese Bread

Yield: 6 to 8 servings.

Cava is the name given to the sparkling wines of Spain. The two cheeses called for in this recipe—manchego and cabrales—are the country's most famous varieties. With garlic and bread, we have equally able partners.

 For a more elaborate dish, make up some of My *Very* Black Bean Sauce (page 213) and speckle it into the fondue. You can also spread some olive tapenade or sun-dried tomato tapenade on the toasts—very comforting.

1 stick (4 ounces) butter

1¹/₂ Spanish onions, peeled and cut into medium slices

2 jalapeño chiles, seeded and thinly sliced

¹/₄ cup Roasted Garlic Power (page 281)

¹/₄ cup flour

1 split (375 ml.) Spanish Cava sparkling wine, or Champagne

1 cup Light Chicken Stock (page 270)

2 cups heavy cream

3 ounces manchego cheese, grated

1¹/₂ ounces cabrales or other blue cheese, very finely crumbled

Salt and freshly cracked white pepper to taste

1 loaf Janet's Pepper-Cheese Bread (page 237) or other loaf, cut into slices

Heat a large, heavy-bottomed saucepan over medium-low heat and melt the butter. Add the onions and jalapeños, and cook until the onions are just translucent, about 5 minutes. Add the roasted garlic and continue to cook for 5 minutes longer, stirring often.

Sift the flour into the saucepan and stir evenly with a wooden spoon, being careful not to let the flour stick or scorch. Cook for about 2 minutes (still over medium-low heat) while stirring constantly. Slowly add the sparkling wine or Champagne, still stirring constantly, and cook for 1 minute. Add the chicken stock and cook, stirring constantly, for about 15 to 20 minutes. Add the cream and reduce the mixture for about 15 minutes, until it coats the back of a spoon.

Combine the cheeses in a large mixing bowl. Strain the cream mixture into the bowl and whisk well. Season to taste. To serve, put the cheese mixture in a warm bowl or a fondue pot.

Toast the sliced bread (or pan-fry in olive oil). Transfer to a serving platter, pass the bread around, and encourage your guests to tear off pieces to dip in the fondue.

Hot-Fried "Caribbasian" Chicken Wings with Sesame, Sriracha, Honey, and Mustard Drizzle

Yield: 10 to 12 servings (30 to 40 wing pieces).

The steady influx of New Yorkers to South Florida and the foods they have brought with them should not be overlooked in the New World Cuisine. In the 1950s, we saw the ascendancy of re-created New York delis. The legendary Wolfie's on Miami Beach still churns out the bagels, briskets, and cheese blintzes (as a very young customer in the winter of '57, I particularly favored the latter, I'm told). In the ensuing decades, another New York tradition—Buffalo wings—became an established part of the cocktail circuit here. I have embellished these wings' flight plan with a little whirlwind tour of the Islands, then on to the Far East, and back again. Their basic character remains the same—they're still hot little critters!

 The drizzle recipe also provides a spicy, rich accent for grilled marinated chicken, spice-crusted seared beef, and meaty fish such as tuna or swordfish. You can also use it as a salad dressing accent with a cobb or chef salad. It'll keep, refrigerated, for up to 1 week.

Sesame, Sriracha, Honey, and Mustard Drizzle
(see recipe)

MARINADE

3 eggs, beaten

1 cup heavy cream

1 jalapeño chile, seeded and thinly sliced

³/₄ tablespoon crushed red pepper

³/₄ tablespoon cayenne

³/₄ tablespoon hot paprika

15 to 20 whole chicken wings (about 3¹/₂ to 4 pounds)

SEASONED FLOUR

2 cups flour

1 tablespoon salt

3 tablespoons black pepper

¹/₄ cup crushed red pepper

4 teaspoons cayenne

Peanut oil for frying

Prepare the drizzle.

Combine all the marinade ingredients in a mixing bowl. Rinse the chicken wings in cool water and pat dry. Cut the top third (wing tip) off and reserve for stock. Cut each wing in half at the joint and immerse in the marinade. Cover and refrigerate overnight.

Combine the seasoned flour ingredients in a mixing bowl.

Remove the chicken wings from the marinade and dredge them in the seasoned flour.

Heat the peanut oil in a deep-fryer to 375 degrees. Drop the wings into the oil, one at a time. Don't deep-fry too many at once as the oil will foam up. Deep-fry each batch for about 4 minutes. Remove with a slotted spoon and drain on paper towels.

Serve the wings on a platter with the drizzle poured over in a zigzag pattern, or serve the drizzle on the side.

SESAME, SRIRACHA, HONEY, AND MUSTARD DRIZZLE

Yield: about 1 cup.

1 egg yolk

1/2 tablespoon honey

2 tablespoons Creole mustard, or another whole-grain mustard

2 tablespoons balsamic vinegar

1/2 cup canola oil

3 tablespoons extra-virgin olive oil

2 teaspoons hot (spicy) sesame oil

1/2 tablespoon hot chile sauce (preferably Sriracha)

Place the egg yolk, honey, mustard, and vinegar in a blender, and mix until well blended. Gradually add the three oils with the machine running, and the chile sauce, and blend until well incorporated. Keep refrigerated.

Calypso Calamari
with Pickled Scotch Bonnet Tartar Salsa

Yield: 4 servings.

It's a simple pleasure, this calamari. And you'll notice that the instructions tell you something you'll hear over and over in a good kitchen: Season as you go. In this case, you add a little of the spice rub at each stage. The rub is inspired by influences described by James Michener in his dependably sprawling work *The Caribbean:* "In the nineteenth century a heavy influx of Hindus and Muslims from India introduced unique influences, making certain islands and regions even more colorful." These immigrants traveling to or through the West Indies brought their spices and recipes with them. Soon the locals were dancing to the heat, hence the name "calypso" that I use for this rub. This blend goes well with foods that can handle strong spicing. I also like to sprinkle it on fresh mango slices for picnics or tailgate parties.

 These calamari are great with a cold beer, and even better with my Hot Lolitas (page 8).

1 cup Pickled Scotch Bonnet Tartar Salsa
(page 50)

Calypso Spice Rub (see recipe)

2 eggs, beaten

*1/4 cup skim milk, or regular milk mixed with a
little water*

3/4 cup flour

3/4 cup yellow cornmeal

Peanut oil, for frying

*8 ounces calamari, cleaned thoroughly and cut
into rings*

1 lemon, cut into wedges, optional

Prepare the salsa and set aside.

Prepare the rub.

In a mixing bowl, whisk together the eggs, milk, and 1 teaspoon of the spice rub. In a separate bowl, combine the flour, cornmeal, and 2 tablespoons of the rub.

In a deep-fryer or iron skillet, heat the peanut oil to 375 degrees. Dip the calamari in the egg wash and coat thoroughly. Remove the calamari and dredge in the flour mixture, shaking off any excess. Carefully lower the calamari into the hot oil; beware hot spattering oil, and stand back! Deep-fry for about 1 minute, until browned. Remove with a slotted spoon and drain on paper towels. Season with the remaining spice rub and transfer (preferably) to baskets lined with absorbent toweling.

Serve the salsa in a small bowl on the side, and garnish the calamari with lemon wedges, if desired.

CALYPSO SPICE RUB

Yield: about 3 tablespoons.

¹/₂ tablespoon cumin seeds

¹/₂ tablespoon black peppercorns

³/₄ teaspoon yellow mustard seeds

³/₄ teaspoon coriander seeds

³/₄ teaspoon whole cloves

³/₄ teaspoon finely ground dried habanero chile

³/₄ teaspoon dried ground ginger

³/₄ teaspoon ground cinnamon

¹/₂ tablespoon brown sugar

³/₄ teaspoon salt

Place the cumin seeds, peppercorns, mustard seeds, coriander seeds, and cloves in a dry skillet and toast over medium heat until fragrant and slightly smoking, about 1 to 2 minutes. Transfer to a spice grinder and grind to a powder. Place in a bowl and mix with the remaining rub ingredients.

Bread with Everything (Pa Amb Recapte)

Yield: 10 to 20 servings.

When you are having company and cocktails after work, it's important to eat. This recipe provides some choices inspired by Colman Andrews's ground-breaking book, *Catalan Cuisine*. He describes *pa amb toma'-quet,* roughly translated as "bread with tomato," which is typical of the Catalan style which uses perfect ingredients wisely. Here, then, is an extension of this idea. The following recipe offers a choice of toppings; it's up to you which you use (each topping yields about 1 cup).

 Several other recipes in this book can be adapted to put a different spin on Bread with Everything. Two examples that I enjoy at Tapas Hour are Salsa Escalivada (page 224) and Pigeon Peas (page 17). If you wish, you can sauté the bread in the oil instead of toasting it in the oven.

CRACKED AND CRUSHED BLACK OLIVE TOPPING

1 cup pitted black olives

1 clove garlic, minced

2 ounces anchovies, rinsed

2 tablespoons capers, drained and rinsed

1 teaspoon Dijon mustard

2 tablespoons fresh lemon juice

2 tablespoons Spanish brandy

¹/₄ to ¹/₂ cup extra-virgin olive oil

Black pepper to taste

GARLIC-POWERED TOMATOES SECA TOPPING

¹/₂ cup Tomatoes Seca (see recipe), or sun-dried tomatoes packed in oil, finely chopped

¹/₂ cup Roasted Garlic Power (page 281)

1 teaspoon balsamic vinegar

Salt and black pepper to taste

1 loaf South Beach Sourdough bread (page 234), or a good-quality bakery bread

1 cup extra-virgin olive oil

Preheat the oven to 350 degrees.

To prepare the olive topping: Place the olives, garlic, anchovies, capers, mustard, lemon juice, brandy, olive oil, and pepper in a food processor or blender and pulse until almost smooth (it should still be a little chunky).

To prepare the tomato topping: Mix together the tomatoes, garlic, vinegar, salt, and pepper in a mixing bowl.

Cut the bread into bite-sized pieces (for example, $1/2$ inch squares, $1/4$ inch thick). If you wish, cut the bread into triangles or circles. Brush the bread liberally with the oil and place on a nonstick sheet pan. Bake in the oven until barely crisp.

Serve the croutons with the toppings; you may wish to spread some additional Roasted Garlic Power on each crouton as a "primer" coat, especially for the olive topping.

TOMATOES SECA

Yield: about 1 pint (2 cups) dried tomatoes.

Seca is Spanish for "dry." I like to make these oven-dried tomatoes in the summer when tomatoes are at their peak. Stored properly, they can be enjoyed during the rest of the year.

Season with kosher salt for a saltier sun-dried taste; you can use them anytime sun-dried tomatoes are called for in a recipe.

6 *large, ripe tomatoes, cored and cut into wedges (about $1/4$ inch thick)*

1 tablespoon roughly chopped thyme leaves

12 basil leaves, chopped

$1/4$ cup extra-virgin olive oil

1 teaspoon salt

1 tablespoon black pepper

Preheat the oven to 225 degrees. Place all the ingredients in a large bowl, mix together, and allow to stand for about 1 hour.

Remove the tomatoes from the bowl and place on a wire rack set over a sheet pan, leaving a little space between the tomatoes. Place in the oven and slowly roast for 5 hours.

Turn the tomatoes over and cook for 2 hours longer. Turn the oven off, and leave the tomatoes in the oven overnight to fully dry. They should look withered and dry; if not, return to the oven until they are.

To store, pack the tomatoes down in a jar, with or without olive oil to cover them. Keep refrigerated until needed.

CHAPTER 2
STARTERS, LITTLE DISHES, ANTOJITOS, TAPAS, AND DIM SUM

The first time, on our way to Germany, we had sat downstairs while our meal was being made. There were big soft leather chairs, and on the dark table was a bowl of the first potato chips I ever saw in Europe, not the uniformly thin, uniformly golden ones that come out of waxed bags here at home, but light and dark, thin and paper-thin, fried in real butter and then salted casually. . . . They were so good that I ate them with the kind of slow sensuous concentration that pregnant women are sup-posed to feel for chocolate-cake-at-three-in-the-morning. I suppose I should be ashamed to admit that I drank two or three glasses of red port in the same private orgy of enjoyment. It seems impos-sible, but the fact remains that it was one of the keenest gastronomic moments of my life.

—M. F. K. Fisher, *The Measure of My Powers*

In 1969, I graduated high school from a small Midwestern town. I went to stay for the summer with my older sister, Jane, in Honolulu. To say that it was magical would be putting it mildly. The "summer of love" never ended for Hawaii's resident youth, and it was blooming in full flower when I arrived. Concerts in the park, body surfing at Makapu and Sandy Beach, hanging out with my sister's college friends. I returned to Hawaii for my sophomore year in college, and it was then that the exotic flavors of Asia began to cast their spell on me. It was here that I learned to appreciate the *dim sum* and the little dishes that sometimes were a meal in themselves.

By early 1973, I had returned to Illinois and started cooking. College was over for me; time to make a living. I got a job in the fanciest restaurant around. They hired me because my mom had worked there a number of years before and they loved her. It was an inn as well as a restaurant in the very wealthy town of Lake Forest. The reigning chef was a Frenchman who retired to his private quarters upstairs in the afternoons with his newspapers, cigars, and Burgundy. I spent many of those afternoons with a kind, funny—and dying—Japanese man named Toké. Toké had been the head chef of the restaurant for many years, but after the cancer hit him, he had no strength for it. His body shrank to a boy's size, which made his head, feet, and hands seem very large.

The kitchen was built down into the ground with no windows. With all the other chefs napping in the bunkhouse behind the restaurant after the morning shift, the hours between three and five were dark, dreamy, and quiet. Toké and I had some chores to do, but we accomplished them quickly so we could sit in the chef's office and drink tea and talk; or Toké would raid the refrigerators and make me some incredible dishes he knew from his travels in the Orient. Many of these were small plates, tastes, appetizers, and I loved that style of eating. On doctor's orders, he ate big bowls of ice cream or drank shakes to try to gain weight, which frustrated him because he missed his own spicy, textured cooking. I was learning why, with the meals he made me, and I was sorry for him. The time I spent with Toké built a foundation that would last the rest of my life.

The dishes in this chapter are also affected by my love of Caribbean, Spanish, French, African, Mexican, and Asian flavors, among others. I find that the first course of a meal can be the most important one, in that it sets the mood and tone for the rest. It's also a course where you'll find guests at their most adventurous. More timid eaters may choose a simple roast or grilled fish as an entrée if the starter is a bit on the unusual side for them, but even those shy types will find that the night has been made special by a dish like those included here. It is the shy ones you have to keep your eye on. They make the best converts, and soon enough they'll be hosting adventurous dinner soirées and cooking their own wild stuff.

A Sushi Kushi with Spicy Raw Tuna and Skewered Grilled Shrimp

Yield: 4 servings.

On a visit to Chicago a few years back I was intrigued to read that *kushi* bars were opening up. Kushi bars are like sushi bars, but the kushi chef prepares skewered and, often, fried kushis with different dipping sauces, vegetable condiments, and seasonings that you can adapt to your liking. Here, I have matched the two ideas, but left out the breading and frying.

 The tuna part of this recipe makes a fine tartare that can be served with rice crackers for a cocktail snack or hors d'oeuvre. You can serve this dish with one of my other sauces, such as the Sesame, Sriracha, Honey, and Mustard Drizzle (page 26).

A Gingery Jus (page 171)

TUNA SUSHI

8 ounces sushi-grade tuna, trimmed of all connective "threads"

1 tablespoon dark roasted sesame oil

1 tablespoon sake

1 to 2 teaspoons hot chile sauce (preferably Sriracha)

1/4 teaspoon soy sauce

Salt and black pepper to taste

SHRIMP

12 large shrimp (about 10 to 12 ounces), peeled and deveined

12 wooden skewers, soaked in water

2 tablespoons Chinese Chile Oil (page 276), or olive oil

2 teaspoons fresh lime juice

1 tablespoon chopped garlic

1 Scotch bonnet chile, seeded and minced

Pinch of salt

1 tablespoon pickled ginger or caviar, optional

1 avocado, sliced, optional

Prepare the jus and set aside.

To prepare the tuna sushi: Thinly hand-slice the tuna against the grain and then chop into fine dice. Reserve in a bowl, cover, and keep chilled until ready to serve.

In a separate bowl, mix the sesame oil, sake, chile sauce, soy sauce, salt, and pepper. Cover and keep chilled.

To prepare the shrimp, place 1 shrimp lengthwise on each skewer so it remains straight while being cooked. (Soaking the skewers in water prevents the skewers from burning up on the grill.) Push the shrimp all the way to the end of the skewer, so it will be easy to eat later. Place the skewers on a platter.

Combine the chile oil, lime juice, garlic, chile, and salt in a bowl, and pour the mixture over the shrimp. Turn the skewers so the shrimp are coated. Cover and keep chilled until ready to cook.

Prepare the grill (or use a broiler). Combine the tuna with the reserved dressing and mix together gently. Allow the tuna to come to room temperature. Mound the tuna at the top of room-temperature serving plates and garnish with a little pickled ginger or caviar, if desired. Grill or broil the shrimp until just cooked through and serve at the bottom of the plate (3 skewers per serving). Serve with the jus and garnish with sliced avocado.

The Painted Birds

Yield: 4 to 8 servings.

Tamarind and Soy Spice Paint on quail makes the birds very crisp. Some Oriental recipes call this "lacquering." The sugars harden the flesh, and with some air circulating around them, the meat turns darker. Once seared and grilled or roasted, the skin becomes deliciously crisp. Duck and chicken breasts can be painted this way too.

 For a more elegant presentation, serve the quail with a mesclun-type salad and a vinaigrette at the center of each plate. To spike the quail with more spice, sprinkle a little Calypso Spice Rub (page 28) over them as soon as they come off the grill.

You can use the spice paint as a very tasty dipping sauce for grilled fish, chicken, meats, or vegetables. Instead of reducing the mixture, just heat it until the sugar dissolves, and serve.

TAMARIND AND SOY SPICE PAINT

¹/₂ cup Light or Dark Chicken Stock (pages 270, 271)

¹/₄ cup unseasoned rice wine vinegar

2-inch length of lemongrass, peeled and cut into ¹/₄-inch slices

1 tablespoon orange zest

2 tablespoons tamarind pulp

5 tablespoons soy sauce

2 tablespoons molasses

¹/₄ cup dark brown sugar

2 tablespoons minced garlic

¹/₂ teaspoon minced ginger

1 jalapeño chile, seeded and minced

1 tablespoon minced cilantro leaves

2 teaspoons hot chile sauce (preferably Sriracha)

Black pepper to taste

8 semi-boneless quail

Peruvian Purple Potato Salad (page 195)

Salt and black pepper to taste

To prepare the spice paint: Combine the chicken stock, vinegar, lemongrass, orange zest, tamarind, soy sauce, and molasses in a saucepan, and bring to a boil. Whisk in the sugar until it completely dissolves. Over high heat, reduce the mixture at a rolling boil to ¹/₂ cup, about 10 to 12 minutes. Remove from the heat and strain into a bowl. Add the remaining spice paint ingredients and reserve.

Rinse the quail quickly in cold water. Trim off the wing bones at the first joint closest to the bird (these can be frozen for a stock). Cut the quail into quarters, taking care to cut at the separations in the meat rather than through them, or you'll waste some of it. Pat the birds dry and place on a wire rack over a nonreactive, nonstick pan. Paint the quail liberally on all sides with the spice paint (you can toss them together in a bowl if you prefer). Transfer to the refrigerator, uncovered. Reapply the spice paint once or twice over the next 12 hours or so.

Prepare the potato salad.

Prepare the grill (or use a broiler).

Remove the quail from the refrigerator. Tip the pan a little and brush the collected juices back over the quail. Season with salt and pepper. Oil the grill or broiler and cook the quail for 4 to 5 minutes, turning often. Transfer to serving plates.

Panfried Peeky-Toe Crabcakes with Salsa Esmeralda

Yield: 6 servings.

"Peeky-toe" is the name the crabbers give to the meat of a particular type of blue crab harvested in Maine's pristine waters. Although you can use any good blue crabmeat for this recipe, you should know about the shy, sweet "peeky-toe."

 If you prefer, you can substitute the Pickled Scotch Bonnet Tartar Salsa (page 50) or the Roasted Garlic Allioli (page 45) for the Salsa Esmeralda.

Cuban Sauce Esmeralda (see recipe)

CRABCAKES

2 egg yolks

2 tablespoons heavy cream

2 tablespoons olive oil

2 tablespoons fresh lemon juice

2 tablespoons Pickapeppa sauce

1 teaspoon Tabasco sauce

$^1\!/_2$ tablespoon dried mustard powder

2 tablespoons minced fresh mixed herbs, such as basil, Italian parsley, cilantro, and thyme

1 pound lump blue crabmeat, picked over for shell or cartilage

1 Scotch bonnet chile, seeded and minced

$^1\!/_2$ cup finely chopped celery

$^1\!/_2$ cup finely chopped red onion or sweet onion

$^1\!/_3$ cup minced red bell pepper

$2\,^1\!/_2$ cups panko crumbs, or seasoned breadcrumbs

$^1\!/_2$ cup chopped toasted pine nuts

Salt and black pepper to taste

$^1\!/_2$ cup flour

1 egg, beaten

$^1\!/_4$ cup milk

1 cup canola or peanut oil, for frying

1 lemon, cut into wedges, for garnish, optional

Prepare the salsa.

To prepare the crabcakes: Whisk together the egg yolks, cream, oil, lemon juice, Pickapeppa and Tabasco sauces, mustard, and herbs in a mixing bowl. Set aside. In a separate large mixing bowl, combine the crabmeat, chile, celery, onion, and bell pepper. Add about 1$^1\!/_2$ cups of the panko and the pine nuts, and mix thoroughly. Pour in the egg yolk–cream mixture, mix together well, and season with salt and pepper. Let chill for 1 hour.

Put the flour in a small bowl. In a separate bowl, whisk the egg and milk together. Put the remaining 1 cup of panko in another bowl or on a plate.

Gently form about $1/4$ cup of the crab mixture into a cake. Lightly dip in the flour, then in the egg wash. Coat with the panko and reserve on a large plate. Repeat for the remaining crab mixture.

Preheat the oven to 400 degrees. Heat a large heavy cast-iron skillet and add the canola or peanut oil. Sauté the crabcakes in batches for 2 to 4 minutes per side, or until golden brown. Drain any excess oil from the pan and finish the crabcakes in the oven for about 2 minutes per batch.

Drain on paper towels and transfer to the bottom part of serving plates. Serve a little of the salsa on top of each crabcake and garnish the plate with a lemon wedge, if desired.

CUBAN SAUCE ESMERALDA

Yield: about $1^{3}/_{4}$ cups.

Elizabeth Lambert Ortiz is a gifted teacher of Latin and Caribbean cuisines, and she was the inspiration for this recipe. Buy her books and taste the world she unveils so well.

3 cloves garlic, finely minced

2 tablespoons small capers, rinsed

4 hard-boiled egg yolks

Pinch of salt

Large pinch of black pepper

Large pinch of cayenne

1 teaspoon Spanish sherry vinegar

2 tablespoons chopped Italian parsley leaves

2 tablespoons chopped cilantro leaves

$1/2$ cup ground toasted almonds

$1/2$ to $3/4$ cup olive oil

Place the garlic, capers, egg yolks, salt, pepper, and cayenne in a bowl and mash with the back of a fork until well crushed. Add the vinegar, parsley, cilantro, and almonds. Mash some more. Add the olive oil and mix in so the texture is like pesto. Reserve until needed.

Baked Clams on the Half Shell with Sausage, Cubanelle Peppers, Culantro, and Lime

Yield: 6 servings.

A "New World Clams Casino" is a simple way of describing this dish to your guests. The cubanelle chiles are mild, with a thick, sweet flesh and just a touch of heat; you can substitute a bell pepper and add a little jalapeño. Culantro is a green, somewhat stiff-leaf herb with small spiky edges that is increasingly available these days. It is (confusingly) spelled almost like *cilantro* and you can substitute cilantro, which tastes very different but does just fine.

When you make this, you'll want to be sure to have some warm bread on hand to sop up the butter and the flavorful juices from the clams.

 The number of clams you serve per person may vary depending on their size. The saltiness of the clams' juice can vary considerably, so taste the dish before adding any more salt.

Any of the prepared butter that you don't use can be rolled in plastic wrap and frozen for another time. Just be sure to mark the package so it doesn't turn into another UFO (Unidentified Freezer Object)!

36 Littleneck clams, scrubbed

4 ounces Norman's Chorizo (page 288), or a good-quality sausage of your choice

1 tablespoon olive oil

1 tablespoon minced garlic

1 cubanelle chile, seeded and diced small

3 tablespoons fresh lime juice

8 ounces butter, slightly softened

¹/₄ cup roughly chopped culantro or cilantro

³/₄ cup breadcrumbs

Salt and black pepper to taste

1 lime, cut into wedges for garnish, optional

Preheat the oven to 425 degrees. Shuck the clams and reserve the juice (liquor). Cover the clams and reserve in the refrigerator.

Strain the clam juice through a fine strainer into a small heavy saucepan. Reduce the clam juice over high heat to 1 tablespoon. Chill and reserve for later.

Remove the sausage casing and crumble the meat. Heat the olive oil in a sauté pan and cook the sausage meat over medium heat until cooked through. With a slotted spoon, transfer the sausage meat to a bowl and reserve.

Add the garlic and cubanelle chile to the pan and sauté for 1 minute. Add the lime juice and boil for 30 seconds. Transfer this mixture to the bowl with the sausage meat, add the reserved clam juice, and chill completely.

When the garlic mixture is cool, mix in the softened butter. Beat in the culantro and $1/2$ cup of the breadcrumbs; season with salt and pepper. Place the clams on a nonstick baking sheet and spoon the prepared butter over each one to amply cover. Sprinkle the remaining $1/4$ cup of the breadcrumbs over the clams.

Bake the clams in the oven for 10 to 12 minutes, or until the butter is hot and bubbly. Transfer to serving plates and garnish with the lime wedges, and additional chopped culantro, if desired.

Tres Quesos Stuffed Eggplant (Escalivada y Allioli)

Yield: 6 to 8 servings.

Vegetarians who eat cheese will appreciate this Spanish cousin of ratatouille. *Escalivada* refers to dishes cooked over an open fire. As you will see from the Salsa Escalivada recipe, we get that smoky flavor without having to use an open fire or a wood-burning oven. If you do have a wood-burning oven, we'll be over around seven.

 Some blue cheeses are relatively salty, so taste first before adding more salt. Add some chopped fresh herbs to the filling if you'd like.

2 cups Salsa Escalivada (page 224)

Roasted Garlic Allioli (see recipe)

1 large eggplant, cut lengthwise into 6 or 8 "planks," each $^1/_3$ inch thick

$^1/_4$ to $^1/_2$ cup olive oil

1 cup ricotta cheese

8 ounces blue cheese

4 ounces manchego cheese (or other semifirm cheese), grated (about 2 scant cups)

Salt and black pepper to taste

Prepare the salsa and the allioli.

Salt and weight the eggplant "planks" (see page xvii). Prepare the grill (or the eggplant may be sautéed). Rinse and drain the eggplant. Pat dry with paper towels and rub with the olive oil. Grill or sauté the eggplant over medium-high heat for about 5 minutes, or until charred and tender. Set aside.

Preheat the oven to 400 degrees. Beat the cheeses together with a mixer until spoonable. Season to taste and reserve.

Lay out the grilled eggplant on a work surface. Place about $^1/_4$ cup of the cheese mixture at the larger end of each eggplant strip and roll up. (The rolled eggplant may be covered and chilled at this point for cooking later; just allow for more warming time).

Spoon the salsa over the bottom of a casserole dish. Place the stuffed eggplant rolls on top of the salsa and bake for 10 to 12 minutes. Spoon some of the salsa and an eggplant roll onto each serving plate and drizzle with the allioli.

ROASTED GARLIC ALLIOLI

Yield: about 1½ cups.

This recipe, a Spanish (Catalan) cousin to the Provençal *aioli,* originally contained no eggs. Times change and the more stable proteins of the egg were added to keep the sauce from breaking.

The roasted garlic makes my allioli a little softer and sweeter; it makes a great all-purpose mayo for tuna, shrimp, and egg salad.

¼ cup Roasted Garlic Power (page 281)

1 egg yolk

1 cup extra-virgin olive oil

1¼ tablespoons fresh lemon juice

Salt and black pepper to taste

¼ cup water

Place the Roasted Garlic Power and egg yolk in a blender or mixer, and blend together. Slowly add the olive oil. As the emulsion thickens, add the lemon juice a few drops at a time until all the oil and juice are incorporated. Season with salt and pepper, and add as much of the water as is needed to thin the consistency to that of mayonnaise. Keep refrigerated.

"Down Island" French Toast

Yield: 4 servings.

This dish has been a "cover girl" for me in several magazines (and she's no modern, skinny thing, that's for sure!). I have seen good eaters like Charlie Trotter, Emeril Lagasse, Colette Rossant, Barbara Kafka, and Maida Heatter go rolly-eyed over this one. The magic perfume of Curaçao comes floating through that sweet brioche and then the citric acidity of the sauce cuts through the richness like a hot knife through foie gras.

 If your budget allows, increase the amount of foie gras. Cutting the brioche into triangles is optional. You can also garnish this dish with the Sour Crema Drizzle (page 69) if you want, as well as orange sections and edible flowers. The caramel sauce can be chilled and reheated slowly.

Citrus-Savory Caramel Sauce (see recipe)

MARINADE

¹/₂ vanilla bean, preferably Tahitian, cut in half lengthwise

1 cup Cointreau, or Curaçao

¹/₂ teaspoon ground mace

¹/₂ teaspoon ground cinnamon

Zest of 1 orange

12 ounces fresh foie gras, cleaned and cut in half

EGG WASH

¹/₂ vanilla bean, preferably Tahitian, cut in half lengthwise

5 eggs, beaten

2 cups half-and-half

¹/₂ teaspoon ground mace

¹/₂ teaspoon ground cinnamon

12 slices Achiote-stained Butter Bread (page 235), or slightly stale brioche, cut into triangles ¹/₃ inch thick

¹/₄ cup clarified butter

Prepare the caramel sauce.

To prepare the marinade: Scrape the seeds from the vanilla bean with the tip of a knife into a mixing bowl, and add the liquor. Add the mace, cinnamon, and orange zest, and whisk together. Put the foie gras into the marinade and cover with plastic wrap. Slosh the marinade around a little and keep refrigerated.

For the egg wash: Scrape the seeds from the vanilla bean with the tip of a knife into a mixing bowl, and add the eggs and half-and-half. Add the mace and cinnamon and beat the mixture together. Soak the brioche slices in the egg mixture and allow them to absorb the flavor. Soaking time will depend on the freshness of the brioche; the softer it is, the shorter the soaking time (sometimes 1 minute is sufficient). Keep covered in the refrigerator until ready to complete the dish.

Preheat the oven to 300 degrees. Remove the foie gras from the marinade and cut the slices about $1/4$ inch to $1/3$ inch thick. Reserve on a chilled plate and discard almost all of the marinade. Remove the brioche from the egg wash and lay the slices on a plate.

Heat the clarified butter in a nonstick skillet, add the bread, and cook over medium heat until golden on both sides. Transfer to a plate and keep warm in the oven.

Reheat the caramel sauce and place 2 tablespoons on each warm serving plate. Heat a nonstick skillet or pan and when hot, sear the foie gras slices over high heat for 15 seconds on each side until seared and very dark brown. Place the foie gras on the brioche in layers: a slice of brioche on the bottom, a slice of foie gras, then brioche, another layer of foie gras, and topped with brioche. Serve with mixed tropical fruits and orange segments, if desired.

CITRUS-SAVORY CARAMEL SAUCE

Yield: 1 to $1^{1}/_{2}$ cups.

Any extra sauce can be chilled and used again. It will keep for up to ten days in the refrigerator.

1 $^{3}/_{4}$ cups Light or Dark Chicken Stock (pages 270, 271)

$^{3}/_{4}$ cup fresh grapefruit juice

$^{1}/_{2}$ cup sugar

2 cups heavy cream

$^{1}/_{4}$ teaspoon light soy sauce

Combine the stock, grapefruit juice, and sugar in a shallow heavy-bottomed saucepan. Cook to the caramel stage; there will be wisps of smoke coming from the center of the pan. Carefully whisk in the cream. Allow the mixture to boil and deepen in color. Reduce the mixture to 1 or $1^{1}/_{2}$ cups, whisking constantly. When it is caramel-dark, add the soy sauce. Strain through a fine-mesh strainer and reserve.

Mashed Yuca–Stuffed Shrimp con Mojo

Yield: 4 servings.

Yuca con Mojo is as Cuban as you can get. Getting the shrimp to carry the yuca really makes this a classy dance team. The mojo scents them both with the healthy glow of garlic. This has turned out to be one of the most popular appetizers at Norman's.

 For a spicier version, toss some more minced chiles into the "Mo J." just as it's getting hot. To cook the yuca, peel, chop, and boil in a saucepan of water for 25 to 30 minutes, until tender.

¹/₂ cup Mo J. (page 226)

*Pickled Scotch Bonnet Tartar Salsa (see recipe),
optional*

*12 jumbo shrimp (about 1 pound), peeled,
deveined, and butterflied*

Salt and black pepper to taste

1 cup cooked and mashed yuca

1 Scotch bonnet chile, seeded and minced

3 cloves garlic, minced

1 cup flour

1 egg

3 tablespoons water

*2 cups panko or breadcrumbs seasoned with
salt and pepper to taste*

¹/₂ cup peanut oil

Prepare the Mo J. and reserve in a saucepan.

Prepare the salsa.

In a mixing bowl, season the shrimp with salt and pepper. Cover and refrigerate. In another mixing bowl, combine the mashed yuca with the Scotch bonnet, garlic, salt, and pepper. Take about ³/₄ tablespoon of the yuca mixture and stuff the cavity of each butterfly-cut shrimp, packing it firmly into place.

Sprinkle the flour on a plate and season with salt and pepper. Beat together the egg and water in a bowl. Dust the shrimp first in the seasoned flour, then in the egg wash, and then in the panko or breadcrumbs.

Heat the peanut oil in a large heavy skillet until very hot. Carefully lay the shrimp in the oil and cook over medium-high heat for about 2 minutes per side, until golden and cooked through. Remove the shrimp with a slotted spoon and allow to drain on paper towels.

Warm the Mo J. in the saucepan until hot. Pour the sauce into a dipping bowl or directly onto the shrimp. Serve with the tartar salsa and garnish with a small mesclun salad.

PICKLED SCOTCH BONNET TARTAR SALSA

Yield: about 1½ cups.

You can make a nonpickled Scotch bonnet version of this salsa with ½ teaspoon minced fresh Scotch bonnet chile. Just make sure you have some extra pickle in there. Fresh herbs and/or a touch of mustard are optional additions.

3 egg yolks

1 tablespoon champagne vinegar

1 teaspoon pickling juice from the Scotch bonnets (see next column)

½ cup virgin olive oil

½ cup canola oil

1½ tablespoons seeded and minced Pickled Scotch Bonnet Chiles (page 283)

3 tablespoons store-bought sweet butter pickles. diced small

2 tablespoons finely diced red onion

1 hard-boiled egg

Salt and black pepper to taste

In a blender, or whisking by hand, beat the egg yolks until they turn pale. Whisk in the vinegar and the Scotch bonnet pickling juice. Whisk in the olive and canola oils very slowly until they are incorporated. Transfer to a bowl (if using a blender) and stir in the Scotch bonnets, pickles, and onion. Finely dice the egg white and sieve the egg yolk through a fine-mesh strainer. Stir both the egg white and yolk into the salsa, and season with salt and pepper. Keep covered in the refrigerator until needed.

"Criolla Mama" Barbecued Shrimp with a Corn and Goat Cheese Torta

Yield: 4 servings.

Literally, *criolla* means "native," but when Caribbean natives say "criolla" they mean "the best"! Anytime you want to add a spicy shellfish flavor to a dish, make sure Criolla Tomato Mama is on the guest list.

 You can serve this dish with rice instead of the torta. If you add a few more shrimp, this dish makes a nice dinner. The Criolla Mama sauce will keep refrigerated for up to a week, and it freezes well.

Criolla Tomato Mama (see recipe)

1 tablespoon butter

2 cloves garlic, minced

$^1/_2$ cup fresh sweet corn kernels

Salt and black pepper to taste

1 tablespoon heavy cream

1 ounce soft chèvre (goat cheese)

Corn Kernel Cakes (page 190)

2 tablespoons virgin olive oil

1 shallot, thinly sliced

12 large shrimp (about 10 to 12 ounces), peeled and deveined

Prepare the Criolla Mama sauce. Preheat the oven to 300 degrees.

Bring a skillet to high heat and add the butter. When it begins to foam, add the garlic. Cook for a few seconds, then add the corn, salt, and pepper. Cook the corn until it begins to blister, about 2 minutes. Add the cream and heat through. Transfer the mixture to a mixing bowl, add the chèvre, and mix well.

Prepare the corn cakes. Arrange eight of them on a work surface and spread four of them with an equal amount of the corn and chevre mixture. Top each with another cake. Place this *torta* on an ovenproof platter and keep warm in the oven.

Heat a large cast-iron skillet over medium-high heat and when very hot, add the olive oil and then the shallot. Season the shrimp with salt and pepper and add to the skillet, stirring rapidly. When the shrimp are just cooked (2 to 3 minutes), add the Criolla Mama sauce, stir, and heat through. Remove the skillet from the heat.

Place a stack of cakes on the center of each serving plate. Prop 3 shrimp around it and spoon the sauce over the shrimp and around the torta. Serve the extra corn cakes on the side.

CRIOLLA TOMATO MAMA

Yield: about 2 cups.

1 tablespoon olive oil

1 ounce smoked bacon, diced

1 Scotch bonnet chile, seeded and minced

2 cloves garlic, minced

1 tablespoon butter

1 teaspoon sugar

1/3 red onion, diced

1 large stalk celery, diced

1 small red bell pepper, seeded and diced

1 small yellow bell pepper, seeded and diced

2 tablespoons Spanish sherry vinegar

1 bay leaf, broken

1/2 teaspoon cayenne

2/3 teaspoon black pepper

1/3 teaspoon salt

2/3 teaspoon Tabasco sauce

1 tablespoon chopped thyme leaves

1 tablespoon chopped basil leaves

1 tablespoon chopped oregano leaves

1 cup Sea Creature Stock (page 274), or clam juice

1 1/2 cups concassé tomatoes (2 large tomatoes)

Heat the olive oil in a large, heavy saucepan and sauté the bacon over medium heat until it is almost cooked. Add the Scotch bonnet and garlic, and sauté for about 1 minute, stirring occasionally.

Add the butter, sugar, onion, celery, and bell peppers. Turn up the heat to medium-high and sauté for 10 to 15 minutes, or until the vegetables just begin to caramelize. Add the vinegar and reduce the heat to medium. Add the bay leaf, cayenne, black pepper, salt, Tabasco, thyme, basil, oregano, and 1/2 cup of the stock, and cook for 3 minutes, stirring occasionally. Add the remaining stock and the tomatoes, and cook for 15 minutes longer, stirring occasionally. Adjust the seasoning and keep warm. (If making ahead of time, keep refrigerated).

Pan Cubano con Camarones al Ajillo (Cuban Bread with Shrimp and Garlic)

Yield: 6 to 8 servings.

Something is always forfeited, if not lost entirely, in translations. So I left this one entirely in her Spanish name. This dish sails west out of Spain, across the Atlantic's stormy waters to dreamy Cuba, and then directly up to garlic, chile, and olive oil heaven!

24 large shrimp (about 1 1/2 pounds), peeled and deveined, shells and heads (if available) reserved

1 cup olive oil

6 to 8 slices (3/4 inch thick) Six O'Clock Cumin Cuban Bread (page 233), or another soft, crusty bread

12 cloves garlic, finely minced

1 to 2 Scotch bonnet chiles, seeded and minced

1/2 cup fresh lime juice (about 4 limes)

1/2 cup coarsely chopped cilantro leaves

1/2 cup coarsely chopped Italian parsley leaves

Salt and black pepper to taste

Pat the shrimp shells and heads dry with paper towels and place in a heavy skillet with the olive oil. Bring to a simmer over medium heat and cook for 5 minutes. Strain off the oil and reserve. Discard the shrimp shells and heads.

Toast the slices of bread and keep warm. Clean out the skillet, add the shrimp-flavored oil, and reheat. Sauté the garlic and chiles over medium-high heat and stir for 45 seconds to 1 minute. Add the shrimp and cook for about 1 minute per side. Remove the shrimp with a slotted spoon and reserve in a warm bowl.

Add the lime juice, herbs, salt, and pepper to the skillet, and stir well. Cook for 30 seconds to 1 minute, until blended together and hot. Place a slice of toast in the center of each soup plate. Top with the shrimp and ladle the flavored oil from the skillet around the toast. Serve with more bread at the table.

CHAPTER 3
BOWLS, BROTHS, STEWS, AND SPOONS

Little Havana Chicken and Plantain Sopa

Ajiaco of Short Ribs, Red Wine, and Tubers

White Bean, Chorizo, and Collard Greens Caldo

No-Roux Black Seafood Gumbo

"Papa's" Rellenas with Oxtails in a Truffled Broth

Gazpacho "B.C."

Grilled-Chilled Christophine Sopa con Rellenitos de Queso Cabrito

Cracked-Hacked Conch Chowder with Saffron, Coconut, and Oranges

Little Saigon Chicken and Noodle Soup

It's easy 'nough to titter w'en de stew is smokin' hot
But hit's mighty ha'd to giggle w'en dey's nuffin' in de pot

—Paul Laurence Dunbar, *Philosophy*

The rain piled up on the streets of Key West faster than snow in Chicago. Key West at its highest is a mere 17 or 18 feet above sea level, and that's at the peak of Solares Hill. The rest slopes to the waterline. After a steady 15 hours of rain, and no sign that it was stopping, I had to get out of our little house. Danny, Ann, and her son, Jermy, decided to come along too. Janet stayed behind with our son, Justin, still an infant then. "I'll get some milk . . . and Pampers too, if I can," I reasoned with her. Danny added helpfully, "And a sixpack!"

The three of us waded the long way around the graveyard. The rain had surpassed anything I'd ever seen. Puddles had become lagoons. The Bottle Lady's famous glass bottle fence was filling with water from both directions. I had to put Jermy on my shoulders by Passover Lane when the water suddenly came up to his chest. There was actually a current running down the brick and rock-pocked street. We locked arms. Cigarette wrappers and leaves swirled past us. I could barely make out the Battleship *Maine* monument less than 50 yards away as we rounded Windsor Lane. The iron-gated pen surrounding the old sailor's graves seemed an extra measure, as if in case the earth might wash them up and cause the caskets to slip their earth-pinned moorings.

It was warm rain, but it looked like snow up against the street lights, swirling as it was in the disorganized tropic wind. Higher up, the mercator projectionlike silhouettes of the Royal Palm fronds dwarfed the lights and gave the "faux snow" a surrealistic edge. I wondered where the cats were that lazed here amidst the stony angels in drier times.

None of us were surprised to see Curry's tiny store closed. The electricity was out, no doubt, all over the island. The crooked wooden houses looked more ghost-haunted than usual. A man walked past us with a transistor radio pressed up against his ear, listening to a baseball game in Spanish. I heard no bats cracking but felt the swish of his body's wake move around us. Little Jermy clung to my head like a ball he dare not drop, blocking any side-to-side vision with his waterlogged blue jeans and the drape of his yellow slicker.

Once home again, we went outside in the back to pull off the weight of our clothing. Janet gave us beach towels to mop ourselves off until we were reasonably dry. I felt my way around the darkened refrigerator and retrieved some wine.

The rain cleared around midnight—25 inches in 24 hours, we learned later. We stayed up, playing Hearts and 31 by candlelight. The power came back on near dawn. We heated some Caldo Gallego soup that we'd made earlier in the week. We ate, and then we caught some sleep. Later, we awoke to the sound of people chugging down the streets in small boats and rafts. I saw a van go by towing a golden retriever on a surfboard. Naturally. Good old Key West . . .

Soups, broths, bowls, and stews are the food universe's equivalent of a hug. I'm glad we had some soup ready that morning.

Little Havana Chicken and Plantain Sopa

Yield: 6 servings.

Discussing Miami's "Little Havana" could be a book of its own. One day, perhaps a filmmaker will do for the era of the 1960s in the area around Eighth Street (*Calle Ocho*) in Miami what Francis Ford Coppola did for Little Italy in *The Godfather II*. The Cubans who came here had fled for their lives and personal freedoms. The city of Miami changed radically. The new citizens embraced democracy and they steadfastly held on to and celebrated their traditions with a religious fervor—perhaps as a means to defeat, at least spiritually, the despotic Fidel Castro.

Part of the tradition of Cuba is her magnificent food. One of the island's most important table foods is plantains, sometimes called cooking bananas. Their starchy qualities give this soup a nice creamy body, while their ripe, sweet flavor makes it equally appealing to adults and children alike.

 If you like, you can garnish the soup with Crispy Fried Plantain Curls (page 188) and Sour Crema Drizzle (page 69).

CHICKEN

1 tablespoon cumin seeds, toasted and ground

2 teaspoons black peppercorns, toasted and ground

Salt to taste

4 boneless, skinless chicken breasts, about 6 to 8 ounces each

¹/₄ cup Annatto Oil (page 275), or olive oil

SOUP

¹/₄ cup olive oil

2 tablespoons butter

2 very ripe plantains, peeled and cut into ¹/₂-inch-thick slices

Pinch of salt

Pinch of sugar

Pinch of cayenne

2 leeks, white part only, diced fine

¹/₂ red onion, diced fine

1 large stalk celery, diced fine

1 large carrot, diced fine

3 cloves garlic, thinly sliced

1 Scotch bonnet or habanero chile, seeded and minced

1 large pinch saffron

1 bunch cilantro, leaves only, finely chopped

1 cup fresh orange juice

4 cups Light Chicken Stock (page 270)

2 cups heavy cream

Salt and black pepper to taste

To prepare the chicken: Mix the cumin, peppercorns, and salt together. Lay the chicken on a plate and season with the spice mixture. Pour the annatto oil over the chicken and turn the breasts over a few times to completely coat. Wrap the chicken in plastic wrap and refrigerate for at least 1 hour to allow the oil to tint the chicken with its dramatic color.

To prepare the soup: Heat the olive oil and butter in a large saucepan over medium-high heat. Add the sliced plantains and season with the salt, sugar, and cayenne. Sauté, stirring occasionally, until nicely browned. Stir in the leeks, onion, celery, carrot, garlic, and chile.

Continue to cook, and when the vegetables are nicely caramelized (about 10 minutes), stir in the saffron, cilantro, and orange juice, and cook for 2 minutes. Stir in the chicken stock and bring to a boil. Reduce the heat slightly to a high simmer and cook for about 12 minutes. Stir in the heavy cream and reduce the soup for 5 minutes.

Transfer the soup to a food processor or blender and purée until smooth. Strain through a medium-sized mesh strainer. Season to taste and keep warm.

Unwrap the chicken breasts. Heat a nonstick pan and, when hot, cook the chicken over medium-high heat until just cooked through. Let the chicken breasts rest a few minutes and cut them into bite-sized pieces. Ladle the soup into warm bowls and garnish with the chicken.

Ajiaco of Short Ribs, Red Wine, and Tubers

Yield: 4 to 6 servings.

Ajiaco is a Taino (Caribbean) Indian word for this stew made with the plentiful tubers and vegetables of the region. They ate ajiaco with yuca bread. The Spanish introduced cattle and other livestock to the New World and added their prized sausages and meats to this previously vegetarian dish. I enjoy the rich broth created by braising short ribs, which makes them my meaty choice for making this "New World" Ajiaco.

 This is a great soup for a dinner main course. Although the dish looks less rustic, you can, if you prefer, remove the rib meat from the bones, chop it up, and return it to the soup.

RIBS

¹/₄ cup flour

Salt and black pepper to taste

3¹/₂ pounds short ribs of beef

3 tablespoons peanut oil

1 red onion, chopped

2 carrots, chopped

3 stalks celery, chopped

1 head garlic, split in half lengthwise

¹/₄ cup toasted cumin seeds

1 tablespoon cayenne

1 bay leaf

1 tablespoon black peppercorns

¹/₂ cup red wine vinegar

2 cups red wine

6 cups Dark Chicken Stock (page 271)

TUBER AND VEGETABLE MIX

3 cups mixed root vegetables (for example, yuca, malanga, potato, yam [ñame], boniato, or sweet potato), peeled and cut into 1-inch dice

3 tablespoons peanut oil

¹/₄ cup flour

Salt and black pepper to taste

1 large ripe plantain, peeled and angle-cut into ¹/₄-inch-thick slices

4 tablespoons butter

1¹/₂ to 2 cups fresh corn kernels (from 2 ears sweet corn)

2 tablespoons olive oil

¹/₂ red onion, chopped

4 cloves minced garlic

2 banana (wax) chile peppers or gueros, seeded and chopped

To prepare the ribs: Mix the flour with salt and pepper on a large plate and roll the ribs in this mixture to coat. Heat the peanut oil in an ovenproof heavy saucepan or Dutch oven over high heat and sear the ribs, turning to brown on all sides. Remove and reserve on a platter.

Add the onion, carrots, celery, and garlic to the saucepan or Dutch oven, stir to coat with oil, and sauté over medium-high heat for about 15 minutes, until browned and caramelized. Add the cumin, cayenne, bay leaf, black peppercorns, red wine vinegar, and red wine. Turn up the heat to high and reduce the liquid by half, about 10 minutes.

Preheat the oven to 300 degrees. Add the stock to the saucepan, bring to a simmer, and skim off any impurities. Add the seared ribs and cover the pot loosely with foil. Bake in the oven for about 2 hours, or until the meat is very tender.

Remove from the oven. Pull out the ribs and place them on a platter to rest. Strain the liquid into a large bowl and quickly chill over an ice bath. When chilled, skim off as much fat as possible. Transfer the liquid to a clean saucepan and reduce by one-quarter over medium-high heat (about 15 minutes). Skim off any impurities, remove from the heat, and set aside.

To prepare the vegetables: Bring a pan of salted water to a boil. Blanch each root vegetable separately, until tender enough to pierce with a sharp knife (cooking times will vary, from about 8 minutes for the carrot, 10 minutes for the sweet potato, and 15 to 20 minutes for the yuca). Drain and reserve.

Heat the peanut oil in a large sauté pan over medium-high heat. Season the flour with salt and pepper, and dredge the plantain in the mixture. Fry the plantain in the hot oil until brown. Remove with a slotted spoon and drain on paper towels.

Wipe out the pan and melt 2 tablespoons of the butter. Add the corn and sauté for about 1 1/2 minutes over high heat. Transfer to a bowl and reserve.

In the same pan over high heat, add the remaining 2 tablespoons of butter and the olive oil. When foamy or sizzling, add the red onion, garlic, and chile peppers, and sauté until the chile peppers blister, about 5 minutes. Keeping the pan over high heat, add the blanched root vegetables. Season to taste with salt and pepper and stir gently once or twice. Add the reserved stock and corn, the meat and plantains, and cook over medium heat for 8 minutes. Serve in soup bowls.

White Bean, Chorizo, and Collard Greens Caldo

Yield: 8 servings.

Collard greens were transported to the New World from Africa by the slave ships, and they became a staple of Southern cooking. Collard greens likewise show up in Brazil in that country's ultimate feast dish, *Feijoada Completa*. They are an integral part of this soup, which is based on the famous Galician (Spanish) soup, *Caldo Gallejo*.

 The beans must be soaked overnight before cooking. An excellent accompaniment for this caldo is my Caribbean Corn Bread (page 240).

3 tablespoons olive oil

8 ounces Norman's Chorizo (page 288), or other spicy sausage

2 tablespoons butter

6 cloves garlic, thinly sliced

1 Scotch bonnet chile, seeded and minced

2 poblano chiles, seeded and diced

1 red onion, diced

12 to 14 ounces dried white beans, soaked overnight

3 quarts (12 cups) Light Chicken Stock (page 270), or water

1 smoked pork hock or ham bone

2 bay leaves, broken

8 ounces beef chuck steak (in one piece), optional

Salt and black pepper to taste

1 red potato, peeled if desired, and cut into large dice

1 turnip, peeled and cut into large dice

2 packed cups collard greens, washed, stems removed, and cut in shreds

Heat the olive oil in a large heavy saucepan. Add the chorizo, piercing the skin in a few places with a sharp knife. Cook over medium heat until brown, turning as necessary. Reduce the heat to low and cook for 10 to 12 minutes longer. Transfer to a plate, let cool, and put in the refrigerator to firm up.

Add the butter to the saucepan and melt over medium heat. Add the garlic, chiles, and red onion. Sauté for 7 to 8 minutes, stirring occasionally. Drain the soaked beans and add to the pan, stirring well. Add the stock or water, pork hock or ham bone, and bay leaves. Raise the heat and bring almost to a boil. Skim off any impurities.

Rub the steak with pepper and leave in one piece, if using. Reduce the heat to low and add the steak. Do not cover the pan. Stir occasionally, checking to make sure the beans do not become stuck to the bottom of the pan. Cook the beans for at least 1 hour, until almost tender; the cooking time will vary according to length of soaking time and size. Season with a pinch of salt and some pepper.

Add the potato, turnip, and collard greens. Cook until the potato is tender, about 45 minutes. Cut the reserved chorizo into $1/2$-inch rounds and add to the soup. Remove the piece of steak and when cool enough, shred into pieces. Turn off the heat and return the shredded beef to the soup. Season to taste and serve.

No-Roux Black Seafood Gumbo

Yield: 4 to 6 servings.

I created this dish for my extraordinary friend Emeril Lagasse, King of the *New* New Orleans cooking. What can I say about him—the man is a force that God sent down to make mouths water and lips laugh. One time, we were cooking at our "Brother" Charlie Trotter's place up in Chicago for a big shindig. Emeril asked me to make the gumbo he had going on *his* menu (his menu, his gumbo). "Well," I said, "Sure . . ." I used to make gumbos a lot in the early 1980s, during my N'Orleans period. Emeril wanted a black roux gumbo; they accurately call this stuff Cajun Napalm—if you splash some on you, it's Burn Unit time! This was a major test. Tickets to the event weren't cheap and the press were making notes. I couldn't let my Brother down. As I finished, I looked up from my stirrin', sweatin', and pan-shakin' to see "Em" appraising my efforts from behind a set of crossed arms, hiding a smile framed under a pair of eyebrows that will one day, I'm sure, be in the Smithsonian. He dipped a spoon in, tasted, and put his head down on his chest. An hour passed in my mind. He put his nose up against mine, his eyes looking serious—*serious*—and suddenly exclaimed: "BAM!"

 I like to serve this in wide soup bowls with a small square of Johnnycake (page 239) in the middle. Having some minced Pickled Scotch Bonnet Chiles (page 283) on hand for some additional incendiary effect should appease any particularly heat-tolerant guests. Feel free to use the seafood of your choice for this recipe; for a less rustic look, you can remove the lobster from the shell.

SOUP BASE

¹/₄ cup olive oil

2 ounces bacon, diced (about ¹/₂ cup)

2 tablespoons butter

6 cloves garlic, minced

2 jalapeño chiles, seeded and minced

1 red onion, diced

2 red bell peppers, seeded and diced small

2 stalks celery, diced small

1 bay leaf

2 teaspoons salt

¹/₂ teaspoon black pepper

¹/₂ teaspoon cayenne

1 tablespoon minced thyme leaves

1 tablespoon minced basil leaves

1 cup sherry

2 cups Sea Creature Stock (page 274), or clam juice

1 cup puréed cooked black beans

3 tomatoes, concassé

Tabasco sauce, to taste

SOUP GARNISH

3 tablespoons extra-virgin olive oil

2 tablespoons butter

3 shallots, thinly sliced

3 cloves garlic, thinly sliced

2 spiny lobsters, or 1 Maine lobster, cut into sections, shell intact

8 ounces large shrimp, peeled and deveined

1 tablespoon roughly chopped thyme leaves

Salt and black pepper to taste

1/2 cup white wine

12 shucked oysters, liquor strained and reserved

12 shucked clams, liquor strained and reserved

Tabasco sauce to taste

To prepare the soup base: Heat the olive oil in a large heavy saucepan and sauté the bacon in the oil over medium heat. When the bacon is about half cooked (about 2 minutes), add the butter. When the butter begins to foam, add the garlic and jalapeños, and stir for 5 seconds. Add the onion, bell peppers, and celery. Stir, and then let caramelize for 30 minutes, stirring only occasionally.

Add the bay leaf, salt, black pepper, cayenne, thyme, and basil. Stir together, add the sherry, and reduce the liquid by half (about 1 minute). Add the stock and reduce the liquid until only about 3/4 cup remains (about 10 minutes). Add the black beans and the tomatoes and remove from the heat. Add the Tabasco and set the soup base aside.

To prepare the soup garnish: Heat the olive oil and butter in a large heavy saucepan. When the butter is foamy, add the shallots and garlic and sauté over medium-high heat for 4 minutes. Add the lobster, shrimp, thyme, salt, and pepper, and cook for 10 minutes, stirring occasionally. Add the wine and cook for 1 minute.

Add the reserved soup base and bring to a simmer. Add the oysters, clams, and their liquors. Return to a simmer and cook for 2 to 3 minutes before serving. Season with the Tabasco sauce.

"Papa's" Rellenas with Oxtails in a Truffled Broth

Yield: 8 servings; or 4 servings as a main-course soup.

This soup is named for the one and only "Papa" Hemingway, a fellow Illinoisian who, like me, fell in love with Key West. The title also doubles for *papas rellenas,* the simple snack of stuffed potatoes sold in the little stands and cafecito joints from Miami down to Key West (not with truffles or broth, mind you!). Papa would have liked the truffles; he would have found the big power alluring despite the violence done to the wallet.

The method for making the rellenas alone can be adapted for all kinds of fillings; they make an excellent snack or cocktail food. If truffles are out of season or out of reach financially, do not despair. This is a very satisfying soup just with the sliced mushrooms.

Sour Crema Drizzle (see recipe)

BRAISED OXTAILS

3 to 4 pounds meaty oxtails, cut into 2-inch lengths

Salt and black pepper to taste

¹/₂ cup flour

¹/₄ cup olive oil

Bean Kit (page 280)

¹/₂ cup red wine vinegar

1 cup Rioja, Cabernet, or Zinfandel red wine

4 cups Dark Chicken Stock (page 271)

RELLENAS

2 pounds red boiling potatoes, diced

1 teaspoon toasted ground cumin

1 teaspoon chile molido, or pure red chile powder

Salt and black pepper to taste

2 eggs, beaten

1 tablespoon water

1¹/₂ cups fresh breadcrumbs

Peanut oil, for deep-frying

TRUFFLE GARNISH

8 ounces button mushrooms, very finely sliced

2 ounces (or as much as the budget allows) white or black truffles, sliced paper thin, or 2 tablespoons truffle oil

Prepare the drizzle.

Season the oxtails with salt and pepper, and dredge in the flour. Heat the olive oil in a heavy saucepan and brown the oxtails on all sides over medium-high heat. Remove the oxtails and set aside.

Bring the bean kit to the ready point and add the vinegar and red wine. Reduce the liquid by half over medium-high heat. Add the stock, bring to a boil, and skim off any impurities. Reduce the heat to very low, return the oxtails to the pan, and cover. Cook for 2 to 2¹/₂ hours.

Remove the oxtails from the stock, and strain the stock through a fine-mesh strainer into a bowl (there should be about 4 cups). Let cool and then chill. Meanwhile, scrape the meat off the bones while they are still warm. Shred the meat as finely as possible.

Reserve 3 cups of shredded meat for this soup and the rest for other uses (such as a risotto, stirfry, or taco filling).

To prepare the rellenas: Bring a saucepan of salted water to a boil and cook the potatoes until just tender, about 10 minutes. Drain off the water, and with the potatoes in the pan, place over medium heat for 30 seconds while shaking the pan to evaporate the remaining moisture. Remove from the heat. Using a ricer, "rice" the potatoes (alternatively, push through a large mesh strainer), and transfer to a bowl. Add the cumin, chile molido, salt, and pepper, and stir gently.

When cool enough to handle, take $1/4$ cup of the potato mixture and roll into a compact ball. Repeat for the remaining mixture. Make a deep well with your finger in each ball and insert about $1/2$ tablespoon of the cooked oxtail meat. Push the hole shut.

Beat the egg and water together in a bowl to form an egg wash, and spread the breadcrumbs on a plate. Roll the stuffed potato balls in the eggwash and then in the breadcrumbs. Cover and refrigerate until ready to serve.

Heat the broth in a saucepan. When the broth reaches a simmer, add the reserved 3 cups of shredded oxtail meat and the sliced mushrooms. Season with salt and pepper, and keep warm.

Heat the peanut oil in a deep-fryer to 350 degrees. Deep-fry the potato rolls for 3 to 5 minutes. Remove with a slotted spoon, drain on paper towels, and keep warm.

Ladle the broth into warm serving bowls and put 1 of the potato rellenas in the center of each. Drizzle the sour crema over the rellenas, sprinkle the broth with the sliced truffles or truffle oil, and serve the remaining potato rellenas on the side.

SOUR CREMA DRIZZLE

Yield: $1/2$ cup.

6 tablespoons sour cream

2 tablespoons heavy cream

Put the sour cream in a small bowl, lightly stir, and add the heavy cream. Stir together to combine.
Spoon the mixture into a squirt bottle and refrigerate until needed.

Gazpacho "B.C."

Yield: 4 servings.

B.C.? Yes, for several reasons. The first is to draw your attention, no small task when you consider that most folks think they already own "the gazpacho recipe" and don't require another. B.C. refers to "Before Columbus." In the Spanish province of Andalusia, gazpachos (yes, plural) were created centuries before the good *capitán* sailed back to Spain from the New World with a fruit the Indians called *tomatl*. It wasn't until the early sixteenth century that the Andalusians allowed the tomato to share the stage with the most popular "ajo blanco" gazpacho made with almonds, or the twelve or more other gazpachos (one of which featured fava beans).

I also call this "B.C." to touch upon its ancient and holy ability to feed. With bread, oil, vinegar, and garlic, the foundations of all gazpachos are laid. Lastly, B.C. stands for "beautiful coconut," in my New World interpretation of this beautiful soup.

 Sliced grapes are a traditional garnish for gazpachos and they would make a nice addition here.

4 ounces stale white (French or Italian) bread, crust removed

Pinch of salt

1/4 cup virgin olive oil

1 1/2 tablespoons champagne vinegar

3/4 cup freshly ground skinless unsalted almonds

1 3/4 cups Coconut Milk (page 7), or canned

2/3 cup ice water

Salt and black pepper to taste

1/2 cup toasted and grated unsweetened coconut meat

Place the bread in a bowl and cover with water for 30 seconds. Drain off the water, squeeze out any excess moisture, and rip the bread into pieces. Transfer to the blender with the salt and olive oil, and purée. Add the vinegar and almonds and blend while adding the coconut milk and enough of the ice water to make the mixture loose but creamy. Season to taste, transfer to a bowl, and chill thoroughly.

When ready to serve, ladle the soup into chilled bowls. Sprinkle the toasted coconut over the soup.

Grilled-Chilled Christophine Sopa con Rellenitos de Queso Cabrito

Yield: 6 servings.

This is my New World version of a chilled cucumber soup and I use a wonderful, sweet squash—christophine—that is also known as chayote and mirliton, depending on which Caribbean island you're on, or which part of the country you're in. It's all the same vegetable, and wherever it's from, it has the same delicate flavor.

 For a simpler presentation, you can serve this soup without the rellenitos. Use a little half-and-half or plain yogurt to thin the soup, if necessary.

If there's any of the goat cheese–cream mixture left over after stuffing the chiles, drizzle it over them for an attractive garnish. The dish can be further garnished with snipped chives, celery leaves, and cracked black pepper, if desired.

RELLENITOS (OPTIONAL)

6 jalapeño chiles, roasted and peeled (stems attached)

2 ounces soft goat cheese

1 tablespoon heavy cream

SOUP BASE

6 tablespoons olive oil

3 tablespoons butter

4 cloves garlic, finely sliced

1 Scotch bonnet or habanero chile, seeded and minced

2 leeks, white part only, diced small

2 small inner stalks of celery, diced small

2 large shallots, finely sliced

Pinch of salt

1 teaspoon black pepper

2 bay leaves, broken

²/₃ cup fresh orange juice

1 cup Light Chicken Stock (page 270)

2 cups heavy cream

2 christophines, peeled and cut lengthwise into ¹/₄-inch-thick slices

1 European or English (hothouse) cucumber, peeled and seeded

1 tablespoon kosher salt

1 ¹/₄ cups buttermilk

1 tablespoon thyme leaves

4 scallions, finely chopped

To prepare the rellenitos: Make a slit down one side of the peeled roasted jalapeños and carefully scrape out the seeds with the point of a knife. Combine the goat cheese and cream in a mixing bowl and spoon the mixture into a pastry bag or zipper-closed plastic bag with a tiny corner cut out of it. Gently squeeze the mixture into the cavities of each jalapeño and close up the slit to return the jalapeño to its original shape. Keep chilled until ready to serve.

To prepare the soup base: In a large soup pot or saucepan, heat 3 tablespoons of the olive oil and the butter over medium heat until slightly foaming. Add the garlic and chile, and stir for 15 seconds. Add the leeks, celery, shallots, salt, pepper, and bay leaves. Reduce the heat to medium-low and cook the mixture until translucent, about 10 minutes.

When the vegetables have just begun to soften, turn up the heat to medium-high and add the orange juice. Reduce the liquid by half, about 7 minutes. Add the chicken stock and reduce again until only about $1/2$ cup of liquid remains, about 15 to 20 minutes. Remove from the heat and pour in the cream. Transfer to a blender or food processor and purée. Strain through a medium-fine-mesh strainer into a large bowl set over ice water. Let chill.

Prepare the grill or heat a griddle.

Season the christophine with the remaining 3 tablespoons of olive oil, and salt and pepper to taste. Grill the slices of seasoned christophine, until they are lightly charred. Put them in a bowl and let cool. When they are cool enough to handle, cut them into short matchstick-sized pieces and reserve.

Cut the cucumber in half and then cut it into long quarters lengthwise. Put the quarters in a colander and sprinkle them with the salt. Let stand for at least 30 minutes; this pulls the excess water out of the cucumber. Rinse the cucumber quickly with cold water, being sure to wash all the salt off, and pat dry with a towel. Thinly slice and reserve.

Remove the bowl containing the chilled purée from the ice bath. Add the buttermilk, thyme, scallions, and the reserved christophine and cucumber. Season with salt and pepper to taste. Cover and store in the refrigerator. Serve the soup in chilled serving bowls and place a rellenito in the center.

Cracked-Hacked Conch Chowder with Saffron, Coconut, and Oranges

Yield: 8 to 10 servings.

This recipe's length may seem daunting, but it's the most popular soup I've ever created. My guests at Norman's would riot in the streets if we ever took it off the menu.

Cracked is the word that traditionally describes the process of removing conch meat from its beautiful spiral shell. It seems odd, considering the shell is not actually cracked or destroyed during these eviction proceedings. That may be of little consolation to the gastropod, but it may make the gastronome more pleased.

 Conch is almost always sold frozen. Check for any freezer burn, and don't buy it if there are ice crystals on the meat. Because conch meat can be extremely tough, it's necessary to tenderize it. Slice the meat as thinly as possible, place between two sheets of plastic wrap, and pound with a rolling pin or mallet. Optional garnishes for this soup are orange sections, toasted coconut, or saffron threads. You can substitute abalone for the conch in this recipe, or make the recipe without conch and garnish with cooked crabmeat or shrimp instead.

SHELLFISH BROTH

¹/₄ cup olive oil

1 Scotch bonnet chile, seeded and minced

6 shallots, thinly sliced

4 cloves garlic, thinly sliced

12 small clams, scrubbed

12 mussels, debearded and scrubbed

1 star anise

1 tablespoon roughly cracked black pepper

3 cups fresh orange juice

2 teaspoons saffron

1 quart heavy cream

1 cup Coconut Milk (page 7), or canned

VEGETABLES

6 new potatoes (about 1 pound), diced

1/2 cup olive oil

2 ounces smoked slab bacon, rind removed if necessary, and diced (about 1/2 cup)

4 cloves garlic, thinly sliced

1 poblano chile, seeded and minced

2/3 cup fresh corn kernels (from 1 ear sweet corn)

1/2 red onion, diced

2 large carrots, diced

1/2 fennel bulb, cored and diced

2 celery stalks, diced

1 red bell pepper, seeded and diced

1/4 cup roughly chopped cilantro leaves

2 bay leaves, broken

Salt and black pepper to taste

CONCH

12 ounces cleaned, pounded conch

Salt and black pepper to taste

1/4 cup flour

2 cups panko crumbs

2 eggs, beaten

1 1/2 tablespoons half-and-half

3/4 cup peanut oil

To prepare the shellfish broth: Heat the olive oil in a large, heavy-bottomed saucepan and sauté the chile, shallots, and garlic over medium-high heat for 1 minute, stirring them around. Add the clams, mussels, star anise, and black pepper. Stir, add the orange juice, and cover the pan.

As the clams and mussels open (after about 3 minutes), remove to a colander set over a bowl to catch the liquid. Take them out as they open, cover the pan again, and keep checking for more open ones. Discard any that do not open after 10 minutes. Return the liquid caught in the bowl to the pan. After all the clams and mussels have been removed, uncover the pan and reduce the liquid until 1 cup remains, about 10 minutes.

Add the saffron, cream, and coconut milk. Bring to a boil, stirring occasionally; take care to prevent the mixture from boiling over. Reduce until the mixture just barely coats the back of a spoon, about 15 to 20 minutes. Turn off the heat and strain the mixture into a bowl. Discard the solids. Remove the clam and mussel meat from the shells and reserve.

To prepare the vegetables: Bring a saucepan of lightly salted water to a boil, add the potatoes, and reduce the heat to a simmer. Cook for 8 to 10 minutes until just underdone. Strain and set aside. In a large, heavy soup pan, heat the olive oil and sauté the bacon over medium-high heat until half cooked. Add the garlic and poblano chile, and stir briefly. Add the corn, onion, carrots, fennel, celery, and bell pepper. Stir to coat. Add the cilantro, bay leaves, salt, and pepper. Stir occasionally and cook until firm, about 8 minutes. Add the cooked potatoes, reserved saffron cream, and the clam and mussel meat. Keep warm.

To prepare the conch: Season it with salt and pepper. Place the flour and panko on separate plates, and whisk the eggs and half-and-half together in a bowl. Dredge the conch in the flour, then in the egg wash, and finally in the panko. Place on a large plate (layer with wax paper or plastic wrap, if you wish). Heat some of the peanut oil in a large skillet and sauté the conch over medium-high heat in batches until nicely browned on both sides. Drain on paper towels and then chop into pieces.

Ladle the soup into warm bowls and scatter the conch over the top.

Little Saigon Chicken and Noodle Soup

Yield: 4 servings.

Having created the Little Havana Chicken and Plantain Sopa in homage to Miami's colorful and exciting enclave that's replete with Cuban spirit, I decided to express my love of Asian flavors with a tasty soup. There are Chinatowns or Japantowns and, more recently, Little Saigons in many cities, and it's always interesting to visit them. Sometimes the communication barrier can be a little daunting, but more often than not, I find I learn something that broadens my horizons.

 You can buy fen noodles in Vietnamese or Oriental stores. They usually need to be pulled apart, but they'll separate in the simmering soup. As an alternative, you can use paparadelle noodles (or a wide fettuccine) cooked al dente.

The soup base can be prepared 1 or 2 days ahead of time if desired. Cover and keep chilled in the refrigerator. You can add chicken pieces to the soup if you'd like it meatier.

SOUP BASE

2 tablespoons dark roasted sesame oil

2 tablespoons virgin olive oil

1 Scotch bonnet chile, seeded and very finely julienned

2 tablespoons minced garlic

1 1/2 tablespoons minced ginger

2 tablespoons butter

1 carrot, thinly sliced

2 celery stalks, thinly sliced

Salt and black pepper to taste

1 tablespoon Thai red curry paste

1 cup sherry

7 cups Light Chicken Stock (page 270)

1 stalk lemongrass, trimmed, peeled, and cut in half lengthwise

SOUP GARNISH

2 tablespoons peanut or canola oil

1 tablespoon dark roasted sesame oil

1 bunch scallions, trimmed and finely minced, including half of the green ends

1 cup sliced shiitake mushrooms, or domestic mushrooms

1 poblano chile, seeded and finely julienned

12 snow peas

12 chives or garlic chives, chopped into 1-inch lengths

10 ounces fresh Oriental noodles, such as fen noodles, or paparadelle or fettuccine, cut into bite-sized lengths

Salt and black pepper to taste

1 tablespoon Oriental fish sauce

To prepare the soup base: Heat the sesame and olive oils in a large saucepan or wok. When hot, add the chile, garlic, and ginger, and stirfry over medium heat for 1 minute. Add the butter, carrot, and celery. Season with salt and pepper and sauté for 5 minutes. Stir in the curry paste and sauté for 30 seconds. Add the sherry and bring to a simmer while stirring the curry paste for 1 or 2 minutes to help it dissolve.

Reduce the heat to low and add the chicken stock and lemongrass. Simmer for 1½ hours, skimming off any impurities as necessary. Strain the soup and discard the vegetables.

To prepare the soup garnish: Heat the oils over medium-high heat in a clean large saucepan or wok. Add the scallions, mushrooms, and chile, and rapidly stirfry for 2 minutes. Meanwhile, blanch the snow peas in boiling water for 30 seconds, shock in ice water, and julienne. Add the reserved chicken soup to the saucepan or wok, and bring to a high simmer. Add the chives, blanched snow peas, and the noodles. Season with salt, pepper, and the fish sauce, and serve in warm soup bowls.

CHAPTER 4
SALADS, SEVICHES, AND SALPICONES

Sea Scallop Seviche *"Ahora Mismo"* with a Peruvian Purple Potato Salad

Smoked Salmon Tortilla Española Ensalada with a
Passion Fruit Vinaigrette

Chopstick Spinach Salad and Asian Tea–Spiced Swordfish with
Mandarin Oranges and a Soy-Scallion Dressing

Cane-Marinated Grilled Quail on Tortillas with Lettuces and
The Redlands Tropical Fruit Chutney

Jerked Chicken with Ripped Lettuces, Raw Mango, Hot Chiles, and
Sweet Onions

Snapper Escabeche Ensalada with Salsa Romesco, Arbequine Olives,
Avocado, Oranges, and Ribbons of Greens

Six O'Clock Cuban Bread Salad with Tomatoes, Herbs, and
Tetilla in an Orange-Sherry Vinaigrette

Salpicón of Everglades Alligator with Greens, Vegetables, Blue Cheese,
Avocado, and Teardrop Tomatoes

Vietnamese Soft Spring Rolls with Paw Paw Slaw and
Peanut Dipping Sauce

Let onion atoms lurk within the bowl
And, scarce suspected, animate the whole.

—Sydney Smith, *"Recipe for Salad"*

It's difficult to point in any one direction as to what may be called a "salad" anymore. To reverse Gertrude Stein's observance, it's a case of "too much here, here."

Salad is an increasingly encompassing term. From a delicate and pale mix of baby bibb and endive to the "Cosmo gal" mesclun, to an athletically endowed *salpicón* of greens, beets, chicken, beans, eggs, chorizo, herbs, and chiles, we have a bountiful body of salads.

Dressing these bodies should be done with an eye to their individual make, shimmy, and shake. I will often use a light vinaigrette to dress one part of a salad, such as the greens, and offer a drizzle of richer, creamy dressing near the edge of the plate to dip some of the salad into. This is much less caloric than a salad dressed only in, say, blue cheese or Caesar dressing, yet it won't seem like inadequate "rabbit food."

In any cuisine, seasonality and freshness are the hallmarks of excellence. With salads, these qualities count in some of the most appreciable and direct ways. Always shop with a flexible frame of reference with the recipes that follow. Let the recipes guide you, but make substitutions that need to be made by the dictates of ripeness.

You have a significant role in helping to shape the range of produce available in our markets. Speak to the managers of your stores and tell them what you would like if it's not carried there. If necessary, remind them how burying produce in layers of plastic is not only wasteful but prevents you from properly assessing the quality of the food. Tell them that the so-called convenience of machine-shaped "baby" carrots are the olfactoral equivalent of a real carrot to the same extent that a magazine's trick blast of perfume is to the scent of a real woman.

Think of memories you may have from traveling to the open-stalled, noisy, colorful, multitongued markets of the Caribbean, Mexico, Italy, France, or the Far East, or even the growing number of great markets now in the United States. As our country becomes increasingly diverse ethnically, we notice new tubers, fruits, fish, and vegetables in our markets. Ask your store managers for print information on recipes and techniques so you can discover more ways to feed yourself, your family, and friends. We'll continue to find even *more* "here, here."

Sea Scallop Seviche "Ahora Mismo" with a Peruvian Purple Potato Salad

Yield: 4 servings.

Ahora mismo means "right now!"—and that's how we make this seviche. Seviches (or *ceviches*) were probably first created in Peru, long before the Spanish arrived. The Incas of the Andes cultivated and developed many varieties of potatoes, including the purple type that are now in vogue. So here we have a pairing that may well have more historical precedent than many folks would have thought.

 These scallops can be paired with many different salads—try what sounds good to you! The potato salad can be made up to 1 day ahead. You can garnish this dish with any citrus fruit. Placing the scallops, well-wrapped, in the freezer for about 20 minutes and then slicing them will make it easier to cut them and make them colder for service, which is a good thing.

3¹/₂ cups (¹/₂ recipe) Peruvian Purple Potato Salad (page 195)

SEVICHE

1 tablespoon fresh lime juice

1 tablespoon fresh lemon juice

2 tablespoons fresh orange juice

1 Scotch bonnet or habanero chile, or 2 serranos, seeded and minced

1 tablespoon minced garlic

Salt and black pepper to taste

12 ounces very fresh large sea scallops, cleaned

1 tablespoon Annatto Oil (page 275), or extra-virgin olive oil

Prepare the potato salad and chill.

To prepare the seviche: Mix together the citrus juices with the chile, garlic, salt, and pepper in a mixing bowl. Cover and chill. Place the scallops in plastic wrap and chill in the freezer for about 20 minutes.

Unwrap the scallops, slice as thinly as possible, and arrange around the inside rim of serving plates. To serve, spoon the reserved liquid evenly over the scallops. Scoop some of the potato salad onto the center of the plates, inside the scallops. Drizzle some of the annatto oil over the scallops and serve.

Smoked Salmon Tortilla Española Ensalada with a Passion Fruit Vinaigrette

Yield: 8 to 10 servings.

In this tortilla salad, the richness of smoked salmon is nicely countered by the exotic acidity of the passion fruit. Although the word *tortilla* usually first brings to mind the thin, round Mexican bread made from corn or flour, in Spanish cuisine it refers to an egg dish very much along the lines of the Italian *frittata*. Tortillas come in as many different forms as omelettes, and they are one of the mainstays of *tapas*. They are usually served at room temperature (as here).

 Many of the recipes that follow call for "handfuls" or "double handfuls" of lettuces and greens. While not necessarily a precise measure, the idea is that you should not be tempted to cram them into a measuring cup and risk damaging them. As a rough guide, a "double handful" is about 2 to 3 cups of loosely packed greens.

TORTILLA

1 cup virgin olive oil

4 red potatoes, cut into quarters lengthwise and sliced 1/8 inch thick

1 red onion, thinly sliced

6 eggs

1/2 cup heavy cream

Salt and black pepper to taste

6 ounces smoked salmon, diced

VINAIGRETTE

1/2 cup fresh or frozen passion fruit juice

1 tablespoon champagne vinegar

1 cup virgin olive oil

1/4 cup extra-virgin olive oil

Salt and black pepper to taste

4 small double handfuls mixed lettuces, such as romaine, red leaf, radicchio, bibb, Belgian endive, and curly endive

To prepare the tortilla: Heat the olive oil in a nonstick pan or well-seasoned skillet over medium heat. When the oil is hot, add the potatoes and onion and stir gently. Cover and let cook for about 20 minutes or until the potatoes are tender, stirring occasionally. Drain in a colander, reserving the oil. Let the potatoes cool.

In a large mixing bowl, whisk together the eggs, cream, salt, and pepper. Add the cooked potatoes and onions, and the smoked salmon. Toss gently, ensuring the egg mixture covers everything. Let sit for 15 to 20 minutes.

Pour 1 tablespoon of the reserved oil into a clean pan set over medium-high heat (save the remaining oil for another use). Add the egg mixture to the pan, and spread out evenly. Shake the pan to prevent the mixture from sticking. Turn on the broiler. After the egg mixture has cooked for 4 minutes, place it about 6 inches under the broiler to slightly set the top. Remove the pan from the broiler, slide a large round platter over the pan and quickly invert it so the tortilla falls onto the plate.

Add another tablespoon of the reserved oil to the pan and heat. Slide the tortilla back into the pan, with the cooked side up, and cook over medium-high heat for 10 minutes longer. Lift up the sides with a wooden spoon occasionally to make sure it's not getting too brown too quickly. Remove the tortilla to a platter to cool (you can serve it warm if you prefer).

To prepare the vinaigrette: Mix the passion fruit juice with the vinegar in a mixing bowl. Whisk in the oils and season with salt and pepper.

To serve: Cut the tortilla into wedges and transfer to large serving plates. Place the lettuces in a large bowl and toss with the dressing. Mound the dressed lettuce attractively next to the tortilla, and serve.

Chopstick Spinach Salad and Asian Tea–Spiced Swordfish with Mandarin Oranges and a Soy-Scallion Dressing

Yield: 4 servings.

If for no other reason, I like chopsticks because they force many of us to slow down. We are living in an era that is consumed with speed, efficiency, and progress. In these days of overnight express mail and faxes, "I need it yesterday" is the common refrain. This pace is literally killing us, and there are so few places where we can take a break and stop to smell the roses—or the sake! A different, tranquil, even ancient Oriental mind-set seems to enter our being when we take some ornately etched chopsticks in our hands. Their aesthetic is so yin compared to the weaponlike yang design of the fork. Chopsticks don't pierce; they gently pinch and softly squeeze. They're long, thin, and ever so slightly tapered. They may be resting on the gentle curve of some teak, pearl, or jade when we first eye their beauty. They may be slow, but watching someone who attracts you delicately convey a small piece of food to their lips with chopsticks can make dinner a prelude to an evening more relaxing than you'd dreamed amidst the daily geometric puzzle of making ends meet.

 Curing is an interesting way of producing enhanced texture as well as flavor, and it's what makes gravlax such a hit. The vinaigrette can be used for other salads and will keep for up to 2 weeks in the refrigerator.

Tea Smokin' Asian Spice Cure (see recipe)

1 pound fresh boneless, skinless swordfish (or tuna)

1 tablespoon olive oil

VINAIGRETTE

1/2 tablespoon fresh lime juice

1 1/2 tablespoons fresh lemon juice

2 tablespoons fresh orange juice

1/2 tablespoon minced ginger

1 tablespoon chopped scallions

2 tablespoons mirin

1 tablespoon soy sauce

1/2 tablespoon sugar

1/2 teaspoon hot chile sauce (preferably Sriracha), optional

6 tablespoons dark roasted sesame oil

Salt and black pepper to taste

SALAD

12 ounces spinach leaves, cleaned and stemmed

Salt and black pepper to taste

2 mandarin oranges, sectioned and cut in half lengthwise

2 scallions, trimmed and finely minced

Prepare the spice cure. Lay the fish on a plate and rub the spice cure over both sides. Cover with plastic wrap. Lay another plate of the same size on top of the fish to create some pressure. Add a little weight to the top plate and refrigerate for 4 to 12 hours.

Unwrap the fish and cut into 4 even pieces. Heat a skillet or wok over high heat and add the olive oil. When hot, cook the fish quickly to the desired doneness (1$\frac{1}{2}$ to 3 minutes). Transfer to a plate, let cool, and then cover with plastic wrap.

To prepare the vinaigrette: Whisk all the ingredients together in a bowl. Transfer to a heavy-bottomed saucepan and warm gently over medium-low heat. Place the spinach in a large bowl, season with salt and pepper, toss, and set aside.

Slice the swordfish against the grain into 1$\frac{1}{2}$ × $\frac{3}{4}$-inch pieces. Arrange around the edge of large serving plates, like the numbers of a clock. Arrange the mandarin orange slices across the swordfish.

When the vinaigrette is warm, pour just enough over the spinach to coat the leaves and let them wilt slightly. Lift the leaves out of the bowl and mound them in the center of the serving plates. Drizzle a little of the vinaigrette over the swordfish, sprinkle the scallions over the spinach, and serve.

TEA SMOKIN' ASIAN SPICE CURE

Yield: 3 tablespoons.

1 tablespoon Lapsang Souchong black loose leaf tea

1 tablespoon sugar

$\frac{1}{2}$ tablespoon salt

$\frac{1}{2}$ tablespoon black pepper

Combine all of the Spice Cure ingredients together in a bowl. If making ahead, store in an airtight container.

Cane-Marinated Grilled Quail on Tortillas with Lettuces and The Redlands Tropical Fruit Chutney

Yield: 4 servings.

Sugarcane is one of the world's most important field crops, but whenever I think of it, I'm reminded of one day in Hawaii in 1971. I was hitchhiking around the Big Island of Hawaii with two buddies, but no one driving by was having anything to do with the three long-haired *haoles* ("round-eyes") that were headed no place in particular but wanting to get there quickly nonetheless. Hours passed.

Eventually, a man in a pickup truck stopped and said, "Hop in back," and we were on our way. The heat and dust of the afternoon roadside was laying thickly on our sun-weathered skins as we bounced happily along, the view unreeling in reverse as we weaved our way along the coastal highway towards Kona, our destination. As we rounded a sharp turn and descended steeply toward a valley, a storm suddenly struck. The wind blew, and it held a wash of rain; but the rain seemed to come backward, more from the land than the sky . . . *up the hill* and toward us. It held the scent of those fields that were full of sugarcane. Like moving wet incense, it enveloped us in its sweetness. It felt like a kiss—a rainy, sweet, sugar-scented kiss from this land of volcanoes, rainbows, waterfalls, kings, queens, and fables.

 The molasses contained in the marinade is derived from sugarcane. You can substitute duck or chicken breasts for the quail, if you prefer, and you can scatter diced avocado and tiny cherry tomatoes around the base of the tortilla stack. The marinade works well for lathering birds for the backyard grill, and also for smoking birds in your home smoker before finishing them off on the grill.

MARINADE

1/4 cup dark molasses

2 tablespoons Spanish sherry vinegar, or apple cider vinegar

1 tablespoon fresh lemon juice

2 tablespoons Creole mustard, or whole-grain mustard

1/4 cup tomato sauce

1 small clove garlic, minced

1/2 Scotch bonnet or habanero chile, or 1 serrano, seeded and minced

1/8 teaspoon cayenne

1/4 teaspoon minced ginger

1/4 teaspoon orange zest

3 sprigs thyme

Pinch of nutmeg

4 semi-boneless quail

2/3 cup The Redlands Tropical Fruit Chutney (page 230), optional

VINAIGRETTE

1/4 cup Spanish sherry wine vinegar

1 tablespoon balsamic vinegar

3/4 cup virgin olive oil

1/4 cup extra-virgin olive oil

8 sage leaves, minced

Salt and black pepper to taste

1/4 cup peanut oil, for frying

3 blue (or yellow) corn tortillas, cut into quarters

4 small single handfuls mixed lettuces, cleaned, spun dry, and cut in ribbons or chiffonade

1/4 cup sour cream (optional)

Mix the marinade ingredients in a bowl. Add the quail and marinate overnight.

Prepare the grill (or use a grill pan). Remove the quail from the marinade, and transfer the marinade to a saucepan. Reduce over medium heat until $\frac{1}{4}$ cup remains, about 5 to 7 minutes, and strain into a bowl.

Grill the quail for about 12 minutes, turning occasionally. When cool enough to handle, remove the meat from the bones and cut into small dice. Add to the reduced marinade.

Prepare the chutney.

To prepare the vinaigrette: Whisk all the ingredients together in a bowl and chill until needed.

In a small nonstick pan, heat the marinade and quail together, and keep warm.

Heat the peanut oil in a skillet and fry the tortillas in batches, until crisp. Drain on paper towels and keep warm. Place a tortilla quarter in the center of a serving plate. Spoon over some of the warm quail mixture, and then add another tortilla quarter and more quail on top. Add another tortilla, more quail mixture, and top with a fourth tortilla quarter. Repeat for the remaining tortillas on the other serving plates.

Dress the lettuce in just enough of the vinaigrette to coat it. Mound in a high arch over the middle of the tortillas. Serve with dollops of the chutney and sour cream.

Jerked Chicken with Ripped Lettuces, Raw Mango, Hot Chiles, and Sweet Onions

Yield: 6 to 8 servings.

Jerked chicken and jerked pork have hit mainstream American restaurant menus over the past few years. They rarely have the punch you'll experience in a Jamaican restaurant! This one does, though.

 The jerk marinade can be used to make a hot chicken dinner too. Just add the side dishes you're in the mood for.

JERK MARINADE

1/4 cup allspice berries

1 cinnamon stick (1 inch long)

1 teaspoon freshly grated nutmeg

2 Scotch bonnet or habanero chiles, seeded

1/2 red onion, chopped

1/2 cup chopped scallions, green and white parts

3 cloves garlic, roughly chopped

3 tablespoons minced ginger

1 tablespoon thyme leaves

1 tablespoon sugar

1 tablespoon soy sauce

2 tablespoons Worcestershire sauce

3 tablespoons fresh lime juice

1/4 cup dark rhum

1 frying chicken, cut into 8 bone-in pieces

Salt and black pepper to taste

3 tablespoons peanut oil

VINAIGRETTE

1/3 cup champagne vinegar

1/4 cup honey

3 cloves garlic, minced

1 teaspoon yellow mustard seeds

1 teaspoon Coleman's English dry mustard

1/4 cup Creole mustard or whole-grain mustard

1/4 cup minced basil leaves

1/2 teaspoon salt

2 teaspoons black pepper

3/4 cup sour cream

1/2 cup buttermilk

1/2 cup heavy cream

SALAD

3 to 4 double handfuls of mixed lettuces, such as romaine, red leaf, radicchio, bibb, Belgian endive, and curly endive

1 cup large-dice mango

1 cup large-dice Vidalia or other sweet onion

3/4 cup large-dice ripe avocado

2 jalapeño chiles, seeded and minced

To prepare the jerk marinade: Toast the allspice in a dry skillet over medium-high heat until warm and fragrant, about 30 seconds. Transfer to a spice grinder and grind with the cinnamon. Put the ground allspice and cinnamon in a food processor and add the remaining jerk ingredients. Blend until smooth.

Season the chicken pieces with salt and pepper and then rub all over with the jerk marinade. Place in a dish and refrigerate for at least 4 hours or overnight.

Preheat the oven to 425 degrees. Heat a dry heavy ovenproof skillet and add the peanut oil. Remove the chicken from the jerk marinade, taking care to leave as much of the marinade on the chicken as possible. Sear the chicken skin side down over medium-high heat for 2 minutes.

Turn the chicken skin side up and roast in the oven for 20 to 25 minutes. Remove the breasts to a plate, and continue to roast the legs and thighs for 15 more minutes. Remove them from the oven and let cool with the breasts. Slice the chicken meat from the bones in bite-sized pieces and reserve, covered, in a bowl. Chill until needed.

To prepare the vinaigrette: Mix together the vinegar, honey, garlic, mustard seeds, dry mustard, Creole mustard, basil leaves, salt, and pepper in a nonreactive bowl. Whisk in the sour cream. Then whisk in the buttermilk, and then the cream. Cover and keep chilled.

To prepare the salad: Put the lettuces in a large bowl and amply coat with the reserved vinaigrette. Add the reserved chicken, mango, onion, avocado, and jalapeños. Toss together and season with more salt and pepper if desired.

Snapper Escabeche Ensalada with Salsa Romesco, Arbequine Olives, Avocado, Oranges, and Ribbons of Greens

Yield: 4 to 6 servings.

There are many kinds of Florida snapper; I like the delicate yellowtail variety, which has a nice texture. The thicker red and mutton snapper will take a little longer to marinate. Choose whichever is freshest. The small black Arbequine olives, from Arbeca in Catalonia, are among the best I've ever tasted. They are so delicate that you may not notice their exquisite flavor immediately, but you soon will.

 The spice rub works magic with fish when you want to "cure" it, and I've also found it to be an effective, quick way to season poultry or pork for grilling or roasting.

Escabeche Spice Rub That Cures (*see recipe*)

FISH

1 to 1 1/4 pounds boneless, skinless snapper fillets

MARINADE

3 cloves garlic, thinly sliced

1/2 red onion, thinly sliced

1/2 bunch cilantro leaves, torn

1/2 cup gold tequila

1/4 cup Spanish sherry wine vinegar

1/4 cup fresh lime juice

1/4 cup fresh orange juice

1/4 cup virgin olive oil

1 to 1 1/2 tablespoons peanut or canola oil

1/2 cup Salsa Romesco (page 220), optional

VINAIGRETTE AND GREENS

1/2 cup fresh orange juice

1/4 teaspoon salt, or to taste

1/4 cup Spanish sherry vinegar

1 cup virgin olive oil

1/4 cup extra-virgin olive oil

2 shallots, thinly sliced

Black pepper to taste

4 small handfuls mixed lettuce, such as romaine, red leaf, radicchio, bibb, Belgian endive, or curly endive, cut into ribbons or chiffonade

2 Valencia or navel oranges, sectioned

1 avocado, peeled, pitted, and sliced

20 to 24 Arbequine (black) olives, pitted or not, as desired

Prepare the spice rub. Lay the snapper on a flat dish. Rub the fish on one side only with the spice rub. Set aside and allow to cure for at least 30 minutes and up to 2 hours.

Combine all the marinade ingredients together in a nonreactive mixing bowl. Set aside in a cool place.

Heat a nonstick or well-seasoned cast-iron pan and add the peanut or canola oil. When the oil is hot and just begins to smoke, add the fillets and sear for 15 seconds on each side. Transfer the fillets to a plate and let cool.

Add the fish to the marinade, cover, and refrigerate. Let marinate for 1 to 3 hours, depending on the thickness of the fish.

Prepare the salsa.

To prepare the vinaigrette: Heat the orange juice in a small heavy saucepan over high heat and reduce to $1/4$ cup. Put the salt in a large mixing bowl, add the vinegar and reduced orange juice, and whisk together. Add the oils, shallots, and pepper, and whisk together thoroughly. Reserve until ready to dress and serve the greens.

Toss the lettuce with the reserved vinaigrette in a bowl, and mound on cool serving plates. Remove the fish from the marinade and neatly slice into fingers. Arrange around the lettuce with the orange sections, avocado, and olives. Dot intermittently with the Salsa Romesco, and serve.

ESCABECHE SPICE RUB *THAT CURES*

Yield: 1 $1/2$ tablespoons.

$1/2$ tablespoon cumin seeds

$1/2$ tablespoon black peppercorns

$1/4$ tablespoon sugar

$1/4$ tablespoon salt

Put the cumin and peppercorns in a dry skillet and toast over medium heat until fragrant and slightly smoking, about 30 seconds to 1 minute. Transfer to a spice grinder and pulverize until not quite finely ground. Place in a bowl, add the sugar and salt, and mix together.

Six O'Clock Cuban Bread Salad with Tomatoes, Herbs, and Tetilla in an Orange-Sherry Vinaigrette

Yield: 4 servings.

I discuss why the bread is called "Six O'Clock" on page 233. The other item in the title you may not be famil-iar with is *tetilla*—a mild cow's milk cheese that originates in the Spanish province of Galicia. It is distin-guished by a slight touch of salt flavor. You can substitute a mild Jack or Muenster cheese.

 You can "pinwheel" a variety of salad options such as olives, avocado spears, red and yellow cherry tomatoes, grilled-chilled mushrooms, or hard-boiled eggs around the let-tuces.

¹/₄ cup Spanish olive oil

*4 slices Six O'Clock Cumin Cuban Bread
(page 233), or other Cuban or French bread,
¹/₂ inch thick and cut into 2 × 3-inch rectangles*

*¹/₄ cup of mixed fresh herbs, such as sage,
rosemary, basil, and thyme (leaves only)*

*1 vine-ripened tomato, cut into 4 slices,
¹/₄ inch thick*

Salt and black pepper to taste

*¹/₄ cup shredded Spanish tetilla cheese, or any
mild cheese such as Muenster, Jack, or
mozzarella*

*4 small single handfuls mixed lettuces, such as
romaine, red leaf, radicchio, bibb, Belgian
endive, or curly endive*

VINAIGRETTE

¹/₂ cup fresh orange juice

Pinch of salt

¹/₄ cup Spanish sherry vinegar

1 cup virgin olive oil

¹/₄ cup extra-virgin olive oil

1 teaspoon freshly toasted and ground cumin

*1 teaspoon freshly toasted and ground black
pepper*

Preheat the oven to 400 degrees. Heat 2 tablespoons of the olive oil in a cast-iron skillet and sauté the bread on both sides over medium-high heat until it is nicely golden. Remove the bread from the pan and wipe the pan with paper towels to remove any oil.

Return the bread slices to the pan and lay the herbs on top of the bread. Layer the tomatoes

on top of the herbs and season with the salt and pepper. Mound the cheese on top of the tomatoes and drizzle the remaining 2 tablespoons of olive oil over the cheese. Place the pan in the oven and allow the cheese to melt, about 5 minutes. When melted, remove the skillet and set aside.

To prepare the vinaigrette: Place the orange juice in a small heavy saucepan and reduce to ¼ cup. Place the salt in a mixing bowl and add the reduced orange juice and vinegar. Whisk together and add the oils, cumin, and pepper. Whisk again and adjust the seasoning to taste.

Place the lettuces in a salad bowl and dress with the vinaigrette. Arrange each warm open-faced Cuban bread sandwich in the center of a serving plate. Mound the dressed lettuces over the sandwich and serve.

Salpicón of Everglades Alligator with Greens, Vegetables, Blue Cheese, Avocado, and Teardrop Tomatoes

Yield: 4 servings.

This is not a Kiplingesque story of how another reptile acquires tears, but about salpicones and their lively spirit. One definition for the word *salpicón* traces its derivation from the Spanish words for salt (*sal*) and to cut (*picar*). Another definitive source tells me it means "hodgepodge" and "splashed" or "spattered." In either case, you will find, in Spanish cookery, meat, fish, and shellfish salpicones with plenty of vegetables, herbs, and spices added for flavor and texture.

Alligator is making inroads into broader markets. It's most often frozen, which isn't all bad news. Alligator meat deteriorates rapidly if sold fresh, *but not fresh enough*. Reputable alligator farmers freeze it immediately after it's cleaned and dressed—usually in 5-pound bags. I defrost the bag in the refrigerator overnight and make arrangements with friends to split it up. The flavor is somewhat sweet, though the texture can be tough—not too surprising for a creature that looks like this one does! No major problem. We just pound it like conch meat or veal scallopine and *make* it tame.

 You can substitute chicken, rabbit loin, or pork tenderloin for the alligator. Other vegetables you can add to the salpicón are thinly sliced red or yellow bell peppers, red onions, cooked potatoes, or cooked artichoke bottoms.

ALLIGATOR

4 alligator tenderloins, about 2 to 3 ounces each

Salt and black pepper to taste

1 tablespoon fresh lime juice

3 tablespoons fresh orange juice

1 tablespoon olive oil

VINAIGRETTE

1 cup virgin olive oil

4 teaspoons red wine vinegar

2 tablespoons Spanish sherry vinegar

4 teaspoons chopped tarragon

2 teaspoons Creole mustard or whole-grain mustard

2 large cloves garlic, minced

Salt and black pepper to taste

12 asparagus spears, trimmed

1 Scotch bonnet or habanero chile, or 2 serranos, seeded and minced

$1/4$ cup flour

1 egg

$1/4$ cup half-and-half

$1/2$ tablespoon canola oil

4 small single handfuls of mixed greens, washed and spun dry, cut into ribbons or chiffonade

$1/2$ cucumber, cut in half lengthwise and thinly sliced

GARNISH

12 teardrop tomatoes, cut in half, or cherry tomatoes, quartered

12 small slices ripe avocado

2 ounces blue cheese, preferably a good-quality Gorgonzola, crumbled

Cut the alligator at the thick end of the tenderloin in a butterfly cut. Make one or two more incisions lengthwise as this will help make pounding easier. Season with salt and pepper. Mix the citrus juices, oil, and the chile in a flat nonreactive dish. Add the alligator and roll it over a few times to thoroughly coat. Cover and refrigerate for 2 to 4 hours.

Remove the marinated alligator and pat dry. Place between 2 sheets of plastic wrap on a work surface and pound it as thinly as you can without tearing it. Place the flour on a large plate and mix with salt and pepper. Dust the alligator on both sides in this mixture. In a bowl, mix the egg with the half-and-half. Dip the alligator in the mixture and set aside in the refrigerator until ready to cook.

Whisk together the vinaigrette ingredients in a small bowl. Blanch the asparagus in a pan of boiling water until al dente, about 30 seconds to 1 minute. Transfer to a bowl of ice water and shock for 30 seconds. Drain on paper towels and keep chilled.

Heat a nonstick sauté pan, add the canola oil, and when hot, carefully lay the alligator in the pan. Sauté over medium-high heat for 1½ to 2 minutes per side, or until golden. Drain on paper towels.

Toss the greens and cucumber slices with the vinaigrette and season to taste. Arrange 3 asparagus spears on each plate like spokes, with the tips pointing to the outside (cut the base if necessary so they will fit on the plate). Arrange clusters of the garnish between the asparagus (one tomato, one slice of avocado, and some cheese between each spear), and drizzle with the vinaigrette. Place the alligator in the center of the plates, covering the base of the asparagus. Top with the tossed greens and serve.

Vietnamese Soft Spring Rolls with Paw Paw Slaw and Peanut Dipping Sauce

Yield: 6 servings.

This striking dish is built around the amazingly versatile rice paper roll, which comes in all different shapes and sizes. Before too long, it wouldn't surprise me to see little kiosks in malls and on street corners next to the hot dog vendors, selling ten different varieties of spring rolls like these, as well as fried spring rolls. By the time that happens, though, you'll have been spoiled by these spring rolls and variations you will want to create using different ingredients or sauces.

 Paw paw is a Caribbean term for papaya (the North American pawpaw fruit is not related). The slaw recipe yields about 2 cups and goes well with a wide variety of Asian dishes as well as Western ones such as grilled chicken or cornmeal-crusted fried fish. Japanese wheat flour somen noodles, the round rice wrappers, and the yaki nori are all available from Oriental stores. For the most dramatic presentation, serve this dish on simple, plain white or black plates.

PAW PAW SLAW

1 tablespoon sugar

2 tablespoons fresh lime juice

1 clove garlic, minced

1 tablespoon minced cilantro leaves

¹/₂ tablespoon hot chile sauce (preferably Sriracha)

2 tablespoons Oriental fish sauce

1 medium carrot, julienned

¹/₂ cup julienned jicama

¹/₂ green papaya, peeled, seeded, and julienned

¹/₂ Granny Smith apple, peeled, cored, and julienned

Peanut Dipping Sauce (see recipe)

Ponzu Dipping Sauce (see recipe)

SPRING ROLLS

1 cup cooked somen noodles

3 tablespoons dark roasted sesame oil

2 tablespoons peanut oil

1 cup julienned mixed vegetables, such as carrots, blanched asparagus, daikon, mushrooms, bell peppers, blanched snow peas, or cabbage

6 round bánh tráng rice wrappers, 8¹/₂ inches across

2 sheets yaki nori (dried seaweed), cut into strips about ¹/₂ inch wide and 4 inches long

Wasabi paste, to taste

To prepare the slaw: Stir the sugar and lime juice together in a mixing bowl until the sugar dissolves. Add the garlic, cilantro, chile sauce, and fish sauce, and mix together to make a dressing. Place the carrot, jicama, green papaya, and apple in a separate mixing bowl, and combine. Add the dressing to the vegetable-fruit mixture, toss together, and chill until needed.

Prepare the peanut and ponzu dipping sauces.

To prepare the spring rolls: Rinse the cooked noodles under cold running water, drain thoroughly, and toss in a bowl with the sesame oil. Heat the peanut oil in a wok over medium-high heat and stirfry the mixed vegetables. When almost cooked, add 5 tablespoons of the ponzu sauce.

Transfer the mixture to a colander set over a bowl to catch the liquid. Return the liquid to the wok and reduce it over medium-high heat to a thick consistency. Pour over the vegetables to coat and let cool.

On a deep platter or in a baking dish, pour enough lukewarm water to come $1/8$ inch up the sides. Place one rice wrapper at a time in the water until it softens and becomes pliable, about 2 to 4 minutes. Transfer the first wrapper to a work surface and pat dry. Lay 2 of the nori strips in a crisscross pattern on the middle one-third of the wrapper. Place one-eighth of the noodles in a horizontal line over the nori, and some of the vegetables on top of the noodles. Fold the top third of the wrapper over this mixture. Fold in both ends and then roll up the wrapper. Reserve the filled spring rolls between slightly moist toweling in the refrigerator. Repeat for the remaining wrappers.

To serve, drain the slaw slightly and mound in the center of serving plates. Transfer the dipping sauce to shot glasses or small Oriental teacups and set toward the top of each plate. Cut off the very ends of each spring roll and cut in the center at a diagonal. Stand the two halves upright at the bottom of each plate. Serve with the wasabi and chopsticks, but encourage your guests to use their hands too!

PEANUT DIPPING SAUCE

Yield: about 1⅓ cups.

For a spicier version, use Norman's Hot 'n' Nasty Nuts (page 13).

¼ *cup dark brown sugar*

⅓ *cup sherry*

2 *teaspoons balsamic vinegar*

2½ *tablespoons mirin*

1 clove garlic, minced

1 tablespoon minced ginger

1 jalapeño chile, seeded and minced

⅓ *cup soy sauce*

1 teaspoon hot chile sauce (preferably Sriracha)

1 cup Spanish peanuts, toasted and skins left on

Place the sugar, sherry, balsamic vinegar, mirin, garlic, ginger, and jalapeño in a food processor, and pulse. Add the soy sauce, chile sauce, and peanuts, and pulse again to a slightly chunky consistency. Reserve until needed.

PONZU DIPPING SAUCE

Yield: about 2½ cups.

Ponzu is a citrusy, tangy sauce used in Japan for sashimi and for fish and seafood dishes. It can be bought bottled in Asian stores.

½ *cup ponzu sauce*

¼ *cup fresh lemon juice*

¾ *cup plus 2 tablespoons fresh orange juice*

2 *tablespoons dark roasted sesame oil*

2 *tablespoons mirin*

2 *tablespoons unseasoned rice wine vinegar*

¼ *cup tamari, or light soy sauce*

½ *tablespoon hot chile sauce (preferably Sriracha)*

3 *tablespoons minced ginger*

1 bunch (5 or 6) scallions, finely sliced

Mix all of the ingredients in a mixing bowl and reserve until needed.

CHAPTER 5
ANCHORS AWEIGH!
FISH AND SHELLFISH

Rhum and Pepper–Painted Grouper with a
Mango-Habanero Mojo and Sweet Panfried Plantains

"Mile Marker 19" Grilled Dolphin Fish with Olive Oil–Roasted New Potatoes,
Caramelized Red Onions, and Anchovy Butter

Grilled Florida Spiny Lobster with an Exotic Fruit–Black Bean Salsa and a
Spicy Cumin Seed Drizzle

Grilled Gulf Swordfish with Big Twist Barbecue Butter and Alligator Pears

Cuban Cookshack Lobster Enchilada with Criolla Tomato Mama

Whole Roasted Pompano with Lemon Butter, Roasted Beets, and Beet Greens

Buttered Snapper Baked in a Banana Leaf with a "Steam" of Clams,
Boniato, Bonnets, Saffron, and Garlic

Hibachi Tuna with Asian "Au Jus" and an Oriental Mushroom Salsa

Pan-Cooked Fillet of Key West Yellowtail with a "Belly" of Mashed Potatoes

Lapsang Souchong Tea and Shallot–Stuffed Salmon Spirals on Sauce Mer Noir

Yuca-Crusted Florida Striped Bass with Florida Sweet Corn

It was only nine o'clock in the morning, but Warren felt like having a drink. Fishing didn't allow for regular hours. Up most of the night, trying to sleep some during the day on a pitching boat beneath the sun; it took a while to settle into a normal routine once you were back on land. Besides, he liked Sloppy Joe's early in the morning. It was quiet, not many tourists, a few fishermen nursing hangovers, and he could sit at the big horseshoe bar and catch the breeze from the wide-open doors and the overhead fans without being blasted by the amplified music that would bring people off the streets later in the day.

He'd have a couple of Bloodys, and then maybe wander up to Shorty's for breakfast before going to the fish house and getting to work on his traps.

He drove the battered pickup through the rain, the fallen red petals from the big poinciana trees squishing beneath his tires, their roots buckling the sidewalk. It was a damn pretty town, and he had always liked it, but it could wear you down. You had to be strong to survive here, or else you found yourself living on a curb along Caroline Street sharing a bottle of Thunderbird if you didn't know when it was time to get out. Maybe now was the time.

—John Leslie, *Blood on the Keys, 1988*

The traders came directly across those waters, fast in the wake of the explorers. They boldly guided their sailing merchant ships past Central America (there was no Panama Canal), down, down, down around the Horn and west, thousands of open sea miles past Hawaii, to the islands they named the Philippines for their Iberian king, beyond again to China . . . and back!

On the way back, they stopped in many of the places in which they had dropped anchor on the way west, and the foods they carried and the way these foods were prepared were scattered like seeds everywhere they went. In those seeds were the genesis of a New World Cuisine.

As the agricultural economies of the Sugar Years waned during the Reconstruction period of the late 1800s in the Caribbean and the Gulf states, many of the women remained in the business of sharecropping while the men took increasingly to the sea, rivers, and lakes to make a living. Fishing and shellfishing in this geographic region, as elsewhere, passed down from father to son, generation to generation. They worked from rustic craft or from the protuberance of piers. Their hooks and nets harvested conch, crabs, grouper, yellowtail, spiny lobsters, shrimp, scallops, clams, snapper, turtles, tuna, swordfish, jewfish, kingfish, dolphin fish, grunts, cobia, wahoo, scamp, snook, and many more. Many of the techniques that fed families in the early part of the twentieth century have changed, but the circadian rhythms of fishermen and fisherboys, moon and tides remain.

Apart from these changes, the most obvious differences over time have occurred in the cooking methods and integration of recipes as reflected through the polyglot and multi-cultural prism of the populations that have made their home in this country. Vietnamese and other Southeast Asian fishing folk comprise a new seaborne nation out on the Gulf and in the Florida shore towns. Their traditional foods and ingredients influence many chefs and home cooks. Ginger, soy, lemongrass, kaffir limes, sticky rice, chile pastes, and coconut milk speckle New World menus as certainly as we were once dominated by hush puppies, black-eyed peas, and fritters. The ingredients and recipes of home cooks from Jamaica to Peru are now becoming increasingly available to cookbook readers and modern travelers. The big benefit of these new styles, after flavor, is health. Battering and deep-frying, mayonnaises, gravies, creams, and butters are being pushed aside by stir-frying and light, tasty dipping sauces.

Fish is getting respect. Beautiful, pristine seafood straight out of Mother Nature's waters inspires me and sets me into motion like few other moments. I absolutely love to hear it when one of my chefs calls out, "Yo! Fish Man's here!"

In a number of the recipes that follow, I call for sauces containing cream or butter. These complement the flavors and textures of the fish, rounding out the dish. However, feel free to substitute any appropriate salsa from Chapter 9.

Rhum and Pepper–Painted Grouper with a Mango-Habanero Mojo and Sweet Panfried Plantains

Yield: 4 servings.

I think many a chef darkly imagines, from time to time, that there is one recipe title of a signature dish that may go on his or her tombstone, just under the name. Here's mine. Garnished with flowers, perhaps?

Probably the first Cuban food that I tasted, in a tiny café in Key West, was sweet panfried plantains. This experience was on my fateful trip in '71 that rang the big bell in my taste buds' alarm box, and set me on the culinary course I now travel. So simple, so pleasurable. It is key to use what the Cubans refer to as "maduro plantains," which are very black and ripe, and bursting with natural fruit sugar. This dish is a perfect example of balancing heat and sweet.

 Keep an eye on the plantains as they get close to done, because they will burn easily if unattended. As an alternative side dish, I would suggest the Caramelized Plantain Mash en Relleno (page 188) which appears in the photograph.

2 cups Mango-Habanero Mojo (page 227)

SWEET PANFRIED PLANTAINS

1 teaspoon black pepper

$^1/_4$ teaspoon salt

$^1/_2$ teaspoon freshly toasted and ground cumin

$^1/_4$ teaspoon ground cinnamon

2 very ripe plantains, peeled and cut into $^1/_4$-inch-thick slices at a diagonal

Vegetable oil, for frying

$^3/_4$ cup Rhum and Pepper Paint (see recipe)

4 black grouper fillets, about 8 ounces each, or dolphin fish (mahi mahi), or red snapper

1 tablespoon peanut oil

4 lime wedges, for garnish

Prepare the mojo.

To prepare the plantains: Combine the pepper, salt, cumin, and cinnamon in a small mixing bowl. Lay the plantain slices on a cutting board and sprinkle on one side only with the spice mix. Heat $^1/_8$ inch of vegetable oil in a sauté pan or skillet over medium-high heat. Place the plantains, spice side down, into the hot oil, and cook for $1^1/_2$ to $2^1/_2$ minutes per side, or until they turn golden brown to slightly black. Remove the plantains from the pan and transfer to a plate lined with paper towels. Keep warm.

Prepare the paint. Preheat the oven to 450 degrees. Spread the paint liberally on the curved side of the fillets. Heat a large cast-iron skillet until almost smoking. Add the peanut oil and carefully lay the fish in the skillet, paint side down. Shake the pan a few times to prevent the fish from sticking. Cook the fish until dark on the painted side, about 2 minutes. Turn the fish over and drain the oil from the skillet. Transfer the skillet to the oven and bake for 7 to 9 minutes.

Warm the mojo through and ladle about ¹/₂ cup onto each serving plate. Remove the fish from the oven and place the fillets on top of the mojo. Serve with the plantains and a wedge of lime.

RHUM AND PEPPER PAINT

Yield: about ¹/₄ cup.

2 teaspoons black peppercorns

4 whole cloves

2 ¹/₂ tablespoons sugar

¹/₄ cup soy sauce

¹/₄ cup white rhum

1 tablespoon grated lemon zest

2 teaspoons fresh lemon juice

Toast the peppercorns and cloves together in a dry skillet over medium-high heat until puffs of smoke begin to appear, about 1 minute. Transfer to a spice grinder and grind roughly.

Place the sugar, soy sauce, rhum, lemon zest, and juice in a small heavy saucepan, and add the powdered spices. Over medium heat, reduce the liquid until ¹/₄ cup remains, about 10 to 12 minutes; it will begin to foam as it reduces.

Remove the pan from the heat and strain through a fine-mesh strainer into a bowl. Let cool to room temperature.

"Mile Marker 19" Grilled Dolphin Fish with Olive Oil–Roasted New Potatoes, Caramelized Red Onions, and Anchovy Butter

Yield: 4 servings.

As you drive down the fabled Florida Keys highway, U.S. 1, you begin to notice (when not caught off guard by the sudden vast expanses of sun-speckled water) little green road markers. They count down the miles you still have left to cover before bawdy old Key West, or, if you choose, some point of idyllic repose in the still laid-back Middle Keys. Some of our friends and family still work in Key West but now live up in sanctuaries off the tourist-busy "Rock." They call us and ask when we're coming back home and giving up the pulsating pace of our lives in Miami. For now, we satisfy our own occasional longing for that peaceful past with a trip to Mile Marker 19 and some sweet dolphin fish cooked over an open fire, where the salt smell of the ocean commingles with the scent of smoke, citrus, anchovy, and sweet onions.

 Dolphin fish is not to be confused with Flipper; it's not the squeaky mammal but a square-headed warm-water fish also known as dorado and mahimahi. I use this marinade for meatier fish and shellfish, such as swordfish, tuna, grouper, salmon, shrimp, and spiny lobster, as well as dolphin fish. It also helps prevent the fish from sticking to the grill.

Macho Fish Marinade (see recipe)

Olive Oil–Roasted New Potatoes (page 196)

Caramelized Red Onions (page 206)

*4 boneless dolphin fish (mahimahi) fillets, about
8 ounces each*

ANCHOVY BUTTER

4 ounces butter, diced and allowed to soften

4 anchovy fillets, rinsed well and minced

1 teaspoon fresh lemon juice

Black pepper to taste

Prepare the marinade.

Prepare the potatoes and caramelized onions.

Prepare the grill. When you're about 20 minutes away from dinnertime, put the dolphin fish in the marinade and let it sit for 10 minutes, turning once or twice.

Meanwhile, to prepare the anchovy butter, mash all the ingredients together in a bowl with a fork.

Remove the fillets from the marinade and grill for 4 minutes on the first side and 2 minutes on the other side. Transfer the fish to serving plates. Mound the onions on top of the fish and spoon some of the anchovy butter on top of the onions. Serve with the potatoes.

MACHO FISH MARINADE

Yield: about 2 cups.

$3/4$ cup olive oil

$1/4$ cup light soy sauce

1 orange, cut in half

1 lemon, cut in half

1 lime, cut in half

2 bay leaves

12 black peppercorns, toasted and crushed

$1/2$ bulb fennel, thinly sliced

$1/2$ red onion, thinly sliced

6 cloves garlic, thinly sliced

1-inch length of ginger, peeled and thinly sliced

2 or 3 sprigs thyme

Pour the olive oil and soy into a large mixing bowl. Squeeze in the juice of the orange, lemon, and lime, and toss in the squeezed rinds.

Add the remaining ingredients and mix well. Set aside.

Grilled Florida Spiny Lobster with an Exotic Fruit–Black Bean Salsa and a Spicy Cumin Seed Drizzle

Yield: 4 servings.

This dish inspires a special Key West memory for me. Back in '89, *Bon Appétit* magazine came down to do a story, and spent the first two days shooting some pictures of the restaurant (Louie's Backyard) and some of my signature dishes, including this one. My favorite shot was the last one they took. It was after a long morning and afternoon of setups, waiting for the light and the everyday restaurant action of running lunch and dinner. I was in this one, in my chef whites with my pant legs rolled up toward my knees, sitting on my brand-new cherry-red motorcycle. The Florida Gulf sky was just slipping into her dusky evening dress behind me. I cradled a tall rhum drink in one hand and waited as the photographer did his work. The ocean was less than ten feet behind me, lapping up gently on the little coral rock and sandy area we called Dog Beach. Diners were just beginning to walk up the wooden steps into the restaurant, and after the lens clicked for a final time I took a moment, took a long drink from the rhum, set it down, got off the bike, and moved to a palm tree. I leaned into its curve, pushed the cooling sand back and forth for a moment with my bare feet, and listened…to the water, to the relaxed laughter of guests sitting down to dinner, and to the late December evening breeze cooling off the heat of another day on that little rock at the end of America. *Then,* I was ready to go in and ride the range for the next 5 hours. This is the dish I cooked for many of our guests who came to dine that evening.

 I think of clawless, warm-water spiny lobsters as really big shrimp rather than comparable to rich, sweet cold-water Maine lobsters. It's a whole 'nother animal, but for the purposes of this dish, they can be substituted. For added presentation, you can keep the lobster tail shell on; to keep it straight while grilling, insert a presoaked wooden skewer through the back inside portion of the shell. A wonderful but optional side dish is the Sweet Potato–Sweet Corn Home Fries *That Kick* (page 201).

MARINADE

¹/₄ cup minced Italian parsley

¹/₄ cup minced cilantro leaves

Juice of 1 lemon

Juice of 1 orange

¹/₄ cup dry Spanish sherry

¹/₄ cup virgin olive oil

¹/₂ cup fresh breadcrumbs

¹/₄ teaspoon ground mace

1 teaspoon hot paprika

¹/₂ teaspoon salt

1 tablespoon black pepper

4 spiny lobster tails, cut in half through the shell lengthwise and deveined

Spicy Cumin-Sichuan Drizzle (see recipe)

3 cups Exotic Tropical Fruit and Black Bean Salsa (page 222)

Mix all the marinade ingredients together in a large mixing bowl. Remove the lobster meat from the tails and place in the marinade. Cover and refrigerate for at least 6 hours for the fullest flavor.

Prepare the drizzle and the salsa.

Prepare the grill. When hot, oil the grill with a brush and cook the lobster through, turning occasionally, about 6 to 7 minutes. Transfer to a cutting board and cut the lobster into even slices, about ¹/₂ inch thick.

Spoon the salsa at the center of the serving plates. Lay the lobster slices around the salsa, spoon some of the drizzle around the edge of the plate, and serve.

SPICY CUMIN-SICHUAN DRIZZLE

Yield: about 1 cup.

¹/₄ cup cumin seeds, toasted and ground

¹/₂ teaspoon Sichuan peppercorns, toasted and ground

2 cups Dark Chicken Stock (page 271)

¹/₄ cup dark roasted sesame oil

¹/₄ cup honey

¹/₄ cup soy sauce

¹/₄ cup unseasoned rice wine vinegar

¹/₄ cup minced ginger

¹/₂ to 1 Scotch bonnet chile, or 1 or 2 serranos, cut in half lengthwise, with stems and seeds

Place all the ingredients in a heavy saucepan and bring to a boil over high heat. Lower the heat to medium-high and reduce for 10 minutes, stirring occasionally. Strain through a fine-mesh strainer back into the saucepan. Return to medium-high heat and reduce the liquid to 1 cup. Set aside.

Grilled Gulf Swordfish with Big Twist Barbecue Butter and Alligator Pears

Yield: 4 servings.

I dedicate this one to my all-time favorite barroom blues entertainer, the late "Big Twist." Twist was from Chicago, and he often came down to Sloppy Joe's Saloon in Key West and *rocked* the joint with his songs about life in the Windy City. Many great black bluesmen went to Chicago from the South in the thirties, forties, and fifties to escape the poverty and with hopes of hitting the big time. They brought with them their instruments, an absolute devotion to Jesus, and (in Twist's case) a universal faith in barbecue. It seems that Twist got "Big" because of his love of great 'cue. One of his memorable talking-bragging blues tunes related the story of a visit to the doctor, who told him the reason he was ailing was Twist's fondness for "*too much barbecue.*" Nearly mortally stung by the quack's advice, he left in a huff, and naturally, went out for some more cold drinks, hot sauce, and barbecue.

 Avocados are sometimes and colorfully known as alligator pears down in the islands. The Big Twist barbecue sauce is textured and fresh flavored, and you can keep it for 2 or 3 weeks; it also freezes well. It's worth making up a big batch if you're going to the trouble of smoking the tomatoes, although you don't *have* to smoke the tomatoes. You can make it spicier by adding some bottled hot sauce or more Scotch bonnets to the Bean Kit. You can use another smoky, spicy, and not-too-sweet barbecue sauce instead of the Big Twist, but add some peeled, seeded, and diced tomatoes. If you are defrosting some of the Big Twist sauce, add a little heavy cream to regain the desired consistency, as defrosting can cause the tomato juices to "weep," making the butter looser than desired.

Optional side dishes for this recipe are my *South* American Fries (page 194) or some homemade crispy fries.

Big Twist Barbecue Sauce (see recipe)

4 swordfish steaks, trimmed (about 7 to 8 ounces each)

1 tablespoon olive oil

Salt and black pepper to taste

Caramelized Red Onions (page 206)

2 tablespoons heavy cream

6 ounces butter, cut into small dice and kept cold

1/2 ripe avocado, pitted, peeled, and cut into 8 thin slices

1 lemon or lime, cut into wedges, for garnish

Prepare the barbecue sauce.

Put the swordfish steaks on a large plate and brush both sides with the olive oil. Season on both sides with salt and pepper. Set aside in the refrigerator.

Prepare the caramelized onions and keep warm.

Prepare the grill.

Place the cream and 1 cup of the barbecue sauce in a saucepan and bring to a simmer over medium heat. When the mixture begins to bubble, gradually whisk in the butter, piece by piece, until it is all incorporated. Season to taste with salt and pepper and keep warm.

Remove the swordfish steaks from the refrigerator and grill for 3 to 4 minutes on the first side and 2 to 3 minutes on the second side. Transfer the swordfish to warm serving plates and spoon some of the sauce around the fish. Place the onions on top of the swordfish and crisscross 2 slices of avocado over the onions on each plate. Garnish with a lemon or lime wedge and serve.

BIG TWIST BARBECUE SAUCE

Yield: about 3 cups.

6 tomatoes. cored and cut in half crosswise

Salt and black pepper to taste

6 tablespoons Spanish sherry vinegar

$1/4$ recipe Bean Kit (page 280)

Prepare the smoker, or use a very low fire with wood chips in a grill. Place the tomatoes, cut side up, in a flat non-reactive dish. Season each tomato half with salt, pepper and $1/2$ teaspoon of the vinegar (you will use 2 tablespoons of vinegar). Smoke the tomatoes for 1 hour, until soft and *really* smoky. Let cool.

Remove the seeds and skins from the tomatoes and place in a bowl. Squeeze the tomatoes with your fingers into another bowl. Strain the liquid from the seeds and skins into the bowl holding the tomatoes, and discard the residue.

Transfer the tomato mixture to a large heavy saucepan, bring to a medium-high simmer, and reduce by about one-third or until quite concentrated, about 30 minutes, stirring occasionally.

Meanwhile, bring the bean kit to the "ready stage." Add the remaining 4 tablespoons vinegar and reduce for 15 to 30 seconds. Stir in the reduced smoked tomatoes, reduce the heat to low, and let the flavors marry for about 5 to 7 minutes. Turn off the heat and let cool.

Cuban Cookshack Lobster Enchilada with Criolla Tomato Mama

Yield: 4 servings.

My friend Maricel Presilla is a fountain of information regarding Latin-Afro cooking, language, and food history. I love to hear her talk and to watch her eyes as she describes the flavors of yuca dishes prepared by the descendants of Arawak Indians along the Orinoco in the Amazon basin, or how the wild guaguao chile, native to Cuba, was prevalent in dishes from that country in days when Cubans ate much spicier food than they do today. Their tastes, she explained, gradually came to resemble the more conservative palate of northern Spain. As a restaurant consultant, Maricel has figured prominently in putting the spice back in Cuban foods here in Miami and also in New York.

The Cuban dishes, *plátanos enchilados,* are not the same as the enchiladas we find in Mexican cooking, but the words and foodstuffs moved rapidly back and forth between Havana and Veracruz on the Spanish galleons that linked the economies of these two cities in the post-Columbian era. Maricel tells me that enchilados/enchiladas always mean chiles, bell peppers, onions, and tomatoes.

 If you prefer, you can remove the cooked lobster meat from the shell and slice it before serving.

4 cups Criolla Tomato Mama (page 52)

Annatto Red Rice (page 202)

4 spiny lobster tails, cut in half through the shell lengthwise and deveined, or 20 jumbo shrimp

Salt and black pepper to taste

1 lime, cut in half

2 tablespoons olive oil

2 tablespoons butter

Prepare the Criolla Mama and the red rice, and keep warm.

Season the lobster tails with salt and pepper and squeeze the lime over them. Heat a large, heavy sauté pan and add the olive oil and butter. When the butter begins to foam, add the lobster, flesh side down, and sauté over medium-high heat until it turns golden brown. Turn over and sauté until cooked through, about 3 to 4 minutes. Add the Criolla Mama, reduce the heat to medium, and cook for 1 to 2 minutes longer.

Place the rice in the center of each serving plate, and the lobster on top. Spoon the sauce around, and serve.

Whole Roasted Pompano with Lemon Butter, Roasted Beets, and Beet Greens

Yield: 4 servings.

In 1988, I had the extreme good fortune to meet and become friends with a special person and one of my heroes—the late Al McClane. Many people knew Al through his work as the author of *The Encyclopedia of Fish Cookery,* his role as editor of *Field and Stream,* or from his contributions to *Esquire.* Al could quote lengthy passages from the classics in his smoke-mellowed voice, and tell fishing and hunting stories from each and every continent. He knew life both in palaces and in pitched tents. Either one was fine with him as long as fishing was not too far away.

Al told me that pompano were "spooky fish" in the water. It was the way they moved. Sometimes they would "walk" around the boat in a semicircle and at other times, they would hurl themselves across the water like skipping stones. Once safely in the kitchen, however, pompano are considered the champagne of saltwater fish. They are found in the waters of Massachusetts south to Brazil, but are especially prevalent in the arc from the Carolinas to Florida and up into the Gulf of Mexico.

 The skin of the pompano has a delicate, rich sweetness and is one of the most delicious parts of the fish. Red snapper makes a good substitute in this recipe.

The "Fish Must Swim Twice" Marinade for Delicate Fish (see recipe)

4 pompano, heads on and cleaned, about 1 to 1 1/2 pounds each

4 beets, or 8 small beets, unpeeled and with their greens attached

Salt and black pepper to taste

LEMON-BUTTER SAUCE

1 lemon, rind and pith removed, quartered

1 cup dry white wine

1 tablespoon champagne vinegar

2 shallots, sliced

1 bay leaf, broken

2 sprigs thyme, roughly chopped

1/4 cup heavy cream

8 ounces butter, diced into small pieces and kept cold

Pinch of salt

1 teaspoon black pepper

2 tablespoons butter

2 shallots, finely sliced

1/4 cup fresh orange juice

2 lemon slices, cut in half, for garnish

Prepare the marinade. Cut 3 or 4 slashes in a crosshatch pattern on each side of the fish, add to the marinade, and let marinate for at least 1 hour and up to 6 hours, turning once or twice.

Remove the green tops from the beets, leaving about 1 inch of the stem remaining. Place the beets in a saucepan of cold water and bring to a boil. Simmer over medium-high heat until they are just cooked through and can be pierced with a knife, about 30 to 40 minutes. Drain the beets and rinse under cold running water. Let cool, peel, cut into halves or quarters, and reserve.

Wash the beet greens well and shake dry. Chop the larger stem portions and shred the greens into $^1/_4$-inch-wide strips. Wrap in a damp towel or in paper towels and keep refrigerated.

Meanwhile, preheat the oven to 450 degrees. Remove the pompano from the marinade, season with salt and pepper, and place in a nonstick baking pan. Bake the pompano in the oven for 35 minutes, basting several times with the marinade to deepen the flavor and make the skin crisper.

To prepare the lemon-butter sauce: Place the lemon quarters in a heavy nonreactive saucepan and add the wine, vinegar, shallots, bay leaf, and thyme. Reduce over medium-high heat until almost no liquid remains, about 12 to 15 minutes. Add the cream and reduce by half, about 2 minutes. Whisk in the 8 ounces of butter, piece by piece. When it is all incorporated, strain the sauce through a fine-mesh strainer and reserve. Season with the salt and pepper and keep warm.

Heat a saucepan and melt the 2 tablespoons of butter over medium-high heat. Add the shallots, stir, and sauté for 1 minute. Add the cooked beets, reserved beet greens, and orange juice, and season with salt and pepper. Cover and cook for 3 minutes.

Spoon some of the lemon butter down on one side of warm serving plates (serve the remaining lemon-butter sauce in a sauce boat on the side). Arrange some of the beet and beet green mixture on top of the butter. Lay the pompano next to the beets, cover each fish eye with a half slice of lemon, and serve.

"FISH MUST SWIM TWICE" MARINADE FOR DELICATE FISH

Yield: 1 to 1¼ cups.

This marinade is for our less assertively flavored swimmers such as pompano, snapper, sole, and flounder, or if I'm using a sauce that I want to be more "center stage." Grilling fish usually involves either oiling the grill or the fish so that it doesn't stick to the bars of the grill. This marinade supplies the nonstick.

¾ cup canola oil, olive oil, or peanut oil

1 orange

1 lemon

1 bay leaf, broken

6 black peppercorns, toasted and crushed

2 sprigs thyme

2 or 3 sprigs basil

Pour the oil into a large mixing bowl. Squeeze in the juice of the orange and lemon, and toss in the squeezed rinds. Add the remaining ingredients and whisk together.

Buttered Snapper Baked in a Banana Leaf with a "Steam" of Clams, Boniato, Bonnets, Saffron, and Garlic

Yield: 4 servings.

Long before cooking *en papillote* (steam-baking inside a parchment paper wrapping) or even "fish in a bag" were developed, natives of many Latin American and Asian countries were using the pliant natural wrapping that banana leaves provide to protect the delicate flavors and textures of their foods. Tamales are becoming increasingly familiar in the United States, and this dish is designed along the same lines, using banana leaves instead of corn husks as a wrapping to keep the fish moist, light, and flavorful. As with tamales, the wrapper is not eaten. Outside the leaf, this recipe offers a melange of flavors. "Steam" is the old Key West term for a stew, and there are local recipes for "steams" of chicken, conch, and turtle. The "chorus" of garlic, chiles, clam liquor, herbs, and saffron make a great dipping broth for the fish, while the boniato gives it a sweet body.

 You can buy banana leaves in Latin American or Asian grocery stores. They're often frozen in 1 pound packages. Just soak the leaves in warm water and wipe them dry before using, and cut out any woody stem. For a simpler dinner, just cook the fish with a simple side and omit the "steam." Alternatively, to vary the steam, add roasted or blistered corn or sautéed mushrooms, or concassé tomatoes at the last minute.

2 tablespoons extra-virgin olive oil

4 tablespoons butter, softened

2 shallots, sliced

1 teaspoon minced garlic

Salt and black pepper to taste

4 to 6 banana leaves

4 snapper fillets, skinned and trimmed, about 7 to 8 ounces each

4 thin lemon slices, cut in half

"STEAM"

1 boniato (or sweet potato), about 1 pound, peeled and diced

1 tablespoon virgin olive oil

2 tablespoons butter

2 shallots, sliced

1 tablespoon finely minced garlic

1 Scotch bonnet or 2 serrano chiles, seeded and minced

24 small clams, scrubbed

1/2 tablespoon thyme leaves

2 bay leaves, broken

1 cup white wine (preferably Chardonnay)

1/2 teaspoon saffron threads

Combine the olive oil, butter, shallots, garlic, salt, and pepper in a bowl. Cut the banana leaves so they will neatly and completely wrap each fish. Use some of the trimmed leaf to make strips to tie the packages shut. Place each fish on top of a banana leaf and divide the butter mixture on top of each fish. Lay 2 sliced lemon halves on each fish. Wrap and tie the fish inside the leaves, and set aside in the refrigerator; make sure you keep the buttered side up.

Preheat the oven to 425 degrees. Cook the boniato or sweet potato in a saucepan of boiling water until just tender, about 5 minutes. Drain well and let cool.

Place the wrapped fish in a nonstick baking pan or dish and place in the oven. Cook for about 20 minutes.

Heat the oil and butter in a large, heavy skillet. When the butter melts, add the shallots, garlic, and chiles, stir, and sauté over medium heat for 30 seconds. Turn up the heat to high and add the clams, thyme, bay leaves, and wine. Cover the skillet and keep checking so you remove the clams as soon as they open; transfer to a bowl and keep them warm. Discard any clams that do not open. Add the saffron threads and cooked boniato and heat through.

Remove the snapper from the oven and place on warm, deep serving plates or in bowls. Cut the top of the wrappers open with scissors and peel back the banana leaves a little to expose the fish. Remove the clam meat from the shells, add to the "steam," and spoon over the fish.

Hibachi Tuna with Asian "Au Jus" and an Oriental Mushroom Salsa

Yield: 4 servings.

Back when I was a student at the University of Hawaii, when my roommates and I moved into a new apartment, we inherited a hibachi grill left behind by the previous tenants. Hibachis are tiny but very efficient, and they keep the heat of cooking outside the house—a definite benefit in tropical latitudes. I loved to watch the lights of Honolulu glitter and glow all around us as we grilled our college bachelor meals; meals that bore little resemblance to the recipe here!

The konbu in the Asian Au Jus is giant kelp. The sea is a primary source of food for the Japanese as their land resources are so limited and precious. The flavor obtained from this seaweed, along with the bonito (dried fish flakes) helps create *dashi,* one of the fundamental flavors of Japanese cuisine. Dashi forms the basis for most clear soups, and reminds me of another liquid that promotes health and well-being—known here in the Miami area as "Jewish penicillin."

 The ingredients for the Jus can be found in Asian stores. I enjoy serving the Asian Au Jus in little cups on the side with grilled fish like tuna.

ASIAN AU JUS

2 cups water

1 piece of dried konbu (giant kelp), about 8 inches long

10 to 12 Sichuan peppercorns, lightly toasted and crushed

¹/₄ cup bonito flakes (optional)

3 tablespoons tamari or light soy sauce

2 tablespoons sake

1 tablespoon unseasoned rice wine vinegar

1 tablespoon mirin

4 loin-cut tuna steaks, about 6 or 7 ounces each

2 tablespoons olive oil

1 to 2 teaspoons freshly toasted and ground Sichuan peppercorns

Salt to taste

1 ¹/₂ cups Oriental Mushroom Salsa (page 222)

To prepare the au jus: Bring the water to a simmer in a saucepan, add the konbu, and simmer over medium heat until 2 cups of liquid remain (about 30 minutes). Remove from the heat. Add the remaining au jus ingredients and let stand for 30 minutes. Strain into a clean bowl, discarding the solids, and reserve until needed.

Prepare a hibachi or regular grill (alternatively, you can use a grill pan). Rub the tuna

with the olive oil and sprinkle with the ground peppercorns and salt. Set aside in the refrigerator.

Prepare the mushroom salsa and keep warm.

Grill the tuna steaks for about 2 minutes per side. Check to see how the inside of the steaks are cooking by gently pulling back a layer of tuna meat with a fork. Grill only to rare or medium-rare, according to your preference; overcooking will result in disagreeably dry tuna.

Transfer the tuna to warm serving plates. Scatter the salsa over the tuna and place the au jus in 4 small teacups. Serve the cups right on the plates, or in saucers beside the plates. Your guests can then sip the au jus between bites or pour it over the tuna if they prefer.

Pan-Cooked Fillet of Key West Yellowtail with a "Belly" of Mashed Potatoes

Yield: 4 servings.

Fish and mashed potatoes? You bet! I learned to cook yellowtail snapper this way in Key West in the late 1970s at the legendary Pier House. The egg batter keeps the delicate yellowtail from drying out, and when the battered fish hits the hot butter it immediately gets a golden lacy color that works very softly with the citrus butter. The "belly" comes to be when we lay one fillet down over the Garlicky Mashed Potatoes; the more potatoes you pile on, the bigger the fish's belly gets!

 It's important the butter is hot when you put the fish in the skillet so the egg batter seals quickly and the fish does not stick to the pan. You can substitute any other thin, delicate fish, such as small snapper, sole, or flounder.

1 egg

¹/₄ cup half-and-half

Salt and black pepper to taste

¹/₄ cup flour

4 yellowtail snapper fillets, about 8 ounces each

Garlicky Mashed Potatoes (page 196)

CITRUS BUTTER SAUCE

¹/₂ cup fresh orange juice

3 tablespoons champagne vinegar

2 shallots, sliced

1 bay leaf, broken

1 teaspoon black pepper

3 tablespoons heavy cream

8 ounces butter, cut into small dice and kept cold

¹/₄ cup clarified butter

1 pound trimmed and peeled asparagus

Salt and black pepper to taste

Orange segments, for garnish

Annatto Oil (page 275), for garnish, optional

In a bowl, beat the egg with the half-and-half, salt, and pepper. Place the flour on a plate. Dust the fillets in the flour, shaking off any excess. Dip into the egg wash and leave them there until ready to cook (this can be done up to 6 hours ahead). Keep refrigerated.

About 45 minutes before dinner, prepare the mashed potatoes.

While the potatoes are cooking, prepare the citrus butter sauce. Place the orange juice, vinegar, shallots, bay leaf, and pepper in a small, nonreactive saucepan and bring to a

simmer over medium heat. Reduce the liquid for about 10 minutes, until only $\frac{1}{3}$ cup remains. Add the cream and bring to a boil. Whisk in the butter, piece by piece, until it is all incorporated. Strain through a fine-mesh strainer into a clean pan and keep warm.

Preheat the oven to 425 degrees. Heat 1 or 2 large cast-iron skillets and ladle in the clarified butter. When the butter is hot, gently remove the fish from the egg wash by hand and lay it in the pan, taking care to let the fish fall away from you to avoid splashing yourself with the hot butter. Gently shake the pan and sauté the fish for 1 to 2 minutes over medium-high heat. When a deep golden color, turn the fillets over with a spatula. Be careful to tilt the pan so the butter runs toward the bottom, and flip the fish away from you to avoid splashing (hot butter makes a nasty burn).

Drain off the excess butter. Transfer to the oven and cook for 7 to 10 minutes, depending on the thickness of the fillets.

While the fish is in the oven, bring a saucepan of salted water to a boil. Add the asparagus, cook for 1 or 2 minutes, drain, and season with salt and pepper.

Place a tall scoop of mashed potatoes on each warm serving plate. Place a yellowtail fillet on top of the potatoes and ladle some of the citrus butter sauce around. Place the asparagus spears attractively on the sauce and garnish with the orange segments. Drizzle with the annatto oil, and serve.

Lapsang Souchong Tea and Shallot–Stuffed Salmon Spirals on Sauce Mer Noir

Yield: 6 servings.

"It wasn't the wine," murmured Mr. Snodgrass in a broken voice, "it was the salmon."

—Charles Dickens, *The Pickwick Papers*

Here, it's both (the wine is in the sauce). It's also got tea, and I'll tell you why. There are, in some wines, flavors and scents that are evocative of tea. I wanted to restate that flavor. I also love a really good, deep, red wine sauce with meaty, rich fish such as salmon. I've been using Lapsang Souchong tea for a long time as a flavoring rub for smoking salmon; it has a woodsy-smoky flavor obtained by withering and slowly drying the leaves over open pine fires in the Fujian province of China. I was holding this tea in my hand one day and it suddenly reminded me of dried tarragon. So I rehydrated it with some wine, vinegar, and shallots, like a béarnaise sauce. This tea became the basis for the mixture coiled up inside the strips of salmon described here. The fish is presented with a red wine reduction sauce, but it would also go perfectly well with a simple lemon butter sauce. Then you'd have another timeless match—tea and lemon.

 If you are short on time, you can substitute the Citrus Butter Sauce (page 131) for the mer noir.

TEA AND SHALLOT STUFFING

$^1/_3$ cup Lapsang Souchong tea leaves

$^1/_3$ cup balsamic vinegar

3 tablespoons butter

10 shallots, thinly sliced

2 tablespoons sugar

Salt and black pepper to taste

12 wooden skewers

$1^3/_4$ to 2 pounds boneless, skinless salmon, cut from a whole side

Mer Noir (see recipe)

Garlicky Mashed Potatoes (page 196), optional

Sizzled Leeks (page 205), optional

1 to 2 teaspoons butter, cut into small dice and kept cold

To prepare the stuffing: Place the tea in a bowl and add the vinegar. Soak for 30 minutes. Heat a shallow saucepan and add the butter. When it begins to foam, add the shallots and stir to coat. Sauté over medium heat for 4 to 5 minutes, until caramelized. Stir in the sugar and the steeped tea-and-vinegar mixture. Reduce until the vinegar has almost evaporated, and season with salt and pepper. Transfer the stuffing mixture to a bowl and let cool. Then finely chop and reserve.

Soak the skewers in water so they won't burn on the grill or under the broiler. Place the salmon on a cutting board and cut lengthwise (the opposite direction than for a fillet) to make "ribbon cuts" a little over 1/2 inch thick and about 18 inches long. Ask your fish store to do this for you, if you prefer. Lay these "ribbons" of salmon on their sides and season lightly with salt and pepper. Take, in pinches, the reserved stuffing mixture and arrange down the center of each "ribbon." Roll up the ribbons in spirals so they resemble cinnamon rolls.

Spear each spiral with 2 skewers—one at the end of the ribbon, straight through the center and out the other side, and the other skewer at right angles to make an *X*. Reserve in the refrigerator.

Prepare the mer noir sauce.

Prepare the grill or broiler.

Prepare the mashed potatoes and leeks.

Grill (or broil) the salmon until done, about 3 minutes on the first side and 2 minutes on the other. Place the mashed potatoes at the center of warm serving plates. Top each serving of potatoes with a salmon spiral, after removing the skewers. Whisk the butter into the reduced mer noir until it is all incorporated, and adjust the seasoning. Spoon around the salmon and serve.

MER NOIR

Yield: about 2 cups.

A broad population of God's creatures inhabit your saucepan when you are making the mer noir sauce, and that's where the power comes from. If you can find squid ink, add 2 tablespoons—it will really make the color jump. I like to add a couple of teaspoons of cold butter when finishing this sauce, for its rich texture and attractive sheen.

1/4 cup olive oil

3 ounces smoked bacon, diced small (about 3/4 cup)

1 pound fish scraps (preferably tuna, salmon, or swordfish)

2 tablespoons butter

1 large onion, diced small

2 leeks, diced small

4 stalks celery, diced small

3 large carrots, diced small

1 head garlic, cut in half crosswise

2 bay leaves, broken

6 thyme sprigs

12 black peppercorns, crushed

12 button mushrooms, diced small

3 cups red wine vinegar

1 bottle (750 ml.) Pinot Noir

2 quarts Dark Chicken Stock (page 271)

18 mussels, scrubbed and debearded

Heat the olive oil in a very large, heavy saucepan and sauté the bacon over medium heat until half cooked. Add the fish scraps, stirring with a wooden spoon to prevent the fish from sticking to the pan. When the fish scraps have darkened around the edges a little, add the butter. Add the onion, leeks, celery, carrots, garlic, bay leaves, thyme, and peppercorns. Stir well and then stir only occasionally until they become nicely caramelized, about 30 minutes.

Stir in the mushrooms and cook for 1 minute longer. Add the vinegar, wine, stock, and mussels. Bring to a boil, and skim off any impurities. Reduce the liquid by half over medium heat, about 1 1/2 hours.

Strain through a fine-mesh strainer into a clean saucepan; the yield should be about 4 cups. Reduce the sauce over medium-high heat to 2 cups, and keep warm.

Yuca-Crusted Florida Striped Bass with Florida Sweet Corn

Yield: 4 servings.

Crusting fish has become relatively commonplace in restaurants these days, and potatoes are one of the ingredients used for crusting. Yuca is a simple, less sticky alternative that makes a nice change. The edgy tang of mustard in this recipe makes an interesting counterpoint to the yuca's soothing earthiness.

 This dish can be prepared using a different type of skinless fillet if you prefer; just omit the steps involving the skin, and serve the yuca crust side up. Equally wonderful! Also: you can garnish the plate with wedges of lemon and freshly snipped chives scattered over the cream.

CORN SAUCE

3 tablespoons butter

2 cloves garlic, thinly sliced

1 or 2 shallots, thinly sliced

1 Scotch bonnet chile or 2 serranos, seeded and minced

1 teaspoon freshly toasted and ground cumin seeds

1 teaspoon freshly toasted and ground black peppercorns

1/2 teaspoon salt

2 cups fresh sweet corn kernels (3 to 4 ears)

4 teaspoons champagne vinegar

1 1/4 cups heavy cream

4 fillets striped bass or red snapper, scaled and skin left on

4 teaspoons Creole mustard or whole-grain mustard

1 medium to large yuca

Salt and black pepper to taste

1/3 cup olive oil

To prepare the sauce: Heat the butter in a saucepan and sauté the garlic, shallots, and chile over medium heat until translucent, about 2 minutes. Stir in the cumin, peppercorns, and salt. Add the corn kernels, increase the heat to medium-high, and sauté until the corn almost blisters, about 6 to 8 minutes, stirring only as needed. Stir in the vinegar and then the cream, and reduce for about 3 minutes, or until the sauce coats the back of a spoon. Remove from the heat and set aside.

Lay the fillets out on a work surface, and using a sharp knife, make 3 or 4 small slits through the skin of each fillet. Turn the fillets over and brush each one with 1 teaspoon of mustard. Peel and grate the yuca, and carefully pack it on top of each fillet to form a crust. Season the yuca with a little salt and pepper.

Heat the olive oil in a large nonstick skillet and sauté the fillets, skin side down, over medium-high heat for 1 minute. Carefully turn the fillets over and cook the yuca side for about 2 minutes or until golden. Remove from the heat.

Reheat the corn sauce and ladle onto the middle of warm serving plates. Place the fillets on the sauce, yuca side down, so the pretty stripes of the bass show. Serve.

CHAPTER 6
LAND HO! BIRDS AND MEATS

Roasted Stuffed Game Hen with Pearl Onions and Sherry

Pan-Roasted Cumin-Rubbed Breast of Chicken with a Plantain–Foie Gras "Mofongo" on My *Very* Black Beans

Bajan-Spiced and Hot-Fried Chicken Dinner

"One-Eyed" Barbecued Ropa Vieja in Home Fries *That Kick*

Grilled Twenty-one-Ounce Chile- and Garlic-Stabbed Gaucho Steaks with Red-Hot Red Onion Rings

Herb-Crusted Grilled T-Bone Steak with Broken Olive Butter and Olive Oil–Roasted New Potatoes

Grill-Roasted Veal Adobo with Creamed Corn Sauce and Charred Corn Salsa

Rioja-Braised Lamb Shanks with Garlicky Mashed Potatoes

Cuban Pork Asado with a Sour Orange Mojo

Mongolian Pork Brochettes with a Confit of Cayenne-Dusted Carambola

Ancho Ham Jam–Glazed and Grilled Pork Chops with *South* American Fries

Palomilla Venison Steak au Poivre with a Tropical Tuber Torta

Tropical America, of course, had always been short of food animals, so there was a long tradition of eating, instead, the insects that abounded.

—Reay Tannahill, *Food in History*

The Taino, Mayan, Arawak, and Carib Indians were among the first inhabitants of the Caribbean. They migrated there centuries before the Europeans and their captives, the African slaves. The Carib Indians came north from the great river basins of South America. Their fierce nature and their hostile environment are reflected in some of the words they coined, and which were later adapted by the Spanish: *cannibal, hurricane, cigar,* and *barbecue.* Roasting, grilling, pan-cooking, boiling, frying, and braising may be other methods of cooking birds and meat, but we should be eternally grateful for the technique of barbecuing that these New World cooks bequeathed.

From neolithic times, the Indians from South America to northern Mexico used earth ovens to efficiently cook such feasts as whole wild pigs—the first *barbacoas.* The traditional preparation of meat dishes in the cattle-raising countries of Argentina, Uruguay, and Brazil have greatly influenced the cooking I have come to love. South American–style *churrasqueriás* are opening in Miami every month. The cowboy heritage of the Argentine *pampas* has also contributed spit-roasting as well as the redefining of generous proportions; hosts serving the grandly celebrated *asado criollo* count on an average of one pound of meat per guest!

The bird recipes in this chapter have been influenced fairly equally by Caribbean, African, and Asian cuisines. The island of Cuba experienced a significant influx of Chinese émigrés by the mid-nineteenth century (most of whom worked on the sugar plantations), in addition to the earlier arrival of Africans. Cuba is typical of many of the islands of the Caribbean, which—some more than others—became something of a tropical culinary laboratory with recipes and ingredients crisscrossing kitchen tables and stoves. In his book *Why We Eat What We Eat,* Raymod Sokolov explains: "Where the native population was small. . . . the exotic foodstuffs brought in by the commerce of the Spanish empire produced an original cuisine . . . with a Spanish gastronomic syntax inspiring new dishes made with ingredients never found all together in one place before."

Sounds like my kinda world!

Roasted Stuffed Game Hen with Pearl Onions and Sherry

Yield: 4 servings.

Cornish game hens are hybrid miniature chickens that weigh up to 2½ pounds. If there's only two or three of us for dinner, I still cook four game hens because they make outrageously good leftovers. I just take all the meat from the bones and shred it, then add a little of the stuffing and any leftover pearl onions and sauce. Enjoy it heated and seasoned in a tortilla or with some toasted bread; some sautéed mushrooms and raw seedless chilled grapes will add a little lusciousness.

 Adding the stock to the stuffing in stages rather than all at once makes it lighter in texture.

STUFFING

½ tablespoon olive oil

1 tablespoon butter

1 small poblano chile, seeded and diced

1 red bell pepper, seeded and diced

4 ounces Norman's Chorizo (page 288), crumbled, or hot Italian sausage

2 cups Caribbean Corn Bread (page 240), or other corn bread

2 tablespoons chopped sage leaves

7 cups Dark Chicken Stock (page 271)

3 tablespoons cumin seeds

3 tablespoons Dried Chiles Mezcla (see recipe), optional

¼ cup Spanish sherry vinegar

½ cup dry Spanish sherry

1 pint (2 cups) pearl onions, root ends removed

4 Cornish game hens, rinsed and patted dry

Salt and black pepper to taste

3 tablespoons peanut oil

To prepare the stuffing: Heat a skillet and add the olive oil and butter. When the butter begins to foam, add the poblano and bell pepper. Toss to coat and sauté over medium-high heat until caramelized, shaking the pan and tossing rather than stirring. Transfer to a mixing bowl.

Brown the chorizo in the same skillet and transfer to the mixing bowl. Add the corn bread and sage. Toss gently to mix. Sprinkle in 1 tablespoon of the chicken stock and toss gently to moisten. Repeat 3 more times (totaling ¼ cup stock) and set the mixture aside.

Heat a large, heavy saucepan and add the cumin. Toast over medium-high heat for 30 seconds. Add the chiles mezcla, vinegar, and sherry, and reduce the liquid by three-quarters (to about ¼ cup), about 2 to 4 minutes. Add the remaining stock and bring to a boil, skimming any impurities as necessary. Reduce, uncovered, for about 50 minutes, or until about 1 to 1½ cups remain, and it is thick enough to coat the back of a spoon. Strain through a fine-mesh strainer into a bowl and set aside.

Meanwhile, bring a saucepan of water to a boil. Add the pearl onions and boil for 30 seconds. Drain in a colander and rinse under cold running water. Pinch the onions to pop off the tough outer skin and reserve the onions.

Preheat the oven to 425 degrees. Season the game hens inside and out with salt and pepper. Stuff the birds with the reserved stuffing mixture. Drape any loose skin over the cavity, cross the legs and tie with butcher's twine. If you wish, rub the breasts with a little butter to keep them moist.

Heat a heavy roasting pan large enough to hold all 4 birds on the top of the stove. Add the peanut oil. When the oil is hot, sear the birds on all sides over medium-high heat. Arrange the birds breast side up in the pan. Place the reserved blanched pearl onions around the edge of the pan and coat with the oil so they caramelize while roasting.

Place the roasting pan in the oven. Baste the birds and onions with the drippings every 10 to 15 minutes. Roast for 40 to 45 minutes or until the juices run clear when the inner thigh is pierced.

Remove the roasting pan from the oven. Transfer the birds to a platter and let rest while keeping warm. Pour the fat from the pan and discard. Place the roasting pan on the stovetop and add the reduced stock sauce to the drippings and onions. Stir gently over high heat for 2 minutes. Add in any juices from the platter on which the birds are resting.

Place 1 bird on each serving plate. Arrange the pearl onions in a circle around the birds and spoon the sauce around.

DRIED CHILES
MEZCLA

Yield: About ⅓ cup.

This is an all-purpose ground chile blend (*mezcla* means "mixed" in Spanish). I like to keep it around to spice up all kinds of dishes.

2 *dried chipotle chiles, seeded*

4 *dried ancho chiles, seeded*

Toast the chiles in a dry skillet over medium heat for about 1 minute. Transfer to a blender or food processor and pulse to roughly process.

Pan-Roasted Cumin-Rubbed Breast of Chicken with a Plantain–Foie Gras "Mofongo" on My *Very* Black Beans

Yield: 4 servings.

Mofongo, despite how it sounds, is not one of the characters in a Disney movie. It's a word that probably was brought from Africa to various Caribbean islands, like Dominica and Puerto Rico. Mofongo, or caramelized plantain mash, is usually given the addition of crushed pork cracklings, which I leave out in favor of foie gras. You can go either route, or neither—your call.

 This dish can also be served with the Crispy Fried Plantains Curls (page 188), draped or stacked around the chicken breasts. The Sesame, Sriracha, Honey, and Mustard Drizzle (page 26) or the Sour Crema Drizzle (page 69) also go nicely, laced over the top of the breasts.

MOFONGO

¹/₄ cup peanut oil

1 very ripe plantain, peeled and cut into ¹/₂-inch slices

2 ounces foie gras, cut into fine (¹/₄-inch) dice

4 tablespoons softened butter

Salt and black pepper to taste

2 cups My Very *Black Bean Sauce (page 213)*

4 ¹/₄ teaspoons Calypso Spice Rub (page 28)

4 boneless chicken breasts, skin intact

¹/₄ cup cornmeal

¹/₄ cup flour

2 tablespoons peanut oil

To prepare the mofongo: Heat the peanut oil in a sauté pan and sauté the plantain slices over high heat for 1 or 2 minutes, turning until browned on both sides. Drain the plantain on paper towels and transfer to a mixing bowl. Add the foie gras, butter, salt, and pepper. Mash together and set aside.

Prepare the black bean sauce, stir in ¹/₄ teaspoon of the spice rub, and set aside.

Preheat the oven to 400 degrees. In the middle of the chicken, cut a pocket sideways into the meat and stuff with the reserved mofongo mixture. Press to close the pocket and season each stuffed breast with 1 teaspoon of the spice rub, rubbing it in.

In a mixing bowl, thoroughly combine the cornmeal, flour, salt, and pepper. Dredge the stuffed chicken breasts in the flour mixture, coating all sides.

Heat the peanut oil in a large, heavy cast-iron skillet and sauté the chicken breasts over high heat, skin side down first. When brown, about 2 minutes, turn over and brown the other side. Place the skillet in the oven and cook for 10 minutes. Remove from the oven and allow the breasts to rest.

Heat the bean sauce through and place about ½ cup on each serving plate. Place the chicken breasts on top of the beans and serve.

Bajan-Spiced and Hot-Fried Chicken Dinner

Yield: 4 servings.

Jessica Harris, a spicy lady herself, has repeatedly inspired me through her books on Afro-American cook-ing, her lectures, and best of all, in person, sitting in a café over a couple of cold Red Stripe beers. We share a passion for the flavors that the cooks conjure up down on Baxter's Road in Barbados. This one's for her!

 This can easily be transformed into a New World traditional chicken dinner, served with the Garlicky Mashed Potatoes (page 196) and some collard greens. For an additional boost of island flavor, offer some Mo J. (page 226) at the table to spritz on the chicken. When frying the chicken, carefully strain off any breadcrumbs that float to the surface of the oil. If you leave them in, they will burn and affect the flavor of the oil and the chicken.

1¹/₂ cups Bajan Spice Paste (page 16)

*2 whole fryer chickens, about 3¹/₂ pounds each,
cut into pieces*

1¹/₂ cups flour

Salt and black pepper to taste

4 eggs

3 teaspoons water

*2¹/₂ teaspoons Matouk's Hot Sauce, Coyote
Cocina's Howlin' Hot Sauce, or your favorite
Caribbean hot sauce*

4¹/₂ cups breadcrumbs

*3 tablespoons Dried Chiles Mezcla (page 143),
or salt and pepper to taste*

Peanut oil, for deep-frying

Prepare the spice paste. With a sharp knife, cut slashes through the chicken skin and partially into the meat. Rub the chicken thoroughly with the spice paste, making sure it fills the slashes you have just made. Transfer to a large plate, cover, and refrigerate for at least 4 to 6 hours.

On another plate, mix together the flour, salt, and pepper. In a bowl, whisk together the eggs, water, and hot sauce. In another bowl, thoroughly mix the breadcrumbs and the chiles mezcla together.

Heat the peanut oil in a deep-fryer or large heavy saucepan to 360 degrees. Preheat the oven to 200 degrees.

Dredge the chicken pieces first in the seasoned flour, then in the egg wash, and finally in the seasoned breadcrumbs, coating thoroughly. Carefully add the chicken to the hot oil, a few pieces at a time. Be careful not to move the pieces around at all for the first few minutes of deep-frying, and only once or twice while they are cooking. Fry until golden brown, about 20 to 25 minutes, or until the juices run clear. Keep the batches of cooked chicken warm on a platter in the oven until ready to serve.

"One-Eyed" Barbecued Ropa Vieja in Home Fries *That Kick*

Yield: 6 servings.

The title of this dish may sound inspired by the barbarous yet colorful days when pirates roamed the seas, but it comes from one of the first dishes I tried in the neighborhood restaurants of Key West in the 1970s: Ropa Vieja. Two gentlemen from Detroit named George and Tony had moved down and bought a long-standing family-owned Cuban restaurant on Duval Street called El Cacique. George and Tony loved the party lifestyle of their newly adopted island, as so many of us did. George was always good for his gossipy pre-tenses of shock, and his bawdy laughter, recapping the previous night's revelries, while Tony would shake his head as gently as if it were an egg with a dangerous crack in it, ready to bust. They had the uncommon sense to leave the restaurant as it had always been and to let the Cuban family continue the cooking and serving. The only thing that changed was that now you could ask questions in English! When I asked George about *ropa vieja*, he told me it meant "old clothes" with a smile and a "hey, it tastes great" shrug. He was right, of course. I have always found the slowly braised flavor of less expensive but tasty cuts of beef to be the most interesting. The egg garnish, traditional for many Spanish dishes, if not this one, led to the dish's "one eyed" nickname.

 This makes an especially tasty Sunday brunch or supper. Even if the clothes are old, they can still be snappy! The barbecued beef also tastes great in burger buns or tortillas.

4 to 5 pounds chuck steak or flank steak

4 teaspoons Escabeche Spice Rub That Cures (page 96), or salt and pepper to taste

2 tablespoons Annatto Oil (page 275), or olive oil

2 tablespoons butter

2 large onions, sliced

12 cloves garlic, sliced

1 cup water

1 cup tomato sauce

3 tablespoons brown sugar

1 teaspoon mustard powder

1/2 cup fresh lemon juice

1/2 cup Spanish sherry vinegar

1/2 cup tomato ketchup

2 tablespoons Worcestershire sauce

1 tablespoon freshly toasted and ground cumin seeds

1 tablespoon black pepper

Sweet Potato–Sweet Corn Home Fries That Kick (page 201)

6 eggs

Place the steak on a work surface and rub in the spice rub evenly on each side. Heat the oil in a large, heavy saucepan or Dutch oven and sear the meat on all sides over medium-high heat. Remove the meat and set aside. Add the butter to the pan and when it begins to foam, add the onions and garlic. Coat thoroughly and sauté until caramelized, about 15 minutes.

Deglaze the pan with 1/2 cup of water, stirring well. Turn the heat down to very low and add the meat. Add the tomato sauce and the remaining 1/2 cup of water. Move the meat around and press down so the liquid and some of the onions cover the meat. Cover the pan and cook for 2 hours. After 1 hour, turn the meat.

Meanwhile, mix together the brown sugar, mustard powder, lemon juice, vinegar, ketchup, and Worcestershire sauce in a small bowl to make a barbecue sauce. When the meat has cooked for 2 hours, uncover the pan, skim off any excess fat, and add the barbecue sauce. Cover the pan and cook for 1 hour longer.

Remove the meat from the pan and let cool. Reduce the sauce over high heat for 10 to 20 minutes, or until it is thick. Shred the meat and discard the bones and fat. Reduce the heat to low and add the meat to the reduced sauce in the pan. Add the cumin and pepper, and cook for 10 minutes longer.

Prepare the home fries. When they are ready, poach or fry the eggs (preferably sunny-side up).

Spoon the home fries onto warm serving plates. If desired, use a circular ring mold to make them uniform in shape. Make a little hollow with the back of a spoon in the home fries and spoon the barbecued ropa vieja on top. Add an egg on top of each serving and season to taste.

Grilled Twenty-one-Ounce Chile- and Garlic-Stabbed Gaucho Steaks with Red-Hot Red Onion Rings

Yield: 4 huge servings.

We all know that *gauchos* are the cowboys of the South American *pampas*. What many North Americans don't realize is that beef is taken as seriously there as it is in many of the finest steakhouses in Chicago, New York, or Los Angeles. When you order the prime rib steaks from your butcher and tell him it's to serve four, he may look at you as though you're crazy, but he *will* respect you at *some* level! You don't have to tell him that the leftovers will support a lunch or two over the next few days.

 You can offer some A Uno, Mi Estilo (page 214), or my Big Twist Barbecue Sauce (page 120), if you have it on hand.

Deep-Fried Red-Hot Red Onion Rings (page 199)

*4 bone-in prime rib steaks. about 21 ounces
each and 1 inch thick*

8 cloves garlic. cut into matchstick-sized strips

*4 jalapeño chiles. seeded and cut into
matchstick-sized strips*

Salt and plenty of black pepper to taste

Prepare the onion rings up to the cooking point.

Prepare the grill (alternatively, use a broiler).

With a sharp knife, make numerous incisions into the steaks, big enough to insert the garlic and jalapeño strips. Lay the steaks out on a work surface and stuff the garlic and jalapeño strips into the incisions. Season liberally with salt and pepper and let the steaks rest for 10 minutes, loosely covered.

Grill (or broil) the steaks over a hot flame to the desired doneness. Finish the onion rings and serve with the steaks.

Herb-Crusted Grilled T-Bone Steak with Broken Olive Butter and Olive Oil–Roasted New Potatoes

Yield: 4 servings.

The olives here are "broken" so we can remove the pits. Then we make a simple butter with them with plenty of herbs, garlic, and spices to rub into the steaks. They are then grilled with nothing more than the primordial powers of the fire working on the seasoned beef. This is a dinner to enjoy with a good bottle of red wine under the canopy of a starry summer evening.

 When grilling the steaks, after the butter is added, take care to cover the grill to limit the amount of oxygen that could cause the flames to get too high and burn the butter.

For the fresh mixed herbs, use any combination of sage, chives, marjoram, oregano, basil, Italian parsley, tarragon, chervil, and thyme. Add salt to the butter carefully, as the olives may have enough by themselves. If you want more spice in the final moment, sprinkle some Dried Chiles Mezcla (page 143) over the steaks.

Olive Oil–Roasted New Potatoes (page 196)

1 cup finely chopped mixed fresh herbs

6 tablespoons olive oil

Salt and black pepper to taste

4 T-bone steaks, about 1¹/₄ pounds each and at least 1 inch thick, with about ¹/₂ inch of fat intact along the edge

Broken Olive Butter (see recipe)

Prepare the potatoes.

In a mixing bowl, thoroughly combine the herbs (all except for 2 tablespoons reserved for the butter), olive oil, salt, and pepper. Cut numerous incisions into the steaks and rub the herb mixture into the slits and all over the steaks. Transfer the steaks onto a platter and let rest, loosely covered, while making the olive butter.

Prepare the grill (alternatively, use a broiler). Grill (or broil) the steaks over a hot flame until just crispy on the outside and very rare on the inside, about 2 minutes per side. Transfer the steaks to a platter and spread one side only with the herbed butter. Return the steaks to the grill, butter side up, and cook for about 2 minutes or to desired doneness.

Transfer to warm serving plates and serve the steaks with the Olive Oil–Roasted New Potatoes.

BROKEN OLIVE BUTTER

Yield: About 1 cup.

¹/₂ cup softened butter

2 tablespoons pitted and finely chopped black olives, such as arbequine or Niçoise

1 tablespoon minced garlic

2 tablespoons chopped fresh mixed herbs

2 tablespoons Spanish sherry vinegar

2 tablespoons Spanish sherry

¹/₂ tablespoon toasted and freshly ground cumin seeds

Salt and black pepper to taste

Combine all the ingredients in a mixing bowl. Keep cool, but not refrigerated, until you have used it for the steak.

Grill-Roasted Veal Adobo with Creamed Corn Sauce and Charred Corn Salsa

Yield: 4 servings.

Grill-roasting is a restaurant technique that can be done at home perfectly well. By beginning cooking on the grill or in a grill pan, you can attractively grill-mark the chops and gain the smoky flavor, then finish them evenly and thoroughly in the oven. This technique also reduces the risk of burning the meat toward the end of the cooking process. You can use this method for cooking any large steaks, birds, or fish.

 Spice up the salsa, if you'd like, with a minced Scotch bonnet chile. Alternative sides for this entrée are simple baked sweet potatoes, or, for a New World treat, Hawaiian Tostones (page 17).

4 rib or loin veal chops, about 1 1/2 inches thick and 12 ounces each

1/2 cup Mexican Adobo Paste (see recipe)

3 to 4 cups Charred Corn Salsa (page 221)

1 tablespoon extra-virgin olive oil

1 teaspoon black pepper

1 cup heavy cream

Juice of 1/2 lime

Lay the chops out on a work surface and rub all over with the adobo paste. Let marinate, covered, in the refrigerator for at least 4 hours and up to 24 hours.

Prepare the salsa. Prepare the grill and preheat the oven to 425 degrees. Place 1 1/3 cups of the salsa in a mixing bowl and stir in the olive oil. Set aside.

Season the veal chops with the pepper and grill over medium-high to high heat for about 4 minutes per side (the cooking time will vary according to thickness). Transfer the chops to a roasting pan and finish in the oven for 10 to 15 minutes.

Place the remaining salsa in a skillet and add the cream. Bring to a boil and add the lime juice. Stir together and keep warm until the chops are cooked.

Transfer the chops to warm serving plates. Spoon the sauce around and top with the reserved salsa in the mixing bowl.

MEXICAN ADOBO PASTE

Yield: 1¹/₂ cups.

Adobo is a word that has been carried from Spain to the Philippines with a major layover in Mexico. It is derived from the word *adobar,* meaning "to pickle" or "to marinate." This paste will keep for several weeks in an airtight container in the refrigerator.

1 clove

10 black peppercorns

1 teaspoon cumin seeds

2 bay leaves, broken

¹/₂ teaspoon ground cinnamon

¹/₂ cup Roasted Garlic Power (page 281)

8 dried ancho chiles, seeded, toasted, rehydrated, and drained (page xix)

4 dried chipotle or morita chiles, seeded, toasted, rehydrated, and drained (page xix)

1 teaspoon fresh oregano leaves

1 teaspoon fresh thyme leaves

1 teaspoon salt

¹/₄ cup Spanish sherry vinegar

Put the clove, peppercorns, and cumin in a dry skillet, and toast over medium heat until fragrant and slightly smoking, about 1 minute. Transfer to a spice grinder, add the bay leaves and cinnamon, and finely grind. Transfer the spice mixture to a food processor or blender and add the Roasted Garlic Power, the drained chiles, oregano, thyme, salt, and vinegar. Purée until smooth and reserve in the refrigerator.

Rioja-Braised Lamb Shanks with Garlicky Mashed Potatoes

Yield: 4 servings.

Braising the lamb shanks transforms them into a fork-tender, meaty, rich meal. The rioja wine gives the dish a Spanish flair, but a good, hearty Californian or Italian red wine would make a suitable substitution. You can roast some red bell peppers, julienne them, and sauté some wild mushrooms for a wonderful, flavorful accompaniment. A final thought: Truffles make this dish *godlike*.

 The lamb can be prepared a day or two in advance if this is more convenient. Because of the richness of the lamb shanks, you should approach this dish with an open mind when it comes to seasoning generously at the table.

¹/₄ cup flour

¹/₂ teaspoon salt

¹/₂ tablespoon black pepper

4 lamb shanks, about 1 pound each

3 tablespoons peanut oil

2 tablespoons butter

3 tablespoons olive oil

1 onion, diced

1 head garlic, cut in half crosswise

1 large carrot, diced

2 large celery stalks, diced

3 sprigs thyme

12 black peppercorns, crushed

2 bay leaves, broken

2 cups Spanish rioja wine

4 cups Lamb Stock (page 272)

RIOJA SAUCE

2 tablespoons butter

2 tablespoons olive oil

1 large carrot, diced small

1 leek, white part only, diced small

1 bulb fennel, diced small

6 cloves garlic, sliced

1 bay leaf, broken

2 sprigs thyme

1 sprig rosemary

¹/₂ cup red wine vinegar

2 cups Spanish rioja wine

Salt and black pepper to taste

Garlicky Mashed Potatoes (page 196)

Preheat the oven to 350 degrees. On a large plate, mix together the flour, salt, and pepper.

Dredge the lamb shanks in the seasoned flour. Heat the peanut oil in a large, heavy roasting pan on the top of the stove. Sear the lamb shanks over high heat. Transfer the lamb to a platter and pour off the fat from the roasting pan. Reduce the heat to medium high and add the butter and olive oil. When the butter begins to foam, add the onion, garlic, carrot, and celery. Sauté until the vegetables caramelize, about 8 minutes.

Add the thyme, peppercorns, bay leaves, wine, and stock. Bring to a high simmer, skimming any impurities as necessary. Add the lamb shanks; they shouldn't be completely immersed by the liquid. Cover the pan with foil, place in the oven, and cook for 1 hour.

Remove the foil, turn the lamb over, and cook for 30 to 40 minutes longer.

Remove the lamb from the braising liquid and transfer to a platter to rest. The meat should just be coming loose from the bone. Strain the broth through a medium-mesh strainer and then through a fine-mesh strainer. Chill completely and reserve (this can be done a day or two in advance).

To prepare the sauce: Heat a heavy saucepan over medium-high heat. Add the butter and oil, and when the butter begins to melt, add the carrot, leek, fennel, garlic, and bay leaf. Stir only occasionally so the vegetables caramelize. When the vegetables are turning very dark at the edges, add the thyme, rosemary, vinegar, and wine. Reduce the liquid by half, about 15 minutes.

Add the reserved lamb broth and bring to a simmer, skimming as necessary. Remove the sprigs of thyme and rosemary and keep the sauce warm.

Prepare the mashed potatoes.

Turn up the oven to 400 degrees.

Place the lamb shanks back in a pan and cover with the rioja sauce. Cook in the oven for 30 to 40 minutes, basting the lamb occasionally.

Place the mashed potatoes at the top of large serving bowls (or plates). Lean the lamb shanks against them. If the sauce is not yet thick enough to coat the back of a spoon, quickly reduce on the top of the stove. Spoon the sauce around the lamb and garnish with mixed fresh herbs, if desired.

Cuban Pork Asado with a Sour Orange Mojo

Yield: 6 servings.

This dish requires some advance planning because the key to the tremendous flavor and tenderness of this pork *asado* (roast) is a nice, slow, long bath in the marinade. The technique I use is to line a large mixing bowl with a plastic bag, and place the ham inside the bag. I add the marinade, tie up or seal the bag, and put it in the refrigerator. Then, whenever I'm getting something out of the fridge, I roll the bag over in the bowl. This way, if the bag punctures, the bowl is there to catch the marinade. The secret of the bag is that it helps hold the marinade close to all sides of the meat.

 The mojo is created with the meat drippings and the marinade, so it's not even an extra step. Optional additional sides are the Crispy Fried Plantain Curls (page 188) and Caramelized Red Onions (page 206).

4 large cloves garlic

5 to 6 pound bone-in pork shoulder, or fresh ham, skin removed and fat intact

MARINADE

³/4 cup fresh sour (Seville) orange juice

¹/4 cup fresh lime juice

³/4 cup virgin olive oil

2 bay leaves, broken

1 tablespoon freshly toasted and ground black peppercorns

1 tablespoon freshly toasted and ground cumin seeds

Sherried Black Beans (page 208)

Basic Saffron Rice (page 204)

Cut two of the garlic cloves into slivers. Make incisions in the pork with a sharp knife and insert a sliver of garlic into each. Slice the remaining 2 garlic cloves, and place in a mixing bowl together with the marinade ingredients. Whisk together. Put a plastic bag big enough to hold the pork inside a mixing bowl. Put the pork and marinade in the bag and tie the bag to secure it. Let the pork marinate in the refrigerator for 2 to 3 days, turning the bag occasionally.

Preheat the oven to 325 degrees. Remove the pork from the bag and the marinade, and place in a Dutch oven or roasting pan, fat side up. Cover and cook in the oven for 1¹/2 hours. Turn the pork fat side down and cook for 1¹/2 hours longer or until the meat is almost falling off the bone. Turn the pork back to fat side up and uncover the pan. Increase the heat to 375 degrees and cook for 30 minutes to brown the pork.

Prepare the black beans and rice in the meantime.

Remove the pork from the oven and transfer to a cutting board to let rest. Pour the juices from the pan into a gravy separator or a clear glass heatproof container. The fat will rise to the top and the natural sour orange "mojo" will sink to the bottom. When the fat has separated, spoon it off and discard. Warm the mojo in a saucepan and serve in a gravy boat. With 2 forks, pull the pork from the bone and serve with the beans, rice, and mojo.

Mongolian Pork Brochettes with a Confit of Cayenne-Dusted Carambola

Yield: 6 to 8 servings.

This dish is flavored with Asian ingredients and is named for the empire that connected Europe and Asia in the Middle Ages. Before 1250, the two continents were linked by the arduous "Silk Road," which snaked overland from China through Baghdad to the Mediterranean coast. The other, watery route went by way of the South China Sea, the Indian Ocean, and the Arabian Sea to Suez. The path of Italian or Frankish traders was often blocked by Muslim Turks beyond the cities of Aleppo, Alexandria, or Damascus, but between 1250 and 1350, this curtain was lifted and caravans made their way to the east. Europe developed a taste for the goods that came back from Asia until the curtain closed again, and the trade was once more interrupted. Then it was the Mongols from Central Asia, the "bad boy" Tartars of thundering hordes fame, who played the role of curtain raisers and restored the trade in the flavors of the Far East to Europe. Come to think of it, the Mongolians, whose vast empire stretched from the Yellow River in China to the shores of the blue Danube during the reign of Kublai Khan, probably deserve a much better place in history. The Silk Road was eventually traveled by the Venetian-born Marco Polo, whose life inspired the imaginations of European explorers and discoverers for the next century. Polo wrote his memoirs from a prison cell in the Italian port city of Genoa; one of those ignited by his spark was a local boy by the name of Christopher.

 This dish is best started the day before you plan to serve it. If carambola (star fruit) is unavailable, substitute fresh plums, mangoes, or peaches. Soaking the wooden skewers helps prevent them from burning up on the grill or splintering. Add some mushrooms or sautéed eggplant to the skewers, if you'd like. Serve with rice or potatoes.

CONFIT SYRUP

Zest of 1 large lime

1-inch length of ginger, thinly sliced (about 1¼ tablespoons)

½ stick cinnamon

6 white peppercorns, toasted and coarsely cracked

1 cup water

1 cup sugar

2 carambolas (star fruit), seeded and cut into ¼-inch-thick slices

2½ pounds boneless pork loin, cut into 1-inch cubes

Pork Marinade (see recipe)

18 to 24 wooden skewers, 6 inches or more long

3 tablespoons virgin olive oil

3 tablespoons butter

1 red onion, cut into 1-inch cubes

2 red bell peppers, seeded and cut into 1-inch cubes

2 yellow bell peppers, seeded and cut into 1-inch cubes

Salt and black pepper to taste

1 tablespoon balsamic vinegar

Cayenne to taste

To prepare the syrup: Combine the lime zest, ginger, cinnamon, peppercorns, water, and sugar in a saucepan, and bring to a simmer. Simmer the mixture for 5 minutes and remove from the heat. Cover and let steep for 10 minutes in a warm place. Strain the liquid into a mixing bowl and add the carambolas. Stir gently and allow to cool. Cover and keep refrigerated overnight.

Place the pork in a large mixing bowl.

Prepare the marinade. Pour the marinade over the pork, cover, and refrigerate overnight. Soak the wooden skewers in water overnight.

Heat the olive oil and butter in a sauté pan and sauté the onion and bell peppers over medium-high heat, stirring occasionally, until blistered slightly, about 15 to 20 minutes (do this in batches, if necessary). Season with salt and pepper, and add the vinegar. Cook until the mixture begins to soften, about 30 seconds. Transfer to a bowl and let cool.

Prepare the grill or broiler. Thread the skewers by alternating pieces of pork, bell peppers, and onion; there should be 3 pieces of pork per skewer. Remove the carambolas from the syrup and lightly dust each piece with cayenne. Set aside, and reserve the syrup.

Lightly oil the grill with a brush so the brochettes won't stick. Grill the brochettes until they are brown on each side and cooked through. Remove from the grill, place on a large, festive platter, and keep warm. Place the carambolas on the grill and heat through (about 30 seconds on each side).

Transfer to the platter, arranged in a circle around the brochettes. Spoon a little of the reserved syrup over the carambolas and serve (this recipe allows for 3 skewers per person).

PORK MARINADE

Yield: About 1 cup.

This marinade also works really well for simply grilled pork or veal.

3 cloves garlic, minced

³/₄ tablespoon minced ginger

1 shallot, minced

1 tablespoon roughly chopped cilantro leaves

¹/₄ cup Spanish sherry vinegar

2 tablespoons hoisin sauce

1¹/₂ tablespoons soy sauce

1¹/₂ tablespoons unseasoned rice wine vinegar

1¹/₂ tablespoons sesame oil

1¹/₂ tablespoons plum sauce

1¹/₂ tablespoons crunchy peanut butter

1¹/₂ tablespoons honey

¹/₂ tablespoon hot chile sauce (preferably Sriracha)

Thoroughly combine all the marinade ingredients in a large nonreactive mixing bowl.

Ancho Ham Jam–Glazed and Grilled Pork Chops with *South* American Fries

Yield: 4 servings.

Here we are, my friends, back in the familiar riptides of "sweet meets heat." The pork chop's meatiness offers a buoy to hang on to while we bob between the fire of chiles and the cool of the jam.

 This dish is still tasty (though less complex in flavor) without the sauce, if you're crunched for time. You can substitute chicken stock for the pork stock if you prefer.

4 center-cut pork chops, about 12 ounces each and 1 inch thick

2 teaspoons Calypso Spice Rub (page 28)

6 large cloves garlic

2 cups Pork Stock (page 273)

2 jalapeño chiles, seeded and cut into thin strips

¹/₂ cup Ancho Ham Jam (see recipe)

South American Fries (page 194)

1 teaspoon butter, diced into small pieces and kept cold

On a plate, coat the pork chops with the spice rub. Cover and refrigerate for 30 minutes.

To prepare the sauce: Blanch the garlic in boiling water for 30 seconds. Remove and cut into thin strips. Combine the stock and jalapeño and garlic strips in a saucepan. Bring to a boil, and reduce over medium-high heat for 15 to 18 minutes until about ¾ to 1 cup remains; it should lightly coat the back of a spoon. Remove the pan from the heat.

Prepare the grill.

Prepare the ham jam and the fries.

Oil the grill with a brush so the chops won't stick. Grill the chops for about 2 to 3 minutes; then turn the chops over. Paint the grilled side with the ham jam. After 2 to 3 minutes, turn the chops once again and paint the newly grilled side as before. Grill for a total of about 15 minutes, until just done, painting and turning from time to time. Transfer the chops to warm serving plates.

Quickly bring the sauce to a boil and whisk in the butter until it is all incorporated. Transfer to a sauce boat and serve with the chops and fries.

ANCHO HAM JAM

Yield: About 2 cups.

This sauce's assertive sweet, hot, one-two punch makes it ideal with ham, hence the name. It goes great with robustly flavored meats and game. It can also be used as a glaze for grilled chicken, or you can add it to a barbecue sauce for some kick. It will keep refrigerated for several months in an airtight container.

1½ quarts water

20 cloves garlic

¼ cup Dried Chiles Mezcla (page 143)

¾ cup honey

¾ cup red currant jelly

¼ cup Spanish sherry vinegar

1 teaspoon salt

4 teaspoons black pepper

In a saucepan, heat the water, garlic, and chiles mezcla. Bring to a boil and over medium-high heat, reduce the liquid until it has almost evaporated, about 1½ hours. The mixture should be just moist. Transfer to a blender or food processor.

In a small saucepan, melt the honey and jelly together. Add to the blender or food processor together with the vinegar, salt, and pepper. Blend the mixture together until smooth. Reserve until needed.

Palomilla Venison Steak au Poivre with a Tropical Tuber Torta

Yield: 4 servings.

An American-Latino-Franco dish! Assuming, that is, you're "game" for the idea of updating the tradition of a *palomilla* steak—it's a tastily marinated but often mighty *thin* slice of beef. I won't knock that tradition, but I was raised in Chicagoland, where thick steaks are the norm. So I blended some ideas from my former home-town with my current one, added a touch of classic French, substituted venison for the beef, and came up with this recipe. Pass the steak knives, *amigo*.

 The steak can be grilled, or pan-grilled without the sauce. You can, by all means, revert closer to the traditional concept of *palomilla* steaks by substituting New York strip steaks for the venison. An alternative side dish is the Cuban French Fries (page 193)

Venison Marinade (see recipe)

4 venison loin steaks. 6 to 8 ounces each and at least 1 inch thick. well trimmed

Tropical Tuber Torta (page 191)

2 tablespoons truffle oil. or virgin olive oil

3 tablespoons coarsely cracked black pepper

4 shallots. thinly sliced

1/4 cup Spanish brandy

2 tablespoons Spanish sherry vinegar

2 cups Dark Chicken Stock (page 271)

1 tablespoon Creole mustard or whole-grain mustard

2 tablespoons butter

Prepare the marinade. Place the venison steaks in the bowl containing the marinade. Let marinate for 4 hours in the refrigerator, turning the steaks once or twice.

Prepare the tuber torta.

Remove the steaks from the marinade, letting them drain for a few seconds. Transfer to a large platter and season with the truffle or olive oil and pepper, pressing the pepper onto

the meat. Heat a large, heavy nonstick or cast-iron skillet until smoking hot. Sear the steaks for 2 minutes on the first side and then 3 minutes on the other for rare to medium-rare. Remove the steaks from the skillet and let them rest in a warm place.

Drain the oil and fat from the pan, add the shallots, and stir for 10 seconds. Add the brandy and vinegar; carefully ignite, and shake the pan. When the flames die down, add the stock and reduce until the liquid becomes thick enough to coat the back of a spoon. Whisk in the mustard, butter, and any collected juices from the resting steaks.

Spoon the sauce onto warm serving plates. Add the steaks and serve with the tuber torta.

VENISON MARINADE

Yield: About 3/4 cup.

1/2 cup Spanish or Californian red wine

1 tablespoon olive oil

6 cloves garlic, cut in half crosswise

1/2 tablespoon black pepper

1/2 tablespoon cumin

1/4 red onion, cut into rings

1 bay leaf, broken

Mix all the marinade ingredients together in a large nonreactive bowl and let the flavors marry for 30 minutes.

CHAPTER 7
PAELLAS, PASTAS, AND NOODLES

Paella Americana

Paella Oriental

Paella de Vegetales a la Parilla

A Savory Paella Rice Pudding with Soft-Shell Crabs and a Mojo Rojo

Fideo Noodles and Fish House Pan Stew

Fettuccine with Spicy Tomato Salsa, Crispy Calamari, and
Roasted Garlic Allioli

Soba Noodles and Sake-Steamed Clam Stirfry with Thai Stick Dip

What was it he read to her once? About how, long ago, the New World was attached to Europe and Africa? Yes, and the continents pulled away slowly, painfully after millions of years. The Americas are still inching westward and will eventually collide with Japan. Celia wonders whether Cuba will be left behind, alone in the Caribbean sea with its faulted and folded mountains, its conquests, its memories.... She finishes chopping the onions and stirs them in a frying pan with a teaspoon of lard. They turn golden yellow, translucent and sweet.

—Cristina Garcia, *Dreaming in Cuban*

I don't know if it's still there, but 20 years ago, flying in an eight-seater airplane into Key West, I noticed, in the choppy motion of descent, a hand-painted sign on the side of a building that stood near the laughably antiquated Key West *International* Airport. It read: ¡BIENVENIDOS A CAYO HUESO! ("Welcome to Key West!").

I was suddenly struck with how I had left the America of my youth. Now I was in a bilingual enclave. I remember smiling out of the window. "*Hola,*" I mouthed to the gathering ground crew below.

The first paella I tasted was probably there in Key West at the Fourth of July restaurant on White Street. Closed now, it used to be festooned with star-spangled banners. I remember being intrigued by the seemingly nonmatching components of paella—"chicken, pork, lobster, vegetables, and rice all in the same pot?" I asked. I ended up being more taken with the rice than the meats and seafood in that first brush with paella. I discovered that the reheating approach often taken to restaurant paellas because of the continuous demands for "fresh paella" ruins the effect. Home cooking allows for paella to be served as soon as it's done. The family or guests come to the table and everything is at its peak.

The rice dishes of Valencia extend beyond paella, and well beyond Valencia itself in terms of what they have inspired. *Asopao* of San Juan is a possible cousin, as are some of the rice dishes found in the Philippines. One of the most interesting of these, *bringhe,* features many of the components of paella, but with coconut milk in lieu of olive oil. One wonders whether the Filipinos or Spanish started or adapted it.

Pastas and noodle dishes in the New World Cuisine have been flavored and influenced, naturally, by the culinary traditions of Italy and the Far East, but it would be remiss of me if I failed to mention that paellas have been made in Spain with fideo noodles for some time. *Canelones* are Spanish meat-filled pastas that were introduced from Italy through the port of Barcelona in the sixteenth century. After the passage of a few centuries, the dish is accepted as thoroughly Spanish, and stores all over the country sell the square-shaped dough for home cooks to fill to their liking.

Noodles and pastas seem to have sprung up independently in cultures as far removed geographically as China and Italy. Some scholars believe that Marco Polo provided the missing link here, but the issue ultimately is not who was first. It is, more keenly, the sentiment that Ken Hom has expressed so concisely: "There is no East or West when pasta lovers meet."

Paella Americana

Yield: 6 servings (or 12 appetizers).

I was discussing with Bobby Flay, the terrific young chef from New York City, the hazards of attempting to overcome culinary misconceptions with your own clientele. We were having lunch at his restaurant, Bolo, which features a new, Spanish-inspired cooking. Bobby recalled taking a few hooks to the chin when opening Bolo and serving authentic paella using the short-grained rice that is the true, genuine rice of Valencia. I enjoyed hearing this because I had been similarly tattooed for years for the same "mistake." We knew *they* were wrong. "What about Penelope Casas's great work, *The Foods and Wines of Spain*," I chimed. "What about eating in Spain—I just got back, for cryin' out loud!" Bobby replied. Bobby recounted how he stood his ground for about a week, and then finally threw up his hands and took the philosophical attitude of "when in America" (not to mention not biting the hand that feeds you). He started serving his paella with long-grained rice and immediately garnered rave reviews. Bobby still has a few tightly sealed bags of the arborio rice around (I hear there are truffles in it!) and he is happy to make it should someone ask. I decided that I would include one paella recipe in this book for everyone who likes paella in this Americanized fashion.

1 chicken, cut into 8 bone-in pieces

¹/₄ cup Dried Chiles Mezcla (page 143), optional

Salt and black pepper to taste

¹/₄ cup Roasted Garlic Oil (page 277), Annatto Oil (page 275), or olive oil

8 ounces Norman's Chorizo (page 288), or other spicy pork sausage, cooked and cut into ¹/₂-inch slices

2 spiny lobster tails, cut through the shell crosswise in 1-inch lengths, deveined

2¹/₄ cups Light Chicken Stock (page 270)

2 tablespoons butter

2 tablespoons olive oil

4 cloves garlic, minced

1 Scotch bonnet chile, seeded and minced, optional

1 onion, diced small

1 carrot, diced small

1 stalk celery, diced small

2 small bay leaves, broken

1¹/₂ cups long-grain rice

1 teaspoon high-quality Spanish saffron

18 Littleneck clams, scrubbed

1¹/₂ cups fresh baby peas

SHRIMP AND GARNISH

1 tablespoon butter

1 tablespoon virgin olive oil

1 shallot, thinly sliced

12 large shrimp (about 10 to 12 ounces), peeled and deveined

Salt and black pepper to taste

2 red bell peppers, roasted, peeled, seeded, and cut into ¹/₂-inch strips

Rub the chicken all over with the chiles mezcla, salt, and pepper. Heat a large, heavy-bottomed, ovenproof pan or paella pan and add the oil. Add the chicken pieces and sauté for 4 to 6 minutes over medium-high heat, turning to brown on all sides. Remove and set aside.

Add the chorizo and lobster pieces, stir around and let brown, about 2 minutes. Remove the lobster and set aside. Cover the pan, reduce the heat to low, and cook the chorizo for 4 or 5 minutes longer. Remove and set aside. Return the chicken pieces to the pan and add the stock. Reduce the heat to a simmer and cover the pan. Cook until tender, about 20 minutes for the breasts, and 30 to 35 minutes for the legs and thighs. Set the chicken aside.

Strain the stock with a fine-mesh strainer and let cool. Scoop up the surface fat and discard it. There should be about 2 cups of stock remaining; add more water or stock if necessary.

Preheat the oven to 300 degrees. Wipe out the pan and add the 2 tablespoons each of butter and olive oil. When the butter foams, sauté the garlic and Scotch bonnet over medium heat for 15 seconds. Raise to high heat and add the onion, carrot, celery, and bay leaves. Stir well, and cook for 5 or 6 minutes until glazed, stirring occasionally.

Stir in the rice and saffron, and season with pepper. Add the reserved 2 cups of stock and stir once. Allow the mixture to almost come to a boil; reduce the heat to medium. Add the clams and peas, and stir in. Cover the pan and cook until all the clams open (this could take up to 12 or 15 minutes). As the clams open, remove to a plate. Once they have all opened, turn off the heat. Discard any that have not opened after 15 minutes. Arrange the chorizo, chicken, lobster, and clams over the rice. Cover the pan tightly with foil and transfer to the oven. Bake for 25 minutes or until the rice is cooked.

Prepare the shrimp and garnish in the meantime.

Heat the butter and oil in a large sauté pan. When the butter melts, add the shallots and sauté over medium-high heat for 30 seconds. Add the shrimp and season with salt and pepper. Sauté until they are just cooked through. Add the roasted bell peppers and sauté briefly.

Remove the paella from the oven. Remove the foil and scatter the shrimp, shallots, and roasted peppers over the dish. Serve in large bowls with some crusty bread.

Paella Oriental

Yield: 4 servings (or 8 appetizers).

If ever there was a dish ripe for cross-culturalization, this might be it, given the mutual love of rice shared by Latins and Orientals.

 I add no salt to the dish as the clams generally supply it, but you can pass the pepper. If the choice comes to mind of adding extras to the paella, such as steamed lobster or grilled shrimp or stirfried squid or even leftover chicken, do it! That's the beauty of paella—it's very friendly.

2 tablespoons butter

5 tablespoons olive oil

2 tablespoons spicy (hot) sesame oil

3 cloves garlic, minced

1 tablespoon minced ginger

2 Thai chiles or 3 jalapeño chiles, seeded and finely minced

1/2 red onion, diced

32 tiny clams, scrubbed

1 piece (9 inches long) lemongrass, cut into 3 pieces

1 cup sake

8 ounces arborio rice (1 cup)

2 1/2 cups Light or Dark Chicken Stock (pages 270, 271)

1 cup warm Mushroom Muscle Power (page 282)

1/4 cup thinly sliced scallions

1 tablespoon soy sauce

1/4 cup roughly chopped cilantro leaves

1 cup bok choy, most of the leaves discarded (to leave mostly stem), and cut thinly on the bias

Heat a large saucepan and add the butter, 2 tablespoons of the olive oil, and the sesame oil. When they are hot, add the garlic, ginger, chiles, and onion, and sauté over medium heat for about 5 minutes. Add the clams, lemongrass, and the sake, and cover the pan. Turn the heat to high and let the clams steam open. Remove the clams as they open and set aside (discard any clams that do not open). Turn off the heat and let the broth rest for about 10 minutes so the flavors can marry. Separate the clam meat from the shells and reserve. Strain the broth into a bowl and set aside.

Wipe out the pan and add the remaining 3 tablespoons of olive oil. Heat the oil over medium heat, add the rice, and stir until well coated. Add 1 cup of the reserved broth to begin with, stirring constantly and allowing the rice to absorb the liquid. Add another

¼ cup of the broth and stir again. Keep adding the broth ¼ cup at a time, and then the stock, stirring, until all the liquid has been absorbed.

Add the reserved clam meat, mushroom power, scallions, soy sauce, cilantro, and bok choy to the rice, and stir well. Serve.

Paella de Vegetales a la Parilla

Yield: 4 servings (or 8 appetizers).

This is a tasty vegetarian paella, but if you're not concerned with keeping it meatless, you can use chicken stock instead of the vegetable stock and add cooked chicken, shellfish, or fish at the last minute. Nuts, cherry tomato halves, or small cubes of cheese are other good additions to make at the end.

 Once the vegetables have been grilled and are set aside, any collecting juices should be saved and added to the stock that is used to make the rice. You can grill the vegetables ahead and keep them in the refrigerator, but make sure they're well wrapped and covered. Check for reseasoning, as the refrigerator is famous for eating spices right out of foods! Serve the paella with grated Parmesan cheese, if desired.

VEGETABLES AND MARINADE

¹/₂ cup broccoli florets

¹/₂ cup cauliflower florets

2 leeks, white and light green parts only, split in half lengthwise

1 small eggplant, partially peeled, cut lengthwise into ¹/₃-inch "planks," salted, and weighted (see page xvii)

1 zucchini, cut lengthwise into ¹/₄-inch-thick "planks"

4 large cremini or other flavorful mushrooms, cut in half

1 ear sweet corn, shucked

1 red bell pepper, roasted, peeled, and seeded

1 cup Roasted Garlic Oil (page 277), or virgin olive oil

3 tablespoons thyme leaves

2 bay leaves, broken

Salt and black pepper to taste

PAELLA RICE

3 tablespoons olive oil

2 tablespoons butter

3 cloves garlic, minced

¹/₂ small red onion, diced

1 poblano chile, seeded and minced

2 bay leaves, broken

8 ounces arborio rice (1 cup)

1 cup white wine

1 large pinch saffron

3¹/₂ cups Vegetable Stock (page 269), or Light Chicken Stock (page 270)

Salt and black pepper to taste

Blanch the broccoli, cauliflower, and leeks in a pan of boiling salted water. Remove the broccoli and cauliflower after 1 to 2 minutes and shock in a bowl of ice water until cool. Blanch the leeks for 1 minute longer and then transfer to the ice water. Drain, and transfer the broccoli, cauliflower, and leeks to a large mixing bowl. Add the remaining vegetables and marinade ingredients. Toss to coat thoroughly with the oil and set aside.

Prepare the grill. Remove the vegetables from the bowl and grill over even heat until lightly charred. Set aside. When they are cool enough to handle, cut the vegetables into bite-sized pieces and cut the corn kernels from the cob. Transfer the vegetables to a non-reactive pan and set aside.

Preheat the oven to 450 degrees. To prepare the paella rice, heat the olive oil and butter in a large saucepan. When the butter foams, add the garlic, onion, and poblano, and sauté over medium heat for 5 minutes. Add the rice and season with salt and pepper. Stir until the rice is well coated.

Add the wine and cook until the liquid has reduced by half. Add the saffron and 1 cup of the stock. Stir constantly until the liquid is almost absorbed by the rice.

Meanwhile, transfer the reserved grilled vegetables to the oven and warm for 10 minutes.

Stir another ¼ cup of stock into the rice until it is absorbed, and repeat until all the stock has been absorbed by the rice. Turn off the heat. Remove the vegetables from the oven and stir into the rice. Serve on warm plates.

A Savory Paella Rice Pudding with Soft-Shell Crabs and a Mojo Rojo

Yield: 4 servings.

The first part of this recipe for the paella rice is great all by itself with some diced cooked shrimp, ham, clams, and lobster tossed in at the very end. Or, you could prepare the Paella Rice Pudding and serve that with a tomatoey fish stew.

 The paella rice can be prepared 1 or 2 days ahead and kept covered in the refrigerator. You can simply use freshly squeezed lemon juice instead of the mojo, if you prefer.

PAELLA RICE

2 tablespoons olive oil

2 tablespoons butter

3 cloves garlic, minced

1/2 small red onion, diced

1 poblano chile, seeded and minced

1 bay leaf, broken

4 ounces arborio rice (1/2 cup)

Salt and black pepper to taste

1/2 cup white wine

1 pinch saffron

1 3/4 cups Light Chicken Stock (page 270)

3/4 cup Mojo Rojo (page 229), or 4 lemon wedges

RICE PUDDING

4 eggs

1/2 vanilla bean, cut in half

1 cup heavy cream

1/2 cup milk

1 teaspoon cornstarch

1 teaspoon cayenne

Salt and black pepper to taste

CRABS

2 eggs, beaten

1/3 cup buttermilk

1 cup panko crumbs

1 cup flour

Salt and black pepper to taste

4 large soft-shell crabs (or 8 small ones), cleaned

Peanut or canola oil, for sautéing

To prepare the paella rice: Heat the olive oil and butter in a large saucepan. When the butter foams, add the garlic, onion, poblano, and bay leaf, and sauté over medium heat for 5 minutes. Add the rice and season with salt and pepper. Stir until the rice is well coated.

Add the wine and reduce it by half. Add the saffron and $1/2$ cup of the stock. Stir constantly until the liquid is almost absorbed by the rice. Stir in another $1/4$ cup of stock until it is absorbed, and repeat until all the stock has been absorbed by the rice, about 20 to 25 minutes. Transfer the rice to a nonstick baking pan or casserole and let cool.

Prepare the mojo rojo and reserve.

Preheat the oven to 350 degrees and set up a water bath large enough to hold 6 lightly buttered 8-ounce custard cups or ramekins.

To prepare the rice pudding: Beat the eggs in a bowl until pale. Scrape out the seeds from the vanilla bean and whisk in, together with the cream, milk, cornstarch, cayenne, salt, and pepper. Beat thoroughly. Add the cooled paella rice and thoroughly combine.

Pour the mixture into the custard cups or ramekins and place them into the warm water bath. Bake in the oven, uncovered, for 35 minutes, or until an inserted toothpick or cake tester comes out clean. Remove the cups or ramekins from the water bath, and run a knife around the inside edge just to loosen. Keep warm while cooking the crabs.

To prepare the crabs: First beat the eggs and buttermilk together in a bowl. Combine the panko, flour, salt, and pepper in another bowl or on a large platter. Dip the crabs in the egg wash and then in the seasoned flour mixture, coating well. Heat enough oil in a large skillet to coat the bottom thoroughly. Sauté the crabs over medium-high heat for about 3 minutes per side. Watch out for spattering hot oil as they cook. Drain on paper towels.

Shake the custard cups a little and invert the rice pudding onto warm serving plates. Place the crabs next to the rice pudding and drizzle some of the reserved mojo on the plate next to the crabs (or squeeze the juice from a lemon wedge over each serving). Garnish with more lemon wedges or fresh herbs, if desired.

Fideo Noodles and Fish House Pan Stew

Yield: 4 servings.

It was a combination of things that caused me to first come upon these Spanish "pasta" noodles, which is typical for me regarding most aspects of Spanish cuisine. In this case, it was reading food writers like Penelope Casas and Colman Andrews, and visiting neighborhood grocery stores in Key West when I used to live there. I learned that fideo noodles were part of the Moorish heritage, and that they should be toasted in some olive oil for a crispy texture rather than boiled like Italian pasta. Loose vermicelli is a good substitute.

 You can embellish the stew with additional vegetables such as roasted red and yellow bell peppers, grilled christophene, or sautéed mushrooms. If desired, serve with roasted garlic bread and some Roasted Garlic Allioli (page 45).

Bean Kit (page 280)

12 mussels, scrubbed and debearded

2 pounds fish scraps, such as swordfish, tuna, and salmon, cut into 2-inch pieces

2 cups soft red wine, such as Merlot

6 tomatoes, concassé

3 tablespoons Fire Power (page 284), or 2 canned chipotle chiles en adobo, chopped, optional

¹/₂ cup tightly packed Italian parsley leaves, chopped

¹/₄ cup Spanish sherry vinegar

¹/₂ cup plus 2 tablespoons olive oil

8 ounces dry fideo noodles, or vermicelli

2 tablespoons butter

4 cloves garlic, finely sliced

12 large shrimp (about 10 to 12 ounces), peeled and deveined

8 ounces snapper, skin on and scales removed, cut into bite-sized pieces

24 tiny clams, cleaned

1 cup dry white wine

Prepare the bean kit to the "ready stage." Add the mussels, fish scraps, and red wine to the saucepan with the bean kit. Cover and cook over high heat for about 5 minutes, or until the mussels steam open. Carefully remove the fish scraps and the mussels, discard any mussels that do not open, and reserve in a colander over a bowl (the mussels and any good meaty scraps can be added back into the stew at the end, if desired). Stir the mixture in the pan gently and cook, uncovered, for another 5 to 8 minutes.

Add the tomatoes, fire power, and parsley to the pan and stew together over medium-low heat for 25 minutes, stirring occasionally. Stir in the vinegar and turn off the heat.

Heat ¹/₂ cup of the oil in a large pan and cook the noodles over medium-high heat. Toss and stir around, using 2 wooden spoons, and shake them out of their bundles. Cook until nicely colored, about 5 minutes. Drain on paper towels and toss the noodles into the stew.

Heat the remaining 2 tablespoons of the oil with the butter in a sauté pan. When the butter foams, add the garlic and sauté for 20 seconds over medium-high heat. Add the shrimp and snapper and sauté for about 3 minutes, until cooked through. Remove with a slotted spoon and gently toss with the stew.

Add the clams to the sauté pan and pour in the wine. Cover the pan and steam the clams until they open, about 5 to 8 minutes. As they open, add to the stew. Discard any clams that do not open. Warm the stew over medium heat and serve.

Fettuccine with Spicy Tomato Salsa, Crispy Calamari, and Roasted Garlic Allioli

Yield: 4 servings.

Given the domination of pasta in these United States, I wrestled with the idea of including a fettuccine recipe in the New World repertoire. Who needs more pasta recipes? But then I realized there were two good reasons for putting a couple in. First, I read how pasta was probably introduced to Spain by the Moors in the eighth century, and that by the 1800s, Italian food was all the rage in Spain. Full circle over a thousand years of history! The second reason was even simpler. I love the way it tastes with the rest of this very Spanish-flavored dish.

 For smokier, spicier calamari, add a little Dried Chiles Mezcla (page 143) to the seasoned flour.

¹/₄ to ¹/₂ cup Roasted Garlic Allioli (page 45)

SPICY TOMATO SALSA

1¹/₂ cups tomato juice

¹/₄ cup balsamic vinegar

1 teaspoon crushed red pepper

2 cups Salsa Escalivada (page 224), or your favorite tomato salsa or sauce

2 eggs, beaten

¹/₄ cup skim milk

³/₄ cup flour

³/₄ cup cornmeal

Salt and black pepper to taste

8 ounces calamari, totally cleaned and cut into rings

8 ounces dried fettuccine noodles, or 1 pound fresh

Peanut oil, for deep-frying

3 tablespoons butter

3 tablespoons extra-virgin olive oil

¹/₂ cup grated Manchego cheese, or to taste

Prepare the allioli and keep refrigerated.

To prepare the salsa: Heat the tomato juice, vinegar, and crushed red pepper in a heavy saucepan and bring to a high simmer. Reduce the mixture to ¹/₂ cup, about 15 minutes. Mix in the salsa Escalivada, remove from the heat, and set aside.

Whisk together the eggs and milk in a bowl. Combine the flour, cornmeal, salt, and pepper on a large plate. Dip the calamari in the egg wash and then dredge in the seasoned flour mixture. Shake off the excess flour and set aside.

Bring a pot of water to a boil and cook the fettuccine. Meanwhile, heat the oil in a deep-fryer or a large saucepan to 375 degrees. Drain the fettuccine well and transfer to a large bowl. Toss the fettuccine with the butter, olive oil, and cheese. Season with salt and pepper.

Carefully lower the prepared calamari rings into the hot oil and fry until they turn deep golden brown, about 1 minute. Drain on paper towels and season to taste. Keep warm.

Scoop the fettuccine into large warm bowls. Top with the reserved salsa and add the calamari on top of the salsa. Drizzle the reserved allioli over the calamari and serve.

Soba Noodles and Sake-Steamed Clam Stirfry with Thai Stick Dip

Yield: 4 servings.

With the Thai stick dip made in advance, you can prepare this dish in one pan or wok.

 Peanut Dipping Sauce (page 106) is a very welcome addition to this party!

Thai Stick Dip (page 215)

STIRFRY

6 asparagus spears

24 snow peas

4 ounces dried soba noodles

1/4 cup virgin olive oil

1 stalk lemongrass, trimmed and cut into thirds

6 cloves garlic, thinly sliced

1 jalapeño chile, seeded and minced

1 tablespoon ginger, minced

2 portobello mushrooms, cleaned, stemmed, and cut into 1/4-inch slices

1/2 cup sake

Salt and black pepper to taste

24 Manila clams, or other small clams such as Littlenecks, scrubbed

1/4 red bell pepper, seeded and julienned

1/4 yellow bell pepper, seeded and julienned

1 packed cup julienned bok choy, stalks and core removed

2 small Japanese eggplants, ends removed and cut lengthwise into 1/4-inch "planks"

Prepare the stick dip and set aside.

To prepare the stirfry: First bring a saucepan of salted water to a boil. Blanch the asparagus for 1 or 2 minutes, shock in ice water, and chill. In the same pan, blanch the snow peas for 30 seconds, shock in ice water, and chill.

In a separate pan of boiling water, cook the noodles until al dente, about 2 to 3 minutes. Rinse under cold running water and chill.

Heat a wok or large skillet until very hot. Add 1 tablespoon of the olive oil and the lemongrass, garlic, jalapeño, and ginger. Stirfry over high heat for a few seconds. Add the mushrooms and sake, and stir gently once or twice. Reduce the heat to low and cook for about 2 minutes. Discard the lemongrass, remove the mixture to a plate, season with salt and pepper, and set aside.

Add the clams to the wok or skillet and return to high heat. Cover and let the clams steam open (about 3 to 5 minutes). Remove the clams as they open (discard any that do not open). When cooled, remove the clams from their shells and reserve with the mushrooms. Reduce the liquid to $1/2$ cup. (The mushrooms will make the liquid grayish, which is fine—the dish will not finish this color.) Strain and reserve in a separate bowl.

Wipe out the skillet or wok and reheat. Add the remaining 3 tablespoons of oil and stir-fry the bell peppers, bok choy, and eggplants over high heat for 3 or 4 minutes. Julienne the reserved asparagus and add it to the skillet or wok with the snow peas, mushrooms, and clams; stirfry for 1 minute. Add the cooked soba noodles, stick dip, and reserved cooking liquid. Toss well to coat and cook for 1 minute.

Transfer all the vegetables and noodles to a bowl, leaving the juices behind. Reduce the juices to $3/4$ cup, still over high heat. Gently transfer to a plate and return the vegetables and noodles to the skillet or wok. Toss again and when hot, transfer to warm serving bowls.

CHAPTER 8
"OVER THE SIDE!" SIDE DISHES

Crispy Fried Plantain Curls

Caramelized Plantain Mash en Relleno

Corn Kernel Cakes

A Tropical Tuber Torta

Cuban French Fries

South American Fries

A Peruvian Purple Potato Salad

Olive Oil–Roasted New Potatoes

Garlicky Mashed Potatoes Times Three

Deep-Fried Red-Hot Red Onion Rings

Sweet Potato–Sweet Corn Home Fries *That Kick*

Annatto Red Rice

Basic Saffron Rice

Sizzled Leeks

Caramelized Red Onions

Sherried Black Beans

Then the static hum of the radio stretched into a languid Latin rhythm, a distant faraway throb of rhumbas and saltwater breakers striking sandy shores. The music from Cuba filled the back room of the groceria with the swish of swaying palm trees. Bang! Justo's grandfather's cane would strike the pine-plank floor. "Niño!" Justo's abuelo called to him. "Mas marquitas y bollos!" Off Justo went running with the single-minded intensity of a bird dog about to jump a covey of quail, returning to Abuelo and the men with bags of fried green plantain bananas and boxes of sweet bollo penny cakes. Abuelo then poured out shots of compuesto. The fiery sugarcane liquor fueled talk of cock-fights and revolutions past and future.

—Thomas Sanchez, *Mile Zero*

I remember walking into a shack of a restaurant (even by Key West standards) in the spring of '71 and being handed a seawater-damp menu with items like turtle steak, jew-fish chowder, fried *bollos, tostones,* guava milkshake, and a meat dish that translated as "old clothes." Coffee was served in plastic thimble-sized cups and called *buches.*

A mix of customers sat around me at the counter that morning: two rummied-out shrimpers eating large steaks piled high with onions; a stiletto-thin, tense young Latin man wearing triple-tinted sunglasses, eating nothing; a "hippie-till-I-die" Janis Joplin–twin Earth Mama feeding her baby; one rock-solid, leather and laced *policía* sergeant finishing a Marlboro and a *café;* a few dead-to-the-world cats; a woman (?) bearing multiple tattoos and a shaved head; and a grand old Mrs. Haversham-type gal, replete with a conch-pink parasol, who offered to read my palm. Instead, I sat down next to a goateed, gentle mountain that I came to know later as Bud Man, who offered me a job cooking ribs, Brunswick stew, chowder, and such in his all-night, open-air barbecue joint called The Midget, about four blocks from the Gulf of Mexico.

Once I got started there, Bud Man introduced me to Bicycle Sammy. Sammy had a voice raspier than Louis Armstrong, and he was just as black. Sammy was trim, almost muscular, despite his 70 years, and he did not suffer fools gladly. Sammy owned a bike that was *his* statement. The basket was large enough to hold a box of plantains or shrimp from the market. The horn was the size of a trumpet and could be heard from some distance. I worked the graveyard shift; Sammy's followed mine. Every morning, he would arrive, sound his horn, park his "steed," and, dressed in freshly bleached and starched chef whites, take over *his* kitchen.

Sammy taught me how to say things like "Adam and Eve on a raft, float 'em," for poached eggs on toast, or "Shipwreck" for scrambled eggs. The thing I appreciated most was when he showed me how to make the side orders of sweet plantains we served with the pork sandwiches. He explained that the bananas had to get very black to turn sweet, not just yellow-black like regular bananas. Then it was simple. You'll find recipes for plantains in various stages of ripeness in this chapter as well as recipes for many of the other tubers, rices, and fruits that I first tasted back in the Cooking School of Bicycle Sammy.

Crispy Fried Plantain Curls

Yield: 4 servings.

The Cubans call these tasty little chips *marquitas*. Call them what you will, I'll bet that you can't eat just one!

 These are great just for munching with cold drinks, but I also like to serve one or two slices over some of my Spanish-inspired dishes as a garnish—for example, with my Little Havana Chicken and Plantain Sopa (page 59), or as chips for Bajan Guacamole (page 15). You can substitute the Calypso Spice Rub (page 28) for the salt and pepper.

Peanut oil, for deep-frying

*2 green plantains, peeled and sliced lengthwise
as thinly as possible*

Salt and black pepper to taste

In a deep skillet, heat the peanut oil to 375 degrees. Drop the plantain slices into the oil one at a time (so they don't stick together) and fry for about 2 minutes or until crisp and golden.

Remove from the skillet and transfer to a bowl lined with paper towels. Season with the salt and pepper, and serve.

Caramelized Plantain Mash en Relleno

Yield: 4 servings.

A "mash" by itself is not the prettiest thing to put on a plate, so here, we package the plantains in a jade-green jewel box of roasted and peeled poblano chile. It also gives us the left-to-right combo jab of sweet to heat.

 The rellenos can be made up to a day or two ahead of time; just cover with plastic wrap and chill in the refrigerator until ready to cook. Bear in mind that if cooked straight from the refrigerator, they'll need a little longer to warm through. You can substitute any mashed tubers—sweet potatoes or boniato, for example—for the plantains.

2 poblano chiles, stems left on, blistered in hot oil and peeled (page xviii)

¹/₄ cup peanut oil, for frying

2 very ripe maduro *(black) plantains, peeled and cut into ¹/₂-inch-thick slices*

2 tablespoons butter

Salt and black pepper to taste

Carefully cut the poblanos (and stems) in half lengthwise and set aside.

Heat the peanut oil in a large skillet and carefully place the plantain slices into the hot oil. Sauté over medium-high heat until very dark golden, about 2 to 3 minutes per side. Turn them over and sauté until brown. Remove the plantains from the skillet and drain on paper towels.

Preheat the oven to 350 degrees. Place the plantains in a bowl and mash with a fork. Mix in the butter, salt, and pepper. Carefully pack the mashed plantains into the poblano chile halves with a spoon. Transfer the chiles onto a baking sheet and place in the oven for about 10 minutes or until they are heated through.

Corn Kernel Cakes

Yield: 15 to 20 3-inch cakes.

Corn was cultivated originally in the New World and figured dramatically in the nourishment of pre-Columbian civilizations. This legacy continues with these tasty cakes.

 Never turn these cakes (or any pancakes) more than once, or they will lose their delicacy. You can substitute blue cornmeal for the yellow cornmeal for a different look and a slightly different taste. I use this recipe for the torta with the "Criolla Mama" Barbecued Shrimp (page 51).

¹/₄ cup yellow cornmeal

¹/₄ cup flour

¹/₄ teaspoon baking powder

¹/₂ teaspoon salt

Black pepper to taste

¹/₄ teaspoon sugar

¹/₄ cup milk

1 cup cooked corn kernels (see Charred Corn Salsa, page 221, for my favorite method)

3 eggs

¹/₂ Scotch bonnet chile, seeded and minced

3 tablespoons melted butter

1 to 2 tablespoons peanut oil, for frying

In a mixing bowl, combine the cornmeal, flour, baking powder, salt, pepper, and sugar together, and set aside. In a blender, cream the milk and ¹/₂ cup of the corn kernels together and set aside.

Separate two of the eggs, placing the whites into a mixing bowl large enough for beating. Place the egg yolks in a separate bowl, add the remaining whole egg, and whisk together. Add the creamed corn mixture, the remaining corn kernels, the Scotch bonnet chile, and butter to the whisked egg mixture, and then stir in the cornmeal mixture. Beat the egg whites until stiff and gently fold them into the cornmeal mixture.

Rub a skillet with a little of the peanut oil. When fairly hot, add 2 tablespoons of batter for each cake and cook for 30 seconds over medium-high heat until golden brown on both sides. Repeat for the remaining cakes. Keep warm in the oven or serve immediately.

A Tropical Tuber Torta

Yield: 12 servings.

Torta means "cake" in Spanish. This *torta* is a multilayered, very visually enticing potatolike cake. I created the parent recipe of this tropical child for my first book, *Norman Van Aken's Feast of Sunlight*. There, I used the combination of sweet potatoes and Idaho potatoes for a less exotic recipe. You could do that here, of course, but if you are curious about things like Peruvian purple potatoes, yuca, boniato, and such, this will be a nice side dish to include in your act.

 The sweet potatoes can be kept covered with a moist towel while layering the torta, but the yuca, boniato, and purple potatoes must be kept soaking. For a taller presentation, you can cut the portions into smaller squares and stack the layers like checkers on the serving plates. This torta makes a great accompaniment with the Palomilla Venison Steak au Poivre (page 164). You can substitute half a baking potato for either the boniato or yuca.

3 tablespoons butter

1 large red onion, sliced

Salt and black pepper to taste

¹/₄ cup Spanish sherry vinegar

³/₄ cup clarified butter

1 large sweet potato, peeled and very thinly sliced

1 boniato, peeled and very thinly sliced

1 yuca, peeled and very thinly sliced

1 cup finely grated Manchego cheese

4 Peruvian purple potatoes, peeled and very thinly sliced

Preheat the oven to 350 degrees. Line a 9 × 13-inch baking pan with parchment paper.

Heat the butter in a saucepan and when melted, add the onion. Toss to coat, and season with salt and pepper. Sauté over medium-high heat until caramelized, about 10 minutes, stirring as necessary. Add the vinegar and reduce until almost no liquid remains, about 1 or 2 minutes. Remove from the heat and set aside.

Lightly brush the baking pan and parchment paper with the clarified butter. Starting with half of the sweet potato, layer the bottom of the pan, overlapping the slices so that it is completely covered. Brush the potato with the clarified butter and season with salt and pepper.

Repeat this process with the half of the boniato, and then evenly distribute half of the caramelized onion over the boniato layer. Layer half of the yuca over the onion, brushing with the butter and seasoning with salt and pepper. Repeat the layering process with the remaining sweet potato, boniato, onion, and yuca.

Add the cheese in a single layer. Top with a layer of purple potatoes. Brush with the clarified butter and season with salt and pepper. Cover with parchment paper and then aluminum foil. Place another (weighted) 9 × 13-inch baking pan (or some other similarly sized pan) on top of the foil to gently compress the torta.

Bake the torta in the oven for about 70 minutes. Remove from the oven and let cool a little. Remove the foil and parchment paper covering, and cut the torta into 3-inch square sections. If desired, you can let the torta cool completely and then reheat the portions you wish to serve.

Cuban French Fries

Yield: 4 servings.

Make these once, and you'll make them again and again. It's the easiest introduction to the tuber pronounced "yoo-kah." The Cuban community adores the tradition of serving these fries with a mojo sauce (the *j* is pronounced like an *h,* don't forget). I've come to love mojo too, but the kind sold in stores usually contains too much salt and preservatives, so I concocted my own twist on mojo. I call it "Mo. J." and you'll find the recipe on page 226. Of course, you may wish to try these fries with something we all love in this wide country of ours: ketchup.

 Use these fries in any recipe or at any time you may ordinarily serve French fries.

2 pounds yuca, peeled and cut into 3-inch-long "planks"

Salt and black pepper to taste

Vegetable or peanut oil, for frying

Place the yuca slices in a large saucepan and cover with water. Bring the water to a boil, lower the heat, and simmer for 15 to 30 minutes (the time can vary a great deal; you want the yuca to still be a little firm). Drain the yuca and let cool slightly on a cutting board. When cool enough to handle, cut the yuca into 3/4-inch strips, discarding any woody core.

Heat the oil in a large skillet or French fryer to 360 degrees and fry the yuca strips until golden brown. Drain on paper towels, season with salt and pepper, and keep warm.

South American Fries

Yield: 4 servings.

One of the best things about becoming a cook, for me, was that I got to eat. Being a young growing boy, this was not a mere perk, but a significant aspect of the job. "American Fries" were part of the menu in the diner where I first started cooking. Potatoes with onions, garlic, and a touch of butter, salt, and pepper are basic and beautiful. The addition of a colorful tuber that comes from the mountainous elevations of Peru takes the look and taste just a notch higher.

 The Peruvian potatoes can be pricey in some markets, and hard to find in others. You can substitute sweet potatoes or small red potatoes for half of the Peruvian potatoes called for in the recipe. If you're preparing a large batch of these fries, I recommend briefly blanching the potatoes first in boiling water. These fries go perfectly with the Grilled Pork Chops (page 162).

2 tablespoons butter

2 tablespoons Roasted Garlic Oil (page 277).
or olive oil

¹/₂ red onion. thinly sliced

8 Peruvian purple potatoes. scrubbed and cut
into ¹/₄-inch slices (skin left on)

Salt and black pepper to taste

In a large skillet, heat the butter and garlic oil. When the butter foams, add the onion, stir once, and sauté over medium-high heat for about 2 minutes, caramelizing them slightly. Add the potatoes and season with salt and pepper. Stir, cover the skillet, and cook for 10 minutes, tossing every few minutes. Uncover and cook for about 5 to 10 minutes, tossing occasionally, until nicely browned and crispy.

A Peruvian Purple Potato Salad

Yield: About 7 cups.

Although true that these purple potatoes taste much like white potatoes, they sure don't look like them. Purple potatoes actually range in color from yellow to red, violet, and black. I enjoy their brilliance for the same reason I like annatto. Their name also helps teach (or remind) people that Peru is the homeland of all potatoes (you'll even find *sun-dried* potatoes in Peru).

 Because Peruvian purple potatoes vary in color, choose the most vividly purple and vibrant ones for the best presentation. Ask your grocer, as nicely as you know how, to see a cut potato so that you can be sure of the color. New or yellow Finnish potatoes can be substituted. I use this salad with the Sea Scallop Seviche *"Ahora Mismo"* (page 83).

12 Peruvian purple potatoes, about 3 pounds

1 red bell pepper, seeded and diced small

1 yellow bell pepper, seeded and diced small

1 red onion, diced small

$^1/_4$ cup coarsely chopped cilantro leaves

$^1/_3$ cup champagne vinegar

$^2/_3$ cup virgin olive oil

Salt and black pepper to taste

Place the potatoes in a large saucepan and cover with water. Bring to a simmer over high heat and cook at a low boil for about 15 to 20 minutes, until just barely cooked through. Drain the potatoes and shock in ice water for 20 seconds.

When cool, drain again and rub the skins off (you can leave them on, if you prefer). Cut the potatoes into $^3/_4$-inch dice and place in a large bowl. Add the bell peppers, onion, and cilantro.

In a separate bowl, whisk together the vinegar and olive oil. Pour the dressing over the potato salad, season with salt and pepper, and gently mix together. Allow the potatoes to cool thoroughly before serving.

Olive Oil–Roasted New Potatoes

Yield: 4 servings.

These herbaceously scented potatoes, with the aroma of warm olive oil perfuming your kitchen, may cause some of your neighbors to wander over and strike up a conversation. You may want to double this recipe! Besides, even if they don't, these spuds still make a very good leftover ingredient for an omelet with, say, my Chorizo (page 288), and maybe some Carmelized Red Onions (page206).

 The olive oil can be reused up to three more times for this recipe; let it cool, strain through a fine strainer, and keep it covered in the refrigerator.

*12 new potatoes (about 1 1/2 pounds), scrubbed,
cut in half and then into wedges*

2 to 3 cups olive oil

2 large sprigs rosemary

3 sage leaves

1 sprig thyme

1 teaspoon coarse sea salt

12 toasted and crushed black peppercorns

Preheat the oven to 425 degrees. Place all the ingredients together in a loaf pan or deep roasting pan. The oil-and-herb mixture should just cover the potatoes (add more oil, if necessary). Transfer to the oven and roast for about 30 to 40 minutes, or until just cooked through. Remove the potatoes from the oil and keep warm until ready to serve. Strain the flavored oil and reserve for another use.

Garlicky Mashed Potatoes Times Three

The first element of this three-part recipe is for simply wonderful mashed potatoes. I think you'll love them so much that you'll be mad at me for tempting you to make them over and over again. The other elements of this recipe give you these sensual spuds in a stacked shape, and then, moving on to the bonus round— Garlicky Mashed *Sweet* Potatoes.

1. GARLICKY MASHED POTATOES

Yield: 4 generous servings.

*6 cups peeled and diced new potatoes (about 12
to 15)*

Large pinch of salt

2 cups heavy cream

$^1/_4$ cup Roasted Garlic Power (page 281)

3 tablespoons butter

Salt and black pepper to taste

Place the potatoes in a large saucepan and cover with cold water. Add the salt and bring the potatoes to a boil. Reduce the heat to medium and simmer the potatoes.

Meanwhile, in a separate saucepan, bring the cream to a boil. Whisk in the garlic power and reduce slightly to 2 cups. Remove from the heat and keep warm until needed.

When the potatoes are just cooked, remove from the heat and strain off the water. Add the butter and mash the potatoes with a fork, potato masher, or the side of a spoon, leaving it a little chunky. Pour enough of the garlic cream into the potatoes to soften them; they should still be firm, and not be too wet. Mash together. Season to taste and serve.

2. GARLICKY MASHED AND STACKED POTATOES

Yield: 4 servings.

This is for very special occasions. The first part of this recipe gives directions for the potato crisps that you use to separate and support the mashed potatoes in a very striking presentation. You can get creative and make squares with the potato crisps to present a faux "box" of mashed potatoes. In the past, I have left the top off of the "box" and added Sizzled Leeks (page 205) so they are jutting out of the mashed potatoes.

$^1/_4$ cup clarified butter, melted

4 new potatoes, peeled

Salt and black pepper to taste

Garlicky Mashed Potatoes (above)

Preheat the oven to 350 degrees. Place the clarified butter in a large bowl. Using a small mandolin slicer, slice the potatoes finely enough that you can see your fingertips through the slices when you hold them up to the light. Scatter the potato slices in the bowl of butter, and gently toss so that each slice is lightly coated.

Line a nonstick pan or baking sheet with parchment paper and arrange the potatoes in 8 pinwheel (or flower petal) shapes. Season with salt and pepper. Cover the pinwheels with parchment paper and weight with another pan or baking sheet placed on top. Roast in the oven for 15 minutes.

Remove from the oven and take off the top pan. *Carefully* peel off the top sheet of parchment paper using a spatula or knife to unstick from the potatoes. Return the pan to the oven for 7 to 10 minutes, until the potatoes are golden brown. Remove from the oven and carefully scoop the potatoes off using a spatula. Reserve on paper towels.

Prepare the Garlicky Mashed Potatoes and keep warm.

To serve, place a large spoonful of the mashed potatoes onto each plate. Place 1 of the potato pinwheels on top of the mashed potatoes and place a layer of mashed potatoes on top of the pinwheel. Top the mashed potatoes with another pinwheel and serve.

3. GARLICKY MASHED SWEET POTATOES

Yield: 6 servings.

This side is just perfect with baked ham, robust game, or spicy chicken dishes.

5 sweet potatoes (about 4 pounds), peeled and diced

Large pinch of salt

1 cup heavy cream

1 tablespoon Roasted Garlic Power (page 281)

1½ tablespoons butter

Salt and black pepper to taste

Place the sweet potatoes in a large saucepan and cover with cold water. Add the salt and bring to a boil. Reduce the heat to medium and simmer the sweet potatoes.

Meanwhile, in a separate saucepan, bring the cream to a boil. Whisk in the garlic power and reduce slightly to 1 cup. Remove from the heat and keep warm until needed.

When the potatoes are just cooked, remove from the heat and strain off the water. Transfer to a large warm bowl. Add the butter and mash the sweet potatoes with a fork, a potato masher, or the side of a spoon.

Pour just enough of the garlic cream into the potatoes to soften them; they should not be too wet. Mash together. Season to taste and serve.

Deep-Fried Red-Hot Red Onion Rings

Yield: 4 to 6 servings.

I have loved onion rings forever. When I became a chile convert, I pumped their power into my "rings" and have been pumped up ever since.

 Use this recipe whenever you feel like robust onion rings; they go particularly well with the Gaucho Steak (page 150).

2 red onions, peeled and cut into ¹/₄-inch-thick rings

1 cup Hot Chile Oil (page 277), or olive oil

1 cup buttermilk

SEASONED FLOUR

2¹/₂ cups flour

2 teaspoons crushed red pepper

2 teaspoons salt

1 tablespoon cayenne

2 teaspoons hot paprika

4 teaspoons black pepper

Peanut oil, for frying

Place the onion rings in a large mixing bowl, add the chile oil, and toss to separate the rings. Cover and refrigerate for at least 2 hours. Add the buttermilk, cover, and chill in the refrigerator for 1 hour longer.

Place all the seasoned flour ingredients in a large mixing bowl and combine thoroughly. Heat the peanut oil in a deep fryer or large saucepan to 365 degrees.

Remove the onion rings from the buttermilk mixture and dredge in the seasoned flour, shaking off any excess flour. Put the onions in the hot oil and deep-fry for 2 to 3 minutes, or until golden brown.

Remove with a slotted spoon and and drain on paper towels. Adjust the seasoning to taste and serve.

Sweet Potato–Sweet Corn Home Fries *That Kick*

Yield: 6 to 8 servings.

Warning! Strong medicine enclosed! These home fries start off sweet and innocent and then, just when you think "What's he mean, *'that kick'*?", a red door in your brain suddenly bangs open. "Why, hello! Hey, who are you?" you ask. "Doctor Bonnet," she replies and, in her chile-spiked heels, ushers you into her back office. *Whoosh,* off comes the mask, and now the smiling good doctor promptly introduces you to a brief but indelible moment in her shock and heat therapies . . .

 You can make this recipe with just sweet potatoes if boniato is unavailable. These fries can be kept warm for up to 30 minutes before serving.

*1 pound sweet potatoes, scrubbed and
quartered (skin on)*

*1 pound boniato, scrubbed and quartered (skin
on)*

Large pinch of salt

1/4 cup Annatto Oil (page 275), or olive oil

1/4 cup butter

6 cloves garlic, thinly sliced

1 Scotch bonnet chile, seeded and minced

1 red onion, sliced

6 scallions, white part only, sliced into rings

2 cups fresh corn kernels (3 or 4 ears)

Salt and black pepper to taste

Place the sweet potatoes and boniato in a large saucepan and cover with water. Add the pinch of salt and bring to a high simmer. Cook for 7 or 8 minutes over medium-high heat; they should still be firm. Drain off the water and let cool.

Peel the cooked sweet potato and boniato and dice them into ¹/₂ × ³/₄-inch cubes. Heat the oil and butter in a very large skillet until the butter melts. Add the garlic and chile, stir, and sauté over medium heat for 1 minute. Turn up the heat to high and add the onion, scallions, and corn kernels. Stir well to coat and season with salt and pepper. Sauté, stirring only occasionally, until the corn is nicely charred, about 5 minutes.

Gently stir in the parboiled sweet potato and boniato cubes, being careful not to crumble them. Reduce the heat to medium and cook for about 10 minutes, until the tubers are browned. Serve.

Annatto Red Rice

Yield: About 3½ cups.

This all-purpose side dish is a simple rice pilaf with the addition of some annatto-infused olive oil, which makes it "simply red."

 The rice can be kept warm for 20 to 30 minutes before serving, if necessary.

2 tablespoons Annatto Oil (page 275)

2 tablespoons butter

½ Scotch bonnet chile, seeded and minced, optional

4 cloves garlic, minced

½ onion, diced small

1 carrot, diced small

1 celery stalk, diced small

2 small bay leaves, broken

1 cup long-grain rice

Salt and black pepper to taste

1¼ cups Light Chicken Stock (page 270)

In a saucepan, heat the annatto oil and the butter. When the butter has melted, stir in the chile and garlic and sauté for 15 seconds over medium heat. Stir in the onion, carrot, celery, and bay leaves, and cook until well glazed, about 10 minutes, stirring frequently.

Stir in the rice, salt, and pepper. Add the chicken stock and stir once. Bring to a boil and immediately reduce the heat to low. Cover the pan and cook for 12 to 15 minutes, or until all of the stock has been absorbed. Serve.

Basic Saffron Rice

Yield: About 3½ cups.

This recipe is identical to the Annatto Red Rice, except that we use olive oil instead of the annatto oil, and saffron. In Key West, old-timers referred to a well-made rice as "one-one" because each grain was distinct from the others.

 This is another all-purpose rice; I use it for the Cuban Pork Asado (page 158). Like the previous recipe, this rice can be kept warm for 20 to 30 minutes before serving, if necessary.

2 tablespoons olive oil

2 tablespoons butter

½ Scotch bonnet chile, seeded and minced
(optional)

4 cloves garlic, minced

½ onion, diced small

1 carrot, diced small

1 celery stalk, diced small

2 small bay leaves, broken

1 cup long-grain rice

Salt and black pepper to taste

1¼ cups Light Chicken Stock (page 270)

1 large pinch high-quality Spanish saffron

In a saucepan, heat the olive oil and butter. When the butter has melted, stir in the chile and garlic and sauté for 15 seconds over medium heat. Stir in the onion, carrot, celery, and bay leaves, and cook until well glazed, about 10 minutes, stirring frequently. Stir in the rice, salt, and pepper.

In a separate pan, warm the chicken stock; add the saffron and let it steep for 5 minutes. Add the stock and saffron to the rice, and stir once. Bring to a boil and immediately reduce the heat to low. Cover the pan and cook for 12 to 15 minutes, or until all of the stock has been absorbed. Serve.

Sizzled Leeks

Yield: 6 servings.

Stack these *high* on many types of savory dishes that call for the oniony taste of leeks, and your guests will be impressed. I like to use them with my Lapsang Souchong Salmon (page 134).

 These babies will turn from white to golden somewhat slowly at first, but they cook very quickly from that point, turning from golden to black (and ruined) quickly . . . so keep your eyes peeled.

Peanut or vegetable oil, for deep-frying

2 leeks, white and light green parts only, finely julienned

Salt and black pepper to taste

Heat the oil in a deep-fryer or large saucepan to 375 degrees. Deep-fry the leeks in large-handful batches, stirring quickly with tongs to keep them separated as they cook. Deep-fry for 2 to 3 minutes, until golden and crisp. Remove from the oil with a slotted spoon and drain on paper towels. Season with salt and pepper, and keep warm until ready to serve.

Caramelized Red Onions

Yield: 4 servings.

I recently watched *Good Morning America*'s resident chef, Sara Moulton, helpfully explain how to make a good dish better without too much trouble. One technique was to save dishes that taste flat because they lacked a little acidity; another was to rescue dishes that look dull because they are monochromatic. Well, these onions will knock out both problems in a wide range of dishes—pronto.

 This recipe can be whipped up an hour or two in advance and then quickly reheated when needed. For a little herb flavor (if you want to accent a dish), add some mixed fresh herbs with the vinegar. This is a versatile side dish that I use with "Mile Marker 19" Grilled Dolphin Fish (page 113) and Grilled Gulf Swordfish (page 119).

2 tablespoons olive oil

2 tablespoons butter

2 red onions. sliced with the lines (lengthwise)

1 tablespoon sugar

¹/₄ cup red wine vinegar

Salt and black pepper to taste

Heat the olive oil and butter in a large sauté pan over high heat. When the butter begins to foam, add the onions and stir once to coat well. Sauté for about 8 to 10 minutes, or until caramelized, stirring only occasionally. Reduce the heat to medium and sauté for another 10 minutes.

Sprinkle the onions with the sugar and stir gently. Cook for 1 minute. Stir in the vinegar and reduce for 1 or 2 minutes, or until the liquid has almost completely evaporated. Season with salt and pepper, and reserve until needed.

Sherried Black Beans

Yield: About 4½ cups.

Black beans are the soul of my New World kitchen. I use them for many dishes; they are a frame of reference for what drives my cooking, as surely as are plantains, chiles, tropical fruits, rice, coffee, and rhum.

 Avoid salting the beans before or during cooking, or they will become tough.

½ recipe Bean Kit (page 280)

1 teaspoon cayenne

¼ cup Spanish sherry vinegar

1 cup Spanish sherry

*1 cup dried black beans, rinsed, soaked
overnight, and drained*

1 ham bone, optional

5 cups Dark Chicken Stock (page 271)

Salt and black pepper to taste

Prepare the bean kit to the "ready stage."

Stir in the cayenne and add the vinegar and sherry. Reduce the liquid by half, about
5 minutes. Add the drained beans, the ham bone, and the chicken stock, and bring to a
boil. Skim off any impurities that come to the surface with a spoon.

Reduce the heat to medium-low and cook the beans, uncovered, until they are just soft,
about 2 hours. Add more stock or water as necessary. Season to taste and serve.

CHAPTER 9
SAUCES AND REDUCTIONS,
SALSAS, MOJOS, AND CHUTNEYS

SAUCES AND REDUCTIONS
My *Very* Black Bean Sauce
A Uno, Mi Estilo
Thai Stick Dip
A Gingery Jus
A Spanish Sherry Reduction
Big Twist Barbecue Essence

SALSAS, MOJOS, AND CHUTNEYS
Salsa Romesco
Charred Corn Salsa
Oriental Mushroom Salsa
Exotic Tropical Fruit and Black Bean Salsa
Salsa Escalivada
West Indian Cocktail Salsa
Mo J.
Mango-Habanero Mojo
Mojo Rojo
The Redlands Tropical Fruit Chutney

It was a moving thing to work with a demon. Nominally the kitchen was mine, but in the course of our cooperations, I felt not only the kitchen, but the whole world in which we were cooperating, pass over into Kamante's hands. For here he understood to perfection what I wished of him, and sometimes he carried out my wishes even before I had told him of them; but as to me I could not make clear to myself how or indeed why he worked as he did.

He had a great memory for recipes. He could not read, and he knew no English so that cookerybooks were of no use to him, but he must have held all that according to some systemization of his own, which I should never know. He had named the dishes after some event which had taken place on the day they had been shown to him, and he spoke of the sauce of the lightning that struck the tree, and of the sauce of the grey horse that died.

—Isak Dinesen, *Out of Africa*

Roman Catholic priest Charles Polzer, speaking at the American Institute of Wine and Food Conference in Washington, D.C., in March 1993, said, "To be American is precisely to be able to share our ethnic diversity, to sustain traditions that have come from elsewhere and to meet the other person on neutral ground—not to force ethnocentrism, not to reject others, but to accept them in all their colors and all their creeds and, I might add, all their flavors."

In this chapter, you will find a world of diversity. When I first learned about cuisine, a sauce was usually three to five ounces of a flavored cream, butter, tomato, vinaigrette, or reduced stock. More often than not, it was very smooth. This was due to the French base on which I had built my learning. As I traveled, read, tasted, and cooked, "sauces" came to mean many other things. They came to be called many things too. I have arranged my "sauces" in the following classification. It is a guide, and some of the recipes could fit into more than one category, especially as their use changes.

Sauces are said to be the place where a chef finds his highest form of expression. No more! Sauces are but one area where we can find a chef best articulating the instruments in the total composition of a dish. Salsas, reductions, broths, essences, oils, drizzles, mojos, madres, chutneys, relishes, and dips have all become part of the tools that modern chefs have in their repertoire. The world is ours in which to search. We have found these now. Who knows what tomorrow brings?

Reductions and *essences* are, usually, intensified protein-rich sauces. With the application of heat, many sauces will reduce in volume and the flavors focus into a tighter field of reference.

Salsas are mixtures of contrapuntual flavors and, often, colors that contrast with the main element of a dish. They are usually textured and are often composed of uncooked or partially cooked elements.

Mojos usually refers to a sauce of Spanish origin, or ingredients that are used in a Spanish-influenced style. The word *mojo* is probably derived from the Spanish *mojar,* which means "to wet." In Cuban cuisine, *mojo* refers to a specific piquant sauce. I decided to broaden the application for my cooking after discovering that the Portuguese word *molho* refers to many different sauces.

Chutneys and *relishes* are fruit and/or vegetable condiments that act as an accent to other foods. They have a greater probability of piquancy than most of the categories listed here; tiny amounts usually act as a bright counterpoint to the main elements of a dish.

Many chefs today are working with these new ways to flavor foods, which is the reason sauces were created in the first place. We are also seeking to satisfy the desire for foods that are lower in fat, less expensive to produce, visually stimulating, and faster to make. The most important reason of all for making these recipes is their *taste.*

SAUCES AND REDUCTIONS

My *Very* Black Bean Sauce

Yield: about 3 cups.

If you're used to cooking beans, it may seem as though I have too much stock in this recipe, but trust me, it's for a very good reason. After the beans are cooked, we reduce the broth to an intense "brew" that contains all the flavors that have been cooked together. It turns what may appear to be a black bean soup recipe into an incredibly flavorful sauce. Even if I were making the classic black beans and yellow rice, I would pump up the flavor of the beans by making them this way.

 These beans are very good refried and added to tacos or enchiladas, or other Southwestern dishes. I use them with the Pan-Roasted Cumin-Rubbed Breast of Chicken (page 144). This recipe makes enough for about 8 entrée side portions. The beans also freeze well.

¹/₂ recipe Bean Kit (page 280)

1 teaspoon cayenne

1 cup dried black beans, rinsed, soaked in water overnight, and drained

¹/₄ cup Spanish sherry vinegar

1 cup Spanish sherry

7 cups Dark Chicken Stock (page 271)

Salt to taste

Prepare the bean kit to the "ready stage."

Add the cayenne, beans, sherry vinegar, and sherry, and reduce the liquid by half over high heat, about 5 minutes. Add the stock, bring to a boil, and skim off any impurities. Lower the heat to medium-low and cook the beans for about 2 hours, or until they are just soft.

Strain the beans through a colander set over a large bowl. Let the broth collect in the bowl and when drained, reserve the beans in a separate bowl. Return the broth to a clean pan (there should be about 2 to 2¹/₂ cups). Reduce by half over high heat, about 10 minutes. Return the thickened broth to the beans and season with salt.

A Uno, Mi Estilo

Yield: 2 to 2½ cups.

This recipe title translates as "A-1, my way." Use it as a dipping sauce for the Palomilla-Venison Steak au Poivre (page 164) or my Gaucho Steak (page 150), brush it on hamburgers as they leave the grill, or use it as a condiment for any robust grilled beef or chicken dish.

 There are a number of flavor variations you can make with a sauce like this. Add some tomato paste for a tomatoey flavor; a cup of chopped caramelized onions for crunchy sweetness; or smoked poultry stock, chipotle chile purée, or fire power for a smokier flavor. This sauce will keep refrigerated and covered for at least 3 weeks, and it can be frozen.

2 tablespoons Roasted Garlic Oil (page 277), or olive oil

2 ounces smoked bacon, rind cut off (about ½ cup)

1 tablespoon butter

1 large clove garlic, finely minced

¼ red onion, diced small

1 stalk celery, diced small

1 carrot, diced small

2 jalapeño chiles, seeded and minced

12 black peppercorns, crushed

2 tablespoons Fire Power (page 284), or 3 canned chipotle chiles, split in half lengthwise

½ cup plus 2 tablespoons Spanish sherry vinegar

1½ cups red wine, such as Zinfandel or Cabernet Sauvignon

1 cup Dark Chicken Stock (page 271), or Light Chicken Stock (page 270)

1 cup (8 ounces) tamarind pulp

1 cup water

2 roasted poblano chiles, peeled and seeded

1 roasted jalapeño chile, peeled and seeded

1 roasted red bell pepper, peeled and seeded

2 tablespoons Creole mustard or whole-grain mustard

2 tablespoons dark molasses

1 tablespoon prepared horseradish, slightly strained

Black pepper to taste

Heat a large, shallow saucepan. Add the garlic oil and cook the smoked bacon over medium heat until almost cooked through. Add the butter and stir in the garlic, onion, celery, carrot, jalapeños, peppercorns, and fire power or chipotles. Turn the heat up to medium-high and caramelize the mixture, stirring occasionally, about 10 minutes.

Add the sherry vinegar and wine, and reduce the liquid by three-quarters, about 10 to 12 minutes. Add the stock and reduce again by three-quarters, about 10 minutes. Strain through a fine-mesh strainer and transfer the liquid to a food processor.

Heat the tamarind pulp with the water in a clean saucepan. Bring to a simmer, whisk vigorously, and strain into the food processor. Add the roasted chiles and bell pepper to the processor, and purée. Mix in the mustard, molasses, and horseradish. Season with pepper to taste and reserve until needed.

Thai Stick Dip

Yield: About 1¼ cups.

This is one of those charmers that can work itself into a variety of roles. I admire its ability to not be simply typecast, and I admire its flavor even more. It works as a dip (at Norman's, I use it with an Asian dish that I call Lobster Thai Sticks, hence its name), and as a reduction. I use it with the Soba Noodles and Clam Stirfry (page 183).

 This dip will keep for weeks in the refrigerator.

1 cup Light or Dark Chicken Stock (pages 270, 271)

½ cup unseasoned rice wine vinegar

½ cup brown sugar

¼ cup soy sauce

¼ cup hoisin sauce

1 teaspoon Oriental hot chile sauce (preferably Sriracha)

1 tablespoon Thai red curry paste

1 tablespoon Oriental fish sauce

Juice of 1 lime

1 tablespoon minced garlic

1 tablespoon minced ginger

1 Scotch bonnet chile, seeded and minced

2 tablespoons roughly chopped cilantro leaves

Combine the stock and vinegar in a saucepan and bring to a boil. Add the remaining ingredients and return to a boil. Whisk vigorously and reduce the mixture by one-third to concentrate the flavors, about 12 minutes. Pour the mixture into a nonreactive container and chill until needed.

A Gingery Jus

Yield: 6 tablespoons.

Jus is French for "juice." The juice inside the ginger is the dominant flavor here. I use it to provide a peppy counterpoint to the richness of Asian-flavored meat and seafood recipes.

 This recipe is best served warm. For larger yields, double or triple the recipe; the jus will keep for up to 1 month in the refrigerator. I use it with the Sushi Kushi (page 35).

¹/₄ cup butter

¹/₄ cup diced ginger

¹/₂ Scotch bonnet chile, seeded and minced

2 tablespoons balsamic vinegar

1 tablespoon tamari

1 tablespoon tomato ketchup

Heat a small saucepan over very low heat and add the butter. When it begins to melt, add the ginger and Scotch bonnet, and simmer for 8 to 10 minutes. Strain with a fine-mesh strainer into a bowl. Discard the ginger and chile. Whisk in the balsamic vinegar, tamari, and ketchup. Reserve until needed.

A Spanish Sherry Reduction

Yield: 2¹/₂ to 3¹/₂ cups.

Too often, sauces are too heavy with stock and meat flavors. This is compounded by the fact that meat sauces are nearly always served with . . . you guessed it, meat. Taste some of these sauces on their own and you may say, "Wow, that's *intense!*" But put a steak on top and it's often past intense and into overwhelming. With a balancing dose of vegetables, wine, and a good wine vinegar, we can create the exquisite flavors that make a dish reach out to higher levels.

This is a very adaptable sauce. You can use alternative wines or vinegars, or even substitute fruit juices to provide the acidity. These choices are determined by other characteristics of the dish. For example, if it's Spanish in style, the sherry vinegar or a red Rioja wine can be used; with the more delicate flavors of birds, a merlot and fruit vinegar reduction might work best.

This sauce can be made a day or two in advance, or frozen up to 3 months. Freeze any leftover sauce or use a little to strengthen a new batch. To give the sauce a beautiful sheen and richness, whisk in a teaspoon or two of cold butter at the end.

2 tablespoons virgin olive oil

2 ounces smoked slab bacon, finely diced (about 1/2 cup)

2 tablespoons butter

1 head garlic, cut in half crosswise

1 onion, diced small

2 leeks, white part only, cleaned and diced small

2 large carrots, diced small

4 large stalks celery, diced small

1 tablespoon black peppercorns, toasted and crushed

2 bay leaves, broken

6 to 8 button mushrooms, diced small

1/4 cup freshly toasted cumin seeds

1/4 cup Dried Chiles Mezcla (page 143)

3/4 cup Spanish sherry vinegar

1 cup Spanish sherry

2 quarts Dark Chicken Stock (page 271)

Heat a large heavy saucepan; add the olive oil and the bacon. Sauté over medium-high heat until the bacon is half cooked. Add the butter; when it begins to foam, add the garlic, and stir. Add the onion, leeks, carrots, celery, peppercorns, and bay leaves. Stir thoroughly and sauté for about 20 minutes, or until caramelized.

Stir in the mushrooms and sauté for 1 minute longer. Add the cumin, chiles mezcla, vinegar, and sherry. Reduce the liquid by three-quarters, about 3 to 4 minutes. Add the stock and bring to a boil. Skim off any impurities and lower the heat to a simmer. Reduce the liquid by half, about 1 hour. Strain into a bowl through a fine-mesh strainer. Chill completely.

Spoon off the accumulated fat and discard. Transfer the liquid to a saucepan. Reduce the liquid down to 3 cups and re-strain. Use immediately or chill again until needed.

Big Twist Barbecue Essence

Yield: About 1 cup.

This recipe is based on the Big Twist Barbecue Sauce recipe on page 120. After you've made the sauce, this recipe is a cinch!

 This is a good example of how you can serve less sauce, yet not lose the chance to serve food with powerful flavors. Drizzle it on grilled chicken or beef. It will keep for up to 2 weeks in the refrigerator.

1 recipe Big Twist Barbecue Sauce

If the barbecue sauce is cold, heat it in a saucepan. When warm, strain through a colander into a clean pan. Reserve the vegetables for another use, such as a pizza topping, an omelete filling, or stirred into a cream sauce for a lively pasta topping. Simmer the strained juice over medium-high heat and reduce to 1 cup, about 30 minutes. Skim any impurities, if necessary. Strain the liquid through a fine chinois strainer and reserve until needed.

SALSAS, MOJOS, AND CHUTNEYS

Salsa Romesco

Yield: About 3½ cups.

It would be logical to think that *romesco* was Italian, but it was created in the Spanish city of Tarragona, which has many ancient monuments from its days of Roman rule. Romesco is used as a salsa, sauce, and as a medium for cooking seafood in particular.

 This salsa will keep up to 3 weeks if refrigerated in an airtight container. It can also be frozen.

2 ripe tomatoes, cored

³/₄ cup extra-virgin olive oil

1 jalapeño chile, seeded and minced

1 poblano chile, seeded and minced

3 dried ancho chiles, seeded, toasted, soaked in water (see page xix), and drained

2 slices country-style white bread

6 cloves garlic, sliced

24 almonds, blanched and roasted

24 hazelnuts, roasted and rubbed with a towel to remove the skins

2 tablespoons minced parsley leaves

2 tablespoons minced cilantro leaves

¹/₄ cup balsamic vinegar

³/₄ tablespoon red wine vinegar

Salt and black pepper to taste

Preheat the oven to 350 degrees. Place the whole tomatoes in a lightly oiled roasting pan or sheet and roast in the oven for 10 minutes. Remove from the oven and let cool.

Heat 1 tablespoon of the olive oil in a pan or skillet and sauté the jalapeño, poblano, and drained anchos over medium-high heat for about 1 minute. Set aside.

Heat 2 tablespoons of the oil in the pan or skillet and fry the bread slices over medium-high heat on both sides until golden brown. Set aside.

Place the cooked chiles and garlic in a food processor or blender and pulse. Add the reserved bread, the nuts, and herbs, and pulse again to mix evenly. In a saucepan on medium-high heat, reduce the balsamic vinegar by half. Skin and seed the roasted tomatoes. Add to the processor or blender and pulse. Add the reduced balsamic vinegar, the red wine vinegar, salt, pepper, and the remaining olive oil. Pulse together to mix.

Charred Corn Salsa

Yield: 3½ to 4 cups.

Corn was initially cultivated by Indians of the New World and has become one of the world's most important food crops. I can instantly recall the aroma of corn roasts from my childhood, tempting in my memory even now in the closed walls of my writing room. The charring takes the just-picked sweet flavor and clasps it with the timeless intoxication of smoke.

 This salsa is best made no more than 3 hours ahead of time. If you want to avoid the hassle of using the grill, blister the corn in a skillet on the stovetop.

3 ears sweet corn, shucked

4½ tablespoons olive oil

Salt and black pepper to taste

½ red onion, diced small

½ red pepper, seeded and diced small

½ yellow pepper, seeded and diced small

2 jalapeño chiles, seeded and minced

3 tablespoons roughly chopped cilantro leaves

3 cloves garlic, minced

1 tablespoon Spanish sherry vinegar

1 teaspoon black pepper

Prepare the grill. Lightly brush the corn with about 1 tablespoon of the olive oil. Season with salt and pepper. Grill the corn until nicely colored. Cut the kernels from the cob and reserve in a bowl.

Heat 1½ tablespoons of the oil in a sauté pan and when hot, quickly sauté the onion and bell peppers over medium-high heat until just soft. Transfer to the bowl of corn and stir in the jalapeños, cilantro, garlic, vinegar, and the remaining 2 tablespoons of the oil. Season with the black pepper and salt to taste. Reserve until needed.

Oriental Mushroom Salsa

Yield: About 1 1/2 cups.

The Asian peoples' long-standing love of mushrooms is well known. They pay enormous sums of money for the mushrooms known as *matsutakes*. Here, I'm using the now commonplace shiitakes. They cost much less too. The complex flavors of this salsa make it ideal for simple grilled fish or meats.

 This salsa can be prepared a few hours in advance and warmed. Store in the refrigerator for up to 2 weeks.

1 tablespoon butter

2 tablespoons dark roasted sesame oil

1/2 Scotch bonnet chile, seeded and minced

2 shallots, sliced

8 shiitake mushroom caps, sliced 1/8-inch thick

1 small tomato, concassé

2 scallions, trimmed and sliced on a bias

2 tablespoons minced cilantro leaves

2 cloves garlic, minced

1 teaspoon minced ginger

2 tablespoons rice wine vinegar

1/4 teaspoon sugar

1 teaspoon Oriental hot chile sauce (preferably Sriracha)

1/2 tablespoon mushroom soy sauce

Salt and black pepper to taste

Heat the butter and sesame oil in a large skillet. When the butter begins to foam, add the Scotch bonnet and shallots, and sauté over medium-high heat for 30 seconds, stirring. Add the sliced shiitakes, stir well, and sauté for 1 minute. Transfer the mixture to a bowl. Add the remaining ingredients and combine thoroughly. Reserve until needed.

Exotic Tropical Fruit and Black Bean Salsa

Yield: About 3 cups.

Researching the materials for my *Exotic Fruit* posters and cookbook (Celestial Arts/Ten Speed Press) was a labor of love and continual discovery. As we all become more knowledgeable about Asian and Latin cooking in the United States, the fruits that have long been a part of these culinary traditions are now nourishing us and becoming interwoven into our recipes. The fruits used here are not nearly as exotic as some that may be available in your local markets; feel free to mix and match as you can!

When making a salsa like this, I like to use my hands to mix the ingredients. They're the most gentle tools we have. This salsa is best used the same day; keep it no longer than the next day after you've made it.

³/₄ cup peeled and seeded papaya, diced small

³/₄ cup peeled and pitted mango, diced small

³/₄ cup peeled and cored pineapple, diced small

¹/₂ cup dried black beans, cooked (1¹/₄ cups cooked beans)

1 Scotch bonnet chile, seeded and minced

¹/₂ cup red onion, diced small

1 tablespoon virgin olive oil

2 tablespoons Spanish sherry vinegar

1¹/₂ tablespoons roughly chopped cilantro

Salt and black pepper to taste

Thoroughly combine all the ingredients in a mixing bowl.

Salsa Escalivada

Yield: About 4 cups.

The word *escalivada* means "grilled over charcoal." I gain the effect of grilling while simplifying the method, preparing the salsa in sauté pans. I still go after that charred, grilled flavor by deeply caramelizing the vegetables.

 While the eggplant should be cut into 1-inch dice, the peppers, chiles, and vegetables should be cut into medium ($\frac{1}{2}$-inch) dice. This salsa can be served warm or cold and it will keep for up to a week in the refrigerator.

1 eggplant, peeled and cut into 1-inch dice

3 tablespoons peanut oil

5 tablespoons butter

1 red onion, diced

1 red bell pepper, seeded and diced

1 yellow bell pepper, seeded and diced

1 poblano chile, seeded and diced

Salt and black pepper to taste

2 celery stalks, diced

1 small fennel bulb, diced

$\frac{1}{2}$ tablespoon sugar

$\frac{1}{4}$ cup Roasted Garlic Oil (page 277), or olive oil

$\frac{1}{4}$ cup red wine

$\frac{1}{4}$ cup red wine vinegar

2 tablespoons tomato juice

$2\frac{1}{2}$ tablespoons chopped basil leaves

2 tablespoons chopped Italian parsley

$\frac{1}{4}$ cup pitted black olives (preferably Niçoise or Arbequine), roughly chopped

2 tablespoons small capers, rinsed and roughly chopped

Salt and weight the eggplant (see page xvii).

Heat 2 tablespoons each of the peanut oil and butter in a large sauté pan. Add the onion, bell peppers, and poblano, season with salt and pepper, and sauté over medium-high heat until they begin to blister and caramelize, about 15 to 20 minutes. Remove with a slotted spoon to a large mixing bowl.

Wipe out the pan with paper towels, add 1 tablespoon each of the peanut oil and butter, and heat. Add the celery and fennel; season with salt and pepper, and sauté over medium-high heat until caramelized, about 8 or 9 minutes. Add the sugar and cook for 1 or 2 minutes, until glazed. Transfer to the bowl containing the cooked vegetables.

Rinse the eggplant and pat dry with paper towels. Wipe out the pan again with paper towels and heat the garlic oil with the remaining 2 tablespoons of the butter. Add the eggplant, season with pepper, and sauté over medium-high heat for 7 to 9 minutes, or until brown. Transfer to the bowl with the cooked vegetables and mix together.

Put the red wine, red wine vinegar, tomato juice, basil, and parsley in a small saucepan, and bring to a medium-high simmer. Reduce the liquid for 4 to 6 minutes, or until $1/2$ cup remains. Add the olives and capers to the pan and transfer immediately to the vegetables in the bowl. Stir together gently.

West Indian Cocktail Salsa

Yield: About 1^2/$_3$ cups.

I use this salsa with the Voodoo Beer-Steamed Shrimp (page 18), but it's a good all-purpose cocktail sauce and makes a damn fine, kick-butt alternative to ketchup for grilled burgers any day!

 This salsa can be stored in the refrigerator for up to 2 weeks. For a sweeter salsa, add 2 tablespoons freshly squeezed orange juice; for a less spicy version, omit the Scotch bonnets and use 1 jalapeño instead.

^{3}/$_4$ *cup tomato ketchup*

^{1}/$_4$ *cup chili sauce (such as Heinz)*

1 Scotch bonnet chile, seeded and minced

3 cloves garlic, minced

^{1}/$_2$ *cup minced red onion*

^{1}/$_4$ *cup roughly chopped cilantro leaves*

Juice of 1 lime

^{1}/$_4$ *cup prepared horseradish*

^{1}/$_4$ *teaspoon Tabasco sauce, or to taste*

^{1}/$_4$ *teaspoon Worcestershire sauce*

Salt and black pepper to taste

Thoroughly combine all the ingredients in a mixing bowl. Keep chilled until needed.

Mo J.

Yield: About 1¼ cups.

This is my version of "mojo criollo," or "mojo naranja agria," the very famous picante dressing that's used in millions of Latin households and restaurants. If you have any question whether mojo is popular, just visit a *grocería* next time you're in Miami. Huge displays and containers of every conceivable size are available. Mojo is used with an enthusiasm similar to that reserved for ketchup in the United States, at least until recently. Unfortunately, most of the store-bought stuff contains the stabilizers and food coloring that's best avoided completely. As you can see, the recipe below is very easy, so you can enjoy a healthy, tasty version in your kitchen any time you want a hit of this lively condiment. It's a natural with Cuban French Fries (page 193) and makes a good spritzer with the Bajan Chicken Dinner (page 146). I also pair it with the Cuban Pork Asado (page 158) and Sea Scallop Seviche (page 83), and it makes a great, fast marinade for flank steak or chicken.

 For a less tart version, use regular oranges instead of the sour type. Add a hefty pinch or two of some chopped mixed herbs, if you like, when you add the oil. It will keep for up to 3 months in the refrigerator.

6 cloves garlic, minced

1 Scotch bonnet or habanero chile, seeded and minced

2 teaspoons freshly toasted cumin seeds

½ teaspoon salt

1 cup olive oil

⅓ cup fresh sour orange juice

2 teaspoons Spanish sherry vinegar

Black pepper to taste

With a mortar and pestle, mash the garlic, chile, cumin, and salt together until fairly smooth. (Alternatively, use a sharp knife and mince very finely on a chopping board.) Transfer to a mixing bowl.

Heat the olive oil in a pan or skillet and when medium-hot, pour over the garlic-chile mixture. Let stand for 10 minutes. Whisk in the orange juice and vinegar, and season with more salt, if desired, and the pepper. Refrigerate until needed.

Mango-Habanero Mojo

Yield: About 2 cups.

This sauce tastes best if not kept warm for too long; the sweet tropical flavor of the mango diminishes if it is overcooked. If you prefer a spicier sauce, add more minced chile—a little at a time—until hot enough.

 Store this mojo in the refrigerator for no longer than 2 or 3 days.

2 ripe mangoes, peeled, pitted, and roughly chopped

¹/₂ cup chardonnay wine

2 tablespoons fresh orange juice

¹/₂ habanero or Scotch bonnet chile, seeded and finely minced

In a blender, purée the mangoes, wine, and orange juice until smooth. Strain through a medium-fine-mesh strainer and stir in the habanero. Keep refrigerated until needed and then serve warm.

Mojo Rojo

Yield: About 1¹/₂ cups.

Mojar means "to wet," I've already told you. You probably know that *rojo* means "red." So this is a brightly colored sauce to liven up a broad variety of your New World dishes.

 Mixing this mojo rojo with some tartar sauce makes a great spread for a fish or soft-shell crab sandwich. The mojo will keep for 2 to 3 weeks refrigerated.

6 cloves garlic, minced

1 Scotch bonnet chile, seeded and minced

2 teaspoons freshly toasted cumin seeds

¹/₂ teaspoon salt

2 red bell peppers, roasted, seeded, and peeled

¹/₂ cup virgin olive oil

2 tablespoons Spanish sherry vinegar

Salt and black pepper to taste

With a mortar and pestle, mash the garlic, chile, cumin, and salt together until fairly smooth. (Alternatively, use a sharp knife and mince very finely on a chopping board.) Transfer to a blender. Add the roasted bell peppers, olive oil, and vinegar, and purée until fairly smooth. Season with salt and pepper, and reserve until needed.

The Redlands Tropical Fruit Chutney

Yield: About 4 cups.

The Redlands, as they are called, and the general area south of Miami to the tip of Florida, is a region of great agricultural activity. It's great to jump in the Jeep, drop out of the city, and visit. Every time I go, I wonder why I don't visit more often. It's *our* Napa or Sonoma valley, but it's flat, and *we* grow fruits and vegetables. The area grows an astonishing variety of mangoes, which are a primary ingredient in this recipe. Attending a festival there, I was stunned to see almost 200 types of mango on display.

 This chutney can be stored in the refrigerator for up to 1 month. If you want to keep it for longer, can it according to manufacturer's instructions.

2 1/2 cups peeled, pitted, and diced mango

1 1/2 cups peeled, seeded, and diced papaya

3 cups peeled, cored, and diced pineapple

2 cups apple cider vinegar

1 cup granulated sugar

1 cup dark brown sugar, tightly packed

1 cup diced red onion

1 to 2 Scotch bonnet chiles, seeded and minced

1 tablespoon minced ginger

1/2 tablespoon ground cinnamon, or canela

1 teaspoon ground allspice

Combine all of the ingredients in a mixing bowl and reserve overnight in the refrigerator.

Transfer to a heavy saucepan and slowly bring to a boil. Reduce the heat and simmer for 1 hour. Let cool. Reserve until needed.

CHAPTER 10
BREADS—THE STAFF THAT DREAMS ARE MADE ON

Con pan y vino se anda el camino. (With bread and wine, you can walk your road.)

—Spanish proverb

Before Columbus, breads in the New World were mainly limited to flatbreads, made from corn or tubers, like manioc (cassava). Arepa bread, johnnycake, and tortillas were the main stars in the constellation of bread before 1492. After the Spanish arrived in the New World, the heavens grew. Wheat and yeast-raised breads were quickly adopted. Europeans continued to innovate and extend their traditions of bread making, but they often used ingredients native to this side of the Atlantic.

Bread making is undergoing a renaissance and a dramatic surge in popularity. Small-scale artisan bakeries are springing up as never before in this country. For now, they mostly represent the French or European style of making breads, which is a laudable place to start anew. It will be interesting when they incorporate some more flavors of the New World to accompany the kinds of regional American foods we are eating these days. In this chapter, you'll have a taste of breads that work well with dishes in this New World Cuisine. Even with the staff of life, variety is the spice of it.

Six O'Clock Cumin Cuban Bread

Yield: 1 loaf.

Cuban bread is made several times during the course of the day in Key West, as it is extremely susceptible to turning stale. This was certainly the case in the "drip–don't dry" humidity of Key West. Bread that was made in the wee small hours of the morning would feel like a whiffle bat by lunchtime. Families going home from work would often stop to pick up a last batch of bread, baked each day around 6 o'clock, just in time for supper. This recipe does not have the problem of getting stale quickly; the problem is that it'll get eaten quickly. I think that's because of the perfume of the freshly toasted cumin seeds.

 Double the amount of yeast if you use fresh rather than dry.

¹/₂ tablespoon dry yeast

5 teaspoons sugar

¹/₄ cup lukewarm water (110 degrees)

6 cups flour

1 tablespoon salt

2²/₃ cups lukewarm water (110 degrees)

1 tablespoon freshly toasted cumin seeds

In a bowl, dissolve the yeast with the sugar and ¹/₄ cup warm water, and let sit for 5 minutes.

Put 5 cups of the flour in the mixer and add the salt. Stir until well blended. Add the 2²/₃ cups warm water and the dissolved yeast mixture. Mix with the dough hook for 10 minutes, gradually working in the remaining 1 cup of the flour (alternatively, mix by hand).

Transfer the dough to a greased bowl and cover with plastic wrap. Let the dough rise in a warm place for about 1¹/₂ to 2 hours, or until it has doubled in volume.

Punch the dough down and turn it out onto a lightly floured work surface. Form into a slightly fat baguettelike loaf. Slash a long thin slit down the center of the loaf. Brush with about 1 teaspoon of water and sprinkle with the cumin seeds. Place the loaf on a baking sheet and transfer to the middle rack of a cold oven.

Set a large pan of hot water on the shelf below and heat the oven to 400 degrees (the bread will continue to rise as this happens). Bake for 40 minutes, or until golden brown. Turn out onto a rack to cool.

South Beach Sourdough

Yield: 2 loaves.

San Francisco rightly lays claim to the title of Sourdough Capital of the Americas. It is believed that Columbus brought a "starter" with him from the Old World. The *biga* in this recipe will provide you with yours, if you do not already own a sourdough starter.

 Instead of making 2 identical loaves, you can transform one into Janet's Pepper-Cheese Bread (page 237) after the first rising. Alternatively, you can refrigerate or freeze any leftover dough. If you freeze it, thaw overnight in the refrigerator, take it out the next morning, and let it sit on your kitchen counter for 24 hours.

Biga (see recipe)

BREAD

¹/₂ tablespoon dry yeast

3 cups lukewarm water (110 degrees)

11 to 12 cups flour

¹/₂ tablespoon salt

Prepare the biga.

To prepare the bread: Dissolve the yeast in ¹/₄ cup of water in a large mixing bowl and let sit for 10 minutes. Add the flour, the remaining water, salt, and 1 cup of the biga; mix together to form a dough. Knead the mixture for 10 minutes until the dough is a little sticky; it should not pull away completely from the sides of the bowl.

Transfer the dough to a greased bowl and cover with plastic wrap. Let the dough rise in a warm place for about 3 hours, or until it has tripled in volume.

Turn the dough out onto a generously floured work surface. Divide the dough in half. Form into rounds by rolling from one side to the other as tightly as possible, dusting with flour as necessary. Turn the dough by 90 degrees and roll the "opposite" sides into as taut a ball as possible.

Line a baking sheet with parchment paper, sprinkle with flour, and place the loaves on the baking sheet. Cover with a damp towel and let the loaves rise for about 1 hour. For more perfect-looking loaves, surround the dough with 10-inch springform pans (the edges only, not the bottoms) before this rising.

Preheat the oven to 425 degrees. Dust the loaves with flour and bake in the oven for 30 to 40 minutes, or until golden brown. The loaves should sound hollow when tapped on the bottom. Turn out onto a rack to cool.

BIGA

¹/₂ teaspoon dry yeast

1 cup lukewarm water (110 degrees)

1¹/₂ cups flour

¹/₃ cup buttermilk

Dissolve the yeast in ¹/₄ cup of the water in a small mixing bowl and let sit for 10 minutes.

Add the remaining ³/₄ cup water and 1 cup of the flour, and mix together with a wooden spoon. Cover loosely with plastic wrap and let this rise at room temperature overnight or for 24 hours.

Mix in the buttermilk and the remaining ¹/₂ cup flour with a wooden spoon. Cover loosely with plastic wrap and let this biga rise again at room temperature for 24 to 72 hours. The longer you let the biga rise, the more sour the bread will be.

Achiote-Stained Butter Bread

Yield: 2 loaves.

Classic brioche is the takeoff point for this colorful bread. I give it a simple twist by incorporating the ground achiote seeds into the dough. The flavor is changed slightly, and the presentation is memorable.

 This bread can be frozen, double-wrapped.

4 packages dry yeast

¹/₄ cup sugar

1³/₄ teaspoons salt

6 tablespoons lukewarm water (110 degrees)

3³/₄ cups flour

5 eggs, at room temperature

1 pound butter, at room temperature

1¹/₂ tablespoons ground achiote seeds

Put the yeast, sugar, and salt in the bowl of an electric mixer. Add the water and mix briefly for 3 to 4 minutes with a paddle attachment at low speed. Let rest for 15 minutes.

Add the flour all at once and mix at low speed. When incorporated, increase the speed to medium and add the eggs one at a time. Mix thoroughly, scraping down the sides of the bowl as necessary. Add the butter 1 tablespoon at a time. When it is all mixed in, continue beating for 1 minute longer. Add the achiote and mix briefly for about 15 seconds. The dough will be sticky and almost like a batter.

Transfer the dough to a greased bowl and cover with plastic wrap. Keep in a warm place (if it is too hot, the butter will separate from the dough). Let the dough rise until it doubles in volume, about 1½ to 2 hours. Punch the dough down, cover, and refrigerate overnight.

The next day, punch the dough down and divide it in half. Butter 2 loaf pans, divide the dough between them, and let it rise for 2 to 3 hours.

Preheat the oven to 375 degrees. Bake the loaves for 40 to 45 minutes, or until they sound hollow when tapped on the bottom. Turn the loaves out to cool on a wire rack.

Janet's Pepper-Cheese Bread

Yield: 2 loaves.

My wife, Janet, is one of eight children, five of whom are males. Growing up, dinner time at her house was in marked contrast to the relative calm I was used to at mine. She learned to cook from her mother, and she learned to turn bread into a meal as an act of self-preservation! This bread is based on the South Beach Sourdough recipe, which is then given a flavor twist.

 For a variation of this bread, substitute the pepper, chile, and cheddar cheese with pesto and tallegio cheese. Alternatively, use prosciutto, smoked ham, salami, different cheeses, or pitted and chopped black olives as fillings. This is a great bread for picnics.

South Beach Sourdough (page 234)

2 tablespoons Roasted Garlic Oil (page 277).
or virgin olive oil

1 tablespoon freshly toasted and cracked black
pepper

1 1/2 tablespoons crushed red pepper. or to taste

3 cups grated sharp cheddar cheese

1 egg

1/2 tablespoon water

1 teaspoon coarse salt

Prepare the sourdough recipe and let it rise for the first time.

Meanwhile, cover a baking sheet or French bread pan with parchment paper and dust with flour. Cut the dough in half and roll out on a well-floured work surface into a 15 × 10-inch rectangle. Brush the dough with the garlic oil and sprinkle with half of the black pepper, crushed red pepper, and cheese. Roll the dough up tightly and place on the prepared baking sheet. Repeat for the other half of the dough. Let the dough rise in a warm place until it doubles in volume, about 1 hour.

Preheat the oven to 375 degrees. Beat the egg and water together in a bowl, and brush the loaves with the egg wash. Make light diagonal slashes in the top of the loaves and sprinkle sparingly with the salt.

Bake in the oven for 40 to 45 minutes, or until the loaves sound hollow when tapped. Turn out to cool on a wire rack.

Sweet Seven-Grain Bread

Yield: 1 large loaf.

My former bread and pastry chef, Kevin Kopsick, worked at a health food bakery as a teenager. He began perfecting this recipe then, and really nailed it in the past few years. It has a sweet note of honey and is heavenly when toasted.

2 tablespoons dry yeast

³/₄ tablespoon sugar

1³/₄ cups lukewarm water (110 degrees)

2 cups stone-ground whole wheat flour

3 cups high-gluten (bread) flour

1¹/₂ cups 7-grain cereal

3 tablespoons vegetable oil

¹/₃ cup honey

2 tablespoons molasses

³/₄ tablespoon salt

1 egg. beaten

¹/₂ tablespoon water

In a large mixing bowl, dissolve the yeast with the sugar and water, and let sit for 10 minutes. Add the whole wheat and high-gluten flours, cereal, oil, honey, and molasses. Then add the salt. Knead for about 10 minutes until the gluten develops.

Transfer to a greased bowl, turn the dough to coat, and cover with plastic wrap. Let rise in a warm place for about 2 hours, or until it doubles in volume.

Punch the dough down and shape into a ball. Place on a greased sheet pan and let the dough rise again for about 1¹/₂ hours. After 45 minutes, make 2 diagonal slashes on top of the loaf.

Preheat the oven to 325 degrees. Beat the egg and water together in a bowl, and brush the loaf with the egg wash. Bake in the oven for about 45 minutes (if 2 loaves) or 1 hour (if a single loaf), or until brown and hollow sounding when tapped.

Johnnycake

Yield: One 9-inch square pan.

There are a variety of recipes for this unleavened cornmeal bread. I wondered why there were so many. Finally, a Caribbean native told me he thought it was because the word *johnny* was probably a corruption of the word "journey," and naturally, you ate *whatever* kind of bread was available on open-boated journeys from one island to the next. Whether in the Caribbean or the swamps and marshes of the deep South or on the wide plains of the Amerindians, johnnycakes filled a lot of hungry travelers' bellies.

3/4 cup yellow cornmeal

1 cup flour

1 teaspoon baking powder

1 teaspoon baking soda

1/2 teaspoon salt

3 tablespoons honey

1 egg, lightly beaten

3 tablespoons butter, melted

1 1/4 cups buttermilk

1 Scotch bonnet chile, seeded and minced

Preheat the oven to 400 degrees. Generously butter a 9-inch square baking pan.

In a large mixing bowl, combine the cornmeal, flour, baking powder, baking soda, and salt. In a separate bowl, beat together the honey, egg, butter, buttermilk, and chile until lightly frothy. Add the dry ingredients and beat until just blended, about 30 seconds. Pour the batter into the prepared baking pan and place on the middle rack of the oven.

Bake for 25 to 30 minutes, or until an inserted toothpick comes out clean. Remove from the oven and let cool for 10 minutes. Turn out onto a wire rack and cut into portions as desired.

Caribbean Corn Bread

Yield: One 8-inch square pan.

Corn is the most important plant of the New World. Bread is the staff of life all over the world. Corn + Bread = Perfection.

1 1/2 tablespoons olive oil

1/2 cup diced red onion

1/2 cup corn kernels, from 1 ear (see page xix)

1 cup flour, sifted

1 cup yellow cornmeal (preferably stone-ground)

1 tablespoon baking powder

3 tablespoons sugar

1 teaspoon salt

2 eggs, well beaten

1 cup milk

1/2 cup buttermilk

1/4 cup melted butter

2/3 cup grated Manchego cheese

1 Scotch bonnet chile, seeded and minced

Preheat the oven to 425 degrees. Line an 8-inch square baking pan with parchment paper and butter the paper and sides of the pan well.

Heat a skillet and when hot, add the oil, onion, and corn. Sauté over high heat until the onion and corn are nicely charred, about 3 to 4 minutes. Set aside to cool.

Sift the flour into a large bowl and add the cornmeal, baking powder, sugar, and salt. In another bowl, beat the eggs, milk, and buttermilk together. Stir in the cooked onion and corn, and the butter, cheese, and Scotch bonnet. Stir in the flour mixture until just mixed.

Pour the batter into the prepared pan and bake in the oven for 35 to 45 minutes, or until an inserted toothpick comes out clean. Remove from the oven and let cool for 10 minutes. Turn out onto a wire rack and cut into portions as desired.

CHAPTER 11
OUR JUST DESSERTS:
"DIG HERE! . . . AND DIG IN"

My Mama's Spanish Cream (The One that Children Dream Of)

A Cubano Bread Pudding Brûlée with Añejo-Espresso Caramel

Key Lime Natilla en Tortilla with Cayenne, Cilantro Sirop, and a
Tropical Fruit Salsa

Havana Bananas with Barbados Rhum, Chiles, and Chocolate Sauce

A Stirfry of Tropical Fruits in Aromatic Spiced Crêpes

Toasted Pecan Caramel Tart with
Jamaican Blue Mountain Coffee Bean Crema

Key Lime Cheesecake with a Toasted Nut Crust

Spanish Olive Oil Cake with Kumquats and Toasted Almonds

The Fallen Chocolate Cake with a Passion Fruit Chantilly

The Duval Street "Café con Leche" Cake with a Hot-Hot Honey

Mandarin Orange Ice with Candied Citrus Zests and
"The Wheel of Good Fortune" Cookies

At home, his mother removes her tunic and slippers. She takes a hammer and rusty chisel and shatters each coconut, scraping the blinding white, perfumed flesh from the shells. Ivanito helps her blend the coconut with egg yolks, vanilla, condensed milk, sugar, cornstarch and salt, and holds the empty tin vegetable-oil containers while she fills them with the mixture. Together they arrange them in the freezer. With the leftover egg whites, she fashions star-shaped meringues, which she serves with the ice cream day after day, for breakfast, lunch, and dinner. His mother believes the coconuts will purify them, that the sweet milk will heal them.

—Christina Garcia, *Dreaming in Cuban*

Desserts have an ability to outdistance every other course of the meal in revealing memories that seem so buried as to have possibly never existed. Do you ever smell a new liqueur or taste a bite of chocolate or pass a bakery that does an Orson Welles "Rosebud" on you? An exhalation and an inhalation, "Roooose . . . buuuud." Images flicker behind your eyes. Time, place, a face—whose? An eight-millimeter home movie entitled "Christmastime, Miami Beach, 1958" begins. The world is fine once again, as fine as spun sugar.

I can see "Knobby" out in the field of white sand from where I am standing, on the hotel balcony overlooking the baby blue and gently rocking ocean. I'm very warm, but a cool breeze washes over me. Warm and cool all at once. I see him raking the sand into millions of neat, wavy rivulets, carefully piling the Portuguese man-of-wars, broken bottles, food wrappers, and seaweed out of the wind into the tucked corner of the sea wall.

Back in the bedroom I see my parents sleeping. My sisters and I are ravenous. We tiptoe out of the dark room and walk down to the vending machines under the hotel's main lobby and push shiny dimes into the machines. We breakfast on Nehi orange drinks and Nutty Buddy ice cream cones.

New reel: We're moving again. Now we're dressed in snazzy vacation wear, our seahorse-adorned sunglasses hug our brightening faces. Our parents are guiding us carefully across a busy boulevard. We go into a building with a flashing, giant Indian's head silhouetted on the top of the door. I can see the Coppertone Girl on a billboard across the street from my spinning stool. My parents look like movie stars to me and smile approvingly and beautifully as we lunge into stacks of French toast, crisp waffles, and strawberry pancakes with pools of maple syrup, pats of butter, and thick cloud banks of powdered sugar. My father lets me taste his coffee and I wash it down by drinking the rich cream from the tiny, thick glass container.

Final scene: We are strolling out in the dazzling sunlight. Knobby is waving. "Ocean today, Missus V, or here by the pool? Hello, Mister V. I'll get the chairs and towels, something to drink?" he asks.

A voice. Cutting through the web of time that says, "Remember me?" "Yes, I do, Knobby, you're here now."

I present you with this final-course chapter to taste and savor some of the flavors drawn from the mists of childhood (as well as some adult ones too). I have described some of my first memories of South Florida. Its magic spell was cast very early in my life. It has changed, just as the world has changed, but I'm certain that those recollections of Miami Beach are a big reason why I live here now.

My Mama's Spanish Cream (The One that Children Dream Of)

Yield: 6 servings.

It may have been a madeleine for some, or an apple pie for others, but this is one recipe that time-travels me back to a night in my childhood with a preternatural force. I eat this and I feel like the boy in the Maurice Sendak classic *In the Night Kitchen*. I wouldn't be surprised to find, in some Jungian unraveling, that this dessert created in me an early confidence in all things Spanish. This would explain why I am, in part, in love with so many Spanish flavors now. Thanks, Ma!

 Adding a dash of cinnamon and/or nutmeg will give a more eggnoggy flavor. If you prefer to store this in the refrigerator overnight, cover the containers with plastic to prevent other odors from spoiling the flavor of the custard.

2 packages gelatin

3 cups cold milk

¹/₂ cup (8 tablespoons) sugar

1 vanilla bean, split in half lengthwise

3 eggs, separated

Place the gelatin in a large mixing bowl and stir in ¹/₂ cup of the milk. Let sit for 5 minutes to allow the gelatin to soften.

Place 1 tablespoon of the sugar on a work surface. Scrape out the vanilla bean seeds onto the sugar and smear around to coat the seeds. Place this sugar-vanilla mixture and the remaining 2¹/₂ cups of milk in a saucepan, and scald (just barely bringing the milk to boiling point). Remove from the heat and allow the mixture to steep for 10 minutes.

In another mixing bowl, whisk together 5 tablespoons of the sugar with the egg yolks until the mixture is thick and pale, about 1 to 2 minutes. Slowly whisk in a small amount of the scalded milk to temper the egg mixture, stirring continuously to prevent the eggs from cooking. Add a little more at a time until the egg mixture is warm. Slowly pour the tempered mixture into the remaining scalded milk and then stir in the softened gelatin. Set aside.

In a large mixing bowl, whisk the egg whites with the remaining 2 tablespoons of sugar until stiff. Using a fine-mesh strainer, strain the egg-milk mixture into the beaten egg whites. Gently fold together.

Pour the cream mixture into your favorite parfait glasses and chill in the refrigerator for about 2 hours, until set.

A Cubano Bread Pudding Brûlée with Añejo-Espresso Caramel

Yield: 6 servings.

I looked at classy crème brûlée and seductive bread pudding and thought, "What a beautiful child they'd make together!" The union took place in Havana and was baptized with the assistance of some local liquids. Ain't she sweet?

 The raisins should be soaked in the rhum overnight, or at least for several hours. Instead of using individual ramekins, you can use a single baking dish.

BREAD PUDDING BRÛLÉE

6 tablespoons raisins

1/4 cup aged añejo rhum

1 cup sugar

1 vanilla bean, split in half lengthwise

1 quart heavy cream

1 whole nutmeg, ground

1 cinnamon stick, ground

10 egg yolks

2 cups cubed slightly stale Cuban or French bread

Añejo-Espresso Caramel (see recipe)

3 tablespoons sugar

To prepare the bread pudding: Soak the raisins in the rhum overnight. Place 1 tablespoon of the sugar on a work surface. Scrape out the vanilla bean seeds onto the sugar and smear around to coat the seeds. Place this sugar-vanilla mixture in a saucepan and add the cream, vanilla bean, nutmeg, cinnamon, and 1/2 cup of the sugar. Bring the mixture to just under a boil. Remove immediately from the heat and let steep for 20 minutes.

In a large mixing bowl, whisk together the egg yolks and the remaining sugar until thick and pale. Slowly whisk in a small amount of the hot cream mixture to temper the egg mixture, stirring continuously to prevent the eggs from cooking. Add a little more at a time until the egg mixture is warm. Slowly pour the tempered mixture into the remaining hot cream and whisk until smooth. Pass through a fine strainer.

Strain the rhum from the raisins, reserving the rhum. Sprinkle the raisins in the bottom of

six 1-cup (8-ounce) ramekins. Add 4 or 5 cubes of the bread to each ramekin, on top of the raisins, and sprinkle the bread with the reserved rhum. Fill each ramekin with the custard. Allow to sit for 15 to 20 minutes before baking. While resting, occasionally push down the bread lightly with the back of a spoon so it absorbs more of the custard.

Meanwhile, preheat the oven to 350 degrees. Place the ramekins in a baking pan lined with a towel (to prevent the ramekins from sliding). Add enough boiling water to the pan to come about halfway up the sides of the ramekins. Cover the pan loosely with aluminum foil.

Bake in the oven for about 40 to 60 minutes, until set but still slightly jiggly. When cooked, remove the ramekins from the water bath and chill for about 2 hours.

Meanwhile, **prepare the añejo-espresso caramel.**

To serve, sprinkle the tops of each ramekin with about ½ tablespoon sugar. Using a handheld propane torch, caramelize the sugar all over the surface (alternatively, place under a very hot broiler or salamander).

Remove the ramekins and allow the tops to harden for a minute. Serve with the warm añejo-espresso caramel in a little side dish.

AÑEJO-ESPRESSO CARAMEL

Yield: About ½ cup.

2 tablespoons cold water

½ cup sugar

5 tablespoons hot water

½ teaspoon fresh lemon juice

2 teaspoons aged añejo rhum

¼ cup freshly brewed espresso

In a heavy saucepan, combine the 2 tablespoons of cold water with the sugar and cook over medium-high heat until golden brown, stirring only occasionally. Whisk in the hot water, taking care, as it will splatter somewhat. Add the lemon juice, rhum, and espresso, and return to a boil. Boil for 1 or 2 minutes, until it lightly coats the back of a spoon. Remove the pan from the heat. (If the caramel seems too thin, boil it for a little longer.)

Key Lime Natilla en Tortilla with Cayenne, Cilantro Sirop, and a Tropical Fruit Salsa

Yield: 6 servings.

Natillas are custards. I think the Spanish word (pronounced nah-tee-yahs) is much prettier! Soft, like the mixture itself. In this recipe, the custard is enveloped in a crispy phyllo "faux tortilla"; it's given an electric-green zap of softly sweetened cilantro herbaceousness as well as a multicolored mix of tropical fruits.

 Feel free to make only the natilla. Serve it in some globe-shaped wineglasses, maybe with a couple of the tortillas broken into large chips and stuck into it. Use less cream for the natillas if you prefer a tarter flavor.

NATILLA

2 eggs plus 2 egg yolks

²/₃ cup plus 1 tablespoon sugar

¹/₂ cup fresh Key lime juice

¹/₂ cup butter, cut into small dice and allowed to soften

¹/₂ cup heavy cream

TORTILLA

4 sheets phyllo

¹/₄ cup melted butter

6 tablespoons sugar

¹/₄ teaspoon cayenne, or to taste

Simple Syrup (see recipe)

CILANTRO SIROP

1 bunch cilantro, stems and leaves

¹/₄ cup Simple Syrup (see recipe)

TROPICAL FRUIT SALSA

2 mangoes, peeled and pitted

1 papaya, halved, seeded, and peeled

¹/₂ pineapple, cored and peeled

To prepare the natilla: Combine the eggs, egg yolks, sugar, and lime juice in a mixing bowl. Place over a double boiler and whisk vigorously and continuously until the mixture becomes thick and pale in color, about 3 to 4 minutes. Remove the bowl from the heat and whisk in the softened butter. Scrape down the sides of the bowl with a rubber spatula and cover with plastic wrap. Refrigerate for at least 2 hours or overnight.

In a mixing bowl, whisk the cream until stiff. Whisk about one-quarter of the cream into the chilled Key lime mixture to lighten it and then carefully fold in the remaining cream with a rubber spatula. Cover and refrigerate.

To prepare the tortilla: Lay 1 of the phyllo sheets out on a work surface and brush liberally with the melted butter. Sprinkle 1$\frac{1}{2}$ tablespoons of the sugar in a thin layer over the butter. Repeat with another phyllo sheet, butter, and sugar, and sprinkle the cayenne powder over. Repeat with 2 more sheets, butter, and sugar (do not add any more cayenne). Place the stacked phyllo in the refrigerator for about 1 hour to chill the butter and ease handling.

Preheat the oven to 350 degrees. Remove the phyllo from the refrigerator and cut into 5-inch circles. Cut each circle in half and place on a parchment-lined baking sheet. Top with another sheet of parchment paper and finally top with another baking sheet, to weight it down.

Place in the oven and bake for about 15 to 20 minutes, until the sugar caramelizes. Remove from the oven and allow to cool; the tortillas can be stored in an airtight container for up to 2 days.

Prepare the syrup.

To prepare the sirop: Place the cilantro in a pan of boiling water and blanch for about 20 seconds. Remove from the boiling water and immediately shock in a bowl of ice water. Transfer the cilantro to a blender with enough syrup (about $\frac{1}{4}$ cup) to obtain a smooth consistency. Refrigerate until needed.

To prepare the fruit salsa: Place the flesh of 1 mango in a blender with enough of the simple syrup to create a smooth saucelike consistency; allow for about 2 parts mango to 1 part simple syrup. Dice the papaya, pineapple, and remaining mango, and stir into the mango purée; the mixture should have a salsalike consistency. Refrigerate until needed.

To assemble the dish, place 1 phyllo half on each plate. Spoon the natilla on top, and place another phyllo half over the natilla. Spoon the fruit salsa around the tortilla, streak sparingly with the sirop, and serve.

SIMPLE SYRUP

Yield: About 1 cup.

$\frac{1}{2}$ cup sugar

$\frac{1}{2}$ cup water

Stir together the sugar and water in a saucepan, and bring to a boil. Remove from the heat and allow to cool. Transfer to the refrigerator to chill.

Havana Bananas with Barbados Rhum, Chiles, and Chocolate Sauce

Yield: 4 servings.

Did I hear the brakes slamming when your eyes saw the word chiles in the recipe title? Chiles in a dessert? Sure! It's what I call an "adult dessert"; just a hint of danger to make it fun. We often overlook the heat of alcohol in desserts, I guess, and here, the chocolate sauce smooths over the rhum like a dusky blanket. Adapted from the New Orleans classic, Bananas Foster, this has been one of the simplest and most popular dishes that I have ever presented.

Chile Jelly (see recipe)

CHOCOLATE SAUCE

4 ounces bittersweet chocolate, cut into small pieces

1 1/2 tablespoons water

2 tablespoons butter

HAVANA BANANAS

4 ripe bananas, peeled and cut into slices 1/4-inch thick

2 1/2 tablespoons butter

1 tablespoon dark brown sugar

3 tablespoons Myers dark rhum

4 scoops vanilla ice cream

Prepare the chile jelly.

To prepare the chocolate sauce: Place the chocolate pieces and water in a stainless steel bowl, and heat over a double boiler until melted, stirring until smooth. Remove from the heat and whisk in the butter. Keep warm until needed.

To prepare the bananas: Heat a skillet and add the bananas, butter, and brown sugar. Stir over medium heat until the butter has melted. Stir in 2 tablespoons of the Chile Jelly and toss the bananas to coat. Add the rhum and carefully deglaze by igniting with a match and letting the alcohol burn off.

To serve, place a scoop of the ice cream in the center of 4 shallow bowls. Arrange the bananas around the ice cream and pour the chocolate sauce over both.

CHILE JELLY

Yield: About 1¼ cups.

The chile jelly can be made weeks in advance, or you can use store-bought, to save time. The jelly also works as a great glaze for hams and roasted chicken.

2 dried ancho chiles, seeded

2 dried chipotle chiles, seeded

1 quart water

6 tablespoons red currant jelly

6 tablespoons honey

2 tablespoons Spanish sherry vinegar

Toast the ancho and chipotle chiles in a dry saucepan over medium-high heat until fragrant, about 1 to 2 minutes. Add the water and bring to a simmer. Continue to simmer over medium heat until the water has almost completely evaporated. Add the red currant jelly, honey, and vinegar, and bring to a boil. Remove immediately from the heat, transfer to a food processor, and purée. Place in a clean bowl and let cool.

A Stirfry of Tropical Fruits in Aromatic Spiced Crêpes

Yield: 6 servings.

Texture and sweet natural flavors were my goal when creating this dessert. I also like the feature of using a savory character (the oil) and role playing (stirfrying) in what is usually the sweet end of the deal.

 Shredded, unsweetened, toasted coconut, and blood orange sections make a very nice garnish. The edge of sweetness to the fruits can be countered with a dollop of unsweetened whipped cream or sour cream.

5 tablespoons Aromatic Dessert Oil (page 278), or grapeseed oil

CRÊPE BATTER

3 eggs, beaten

1 cup milk

1 cup flour

1/8 teaspoon salt

1 teaspoon ground cinnamon

1 teaspoon ground cloves

2 tablespoons melted butter

STIRFRY

1 banana, peeled and diced

1/2 mango, peeled, pitted, and diced

1 star fruit (carambola), thinly sliced and quartered

1 cup diced pineapple

1 cup seeded and diced watermelon

1 tablespoon spiced rhum, such as Captain Morgan's

1 cup apple cider or apple juice

Juice of 1 lemon

1/2 cup honey

Prepare the dessert oil, if using.

To prepare the batter: Whisk the eggs and milk together in a large mixing bowl. Beat in the flour, salt, cinnamon, cloves, melted butter, and 2 tablespoons of the dessert oil until the batter is smooth. Set aside.

To prepare the stirfry: Heat the remaining 3 tablespoons of the dessert oil in a large skillet or wok. When the oil is hot, add the banana, mango, star fruit, pineapple, and watermelon, and sauté until just softened, about 2 minutes, stirring occasionally. Remove the fruit from the skillet with a slotted spoon and place in a bowl.

Add the rhum and carefully deglaze by igniting with a match and letting the alcohol burn off over medium-high heat. When the rhum has thoroughly burned off, add the apple cider, lemon juice, and honey, and reduce the mixture to a syrup, about 15 to 20 minutes. Keep the syrup warm until needed. If the mixture becomes too thick, just whisk in a little more apple cider or juice.

To make the crêpes: Heat a nonstick crêpe pan or skillet over medium-high heat. Add 3 tablespoons of the batter and cook the crêpe for 20 seconds for the first side, and 10 seconds for the second side, or until brown spots appear on the pan side of the crêpe. Keep warm, and repeat for the remaining crêpes (you will need 12 crêpes).

Spoon about 1½ tablespoons of the reserved stirfry fruit mixture into one quadrant of each crêpe. Fold the crêpe in half, and then in half again, so that it is in a quarter-circle shape. Place 2 crêpes on each serving plate and drizzle with the warm fruit syrup.

Toasted Pecan Caramel Tart with Jamaican Blue Mountain Coffee Bean Crema

Yield: One 10-inch tart (10 to 12 servings).

Intense and homey are usually antonyms, but I don't know of another way to describe this nut-rich wedge of honeyed crunch. The toasty, bitter flavors of the coffee lash the sweetness back into place to make this one of my most favorite desserts.

 Use your favorite pie crust recipe, if you prefer.

PÂTÉ BRISÉE TART CRUST

1¼ cups flour

¼ teaspoon baking powder

¼ teaspoon salt

¼ cup butter

¼ cup shortening (such as Crisco)

¼ cup cold milk

FILLING

1 cup butter

1 cup firmly packed brown sugar

3 tablespoons granulated sugar

¾ cup honey

1 pound whole, shelled pecans, toasted

¼ cup heavy cream

Coffee Bean Anglaise (see recipe)

To prepare the tart crust: Place the flour, baking powder, salt, butter, and shortening in a mixing bowl, and cut with a fork or pastry cutter to the texture of coarse meal. Stir in the milk with a fork until the mixture forms a ball. Cover in plastic wrap and refrigerate for 1 hour.

Shortly before removing from the refrigerator, preheat the oven to 475 degrees. Unwrap the tart crust dough and roll out so that it fits into a 10-inch tart pan. Line the tart crust with parchment paper and place beans or weights to the top of the paper. Bake the crust in the oven for 10 minutes, until just half-baked. Remove from the oven and set aside. Turn down the oven to 350 degrees.

To prepare the filling: Melt together the butter, brown sugar, granulated sugar, and honey in a saucepan over medium-high heat. While stirring constantly, bring to a full rolling boil. Keep boiling for 3 minutes. Remove from the heat and stir in the pecans and heavy cream. Pour into the half-baked tart crust and bake in the oven for 20 to 25 minutes. Place a cookie sheet or foil under the tart to catch any drippings. The tart will bubble up through the middle while baking. Remove the tart from the oven and let cool completely.

Prepare the coffee anglaise and serve with the tart.

COFFEE BEAN ANGLAISE

Yield: About 3 cups.

3/4 cup sugar

1 vanilla bean, cut in half lengthwise

2 cups heavy cream

1 tablespoon Jamaican Blue Mountain coffee beans, or any good-quality espresso beans

4 egg yolks

Place 1 tablespoon of the sugar on a work surface. Scrape out the vanilla bean seeds onto the sugar and smear around to coat the seeds. Place this sugar-vanilla mixture and half of the remaining sugar in a saucepan, add the cream and coffee beans, and scald over medium-high heat (just barely bringing the milk to boiling point). Remove from the heat.

Meanwhile, in a mixing bowl, whisk together the egg yolks and the remaining sugar together until thick and pale, about 1 to 2 minutes. Slowly whisk in a small amount of the hot cream mixture to the egg yolk mixture to temper, stirring continuously to prevent the eggs from cooking. Add a little more at a time until the egg mixture is warm.

Slowly whisk the tempered mixture back into the remaining scalded cream mixture. Cook over low heat while stirring with a wooden spoon for about 1 to 2 minutes, until the mixture coats the back of the spoon. Using a fine-mesh strainer, strain the custard and keep warm.

Key Lime Cheesecake with a Toasted Nut Crust

Yield: One 10-inch cheesecake (8 to 10 servings).

Key limes are another distinguishing facet of recipes from the New World Cuisine. We're fortunate to get wonderful fresh limes here in South Florida. What is not widely known is that the Key (or Mexican) lime is the true lime, while the larger green Persian or Tahitian lime is really an anomalous hybrid of the lemon. I recommend serving this cheesecake with espresso. However, a twist of lemon will not be needed for the coffee, I assure you.

 Bottled Key lime juice is widely available at gourmet food stores. You can serve this cheesecake with a coulis of fresh berries or your favorite fresh fruit.

CRUST

1 cup graham cracker crumbs

3/4 cup toasted and ground almonds, or nuts of your choice

1/3 cup sugar

1 teaspoon ground cinnamon

1 teaspoon ground nutmeg

1/3 cup melted butter

FILLING

3/4 cup plus 2 tablespoons sugar

1 pound cream cheese

4 eggs, separated

1 cup sour cream

1/2 teaspoon pure vanilla extract

1/4 cup fresh Key lime juice

To prepare the crust: Thoroughly combine all the ingredients in a 10-inch springform pan and press firmly to mold over the bottom and up the sides. Preheat the oven to 350 degrees.

To prepare the filling: Cream together ¾ cup of the sugar and the cream cheese in the bowl of an electric mixer. Add the egg yolks and mix for 5 minutes. When incorporated, add the sour cream and blend. Then add the vanilla and lime juice, and mix until blended.

In a separate mixing bowl, beat together the egg whites and remaining 2 tablespoons of the sugar until just stiff. Fold into the cream cheese mixture. Pour the filling into the prepared crust and bake in the oven for 1 hour.

Remove the cheesecake from the oven and run a thin knife around the inside edges to loosen the cheesecake. Let rest for 10 minutes, and then carefully release the springform and allow to cool before serving.

Spanish Olive Oil Cake with Kumquats and Toasted Almonds

Yield: One 9-inch cake (about 8 servings).

The healthy richness of olive oil is lightened by the citrus flavor of the kumquats in this almond cake. Almonds probably originated in Asia Minor and were introduced to Spain and Portugal by the Moors. I created this dessert for the Spanish Olive Oil Council, which was delighted to see olive oil used in a dessert. I think you'll see why.

 This cake is simple to prepare and is ideal for picnics or tailgate parties. The Chocolate Sauce (page 251) makes a wonderful topping.

6 kumquats, cut in half

²/₃ cup Spanish (or other) virgin olive oil

1 orange

1 lemon

1 mango, peeled, pitted, and diced small

1 cup flour

1 tablespoon baking powder

4 eggs

1 ¹/₂ cups sugar

³/₄ cup blanched and toasted almonds, finely ground

Place the kumquats and olive oil in a saucepan and bring to a simmer. Continue simmering for 3 minutes and then remove from the heat. Let steep for 1 hour. Strain the fruit from the olive oil. Reserve the oil and discard the fruit.

Place the (uncut) orange and lemon in a saucepan and cover with water. Simmer for 30 minutes. Drain and let cool. Cut off the stem end of the citrus fruits and then cut in half. Scoop the pulp and seeds from the lemon and discard. Finely mince the lemon rind.

Squeeze out as much of the orange juice as you can, reserving for another use, and discard the seeds. Chop the orange skin and pulp very finely, mix with the lemon and mango, and reserve (discard any part of the rinds that have not softened).

Preheat the oven to 350 degrees. Sift the flour and baking powder together into a mixing bowl. In the bowl of an electric mixer, beat the eggs until thick and pale, about 4 to 5 minutes. Continue beating while adding the sugar. Stir in the flour mixture just until blended. Gently add the reserved fruit, almonds, and infused oil. Pour the batter into a very lightly oiled 9-inch springform pan.

Bake in the oven for about 50 minutes, or until a knife inserted comes out clean. Remove from the oven and place on a wire rack. Run a knife around the inside edge of the pan and let cool for 15 minutes. Release the springform and allow to cool completely before serving. Cut the cake into wedges and serve.

The Fallen Chocolate Cake with a Passion Fruit Chantilly

Yield: One 9-inch cake (about 10 servings).

Inside the oven, this supermoist chocolate cake rises slowly heavenward, trembling under her cocoa-colored weight. Coming out of the oven is too much, though, and her destiny is realized with a slow but steady fall. While the physics may be terrestrial, the flavors belong to the celestial realm.

 If you like, serve with puréed raspberries.

CAKE

10 ounces semisweet chocolate, chopped

2 ounces bitter chocolate, chopped

12 ounces (1 1/2 cups) butter

1/3 cup spiced rhum, such as Captain Morgan's

1 cup sugar

6 eggs, separated, and yolks beaten

PASSION FRUIT CHANTILLY

1 cup heavy cream

2 tablespoons sugar

Juice of 2 ripe passion fruits, strained

Preheat the oven to 300 degrees. Lightly butter and flour a 9-inch springform pan.

To prepare the cake: In a double boiler, melt both chocolates with the butter. Remove from the heat and let cool for 30 minutes. Whisk in the rhum, ³⁄₄ cup of the sugar, and the beaten egg yolks until smooth.

In a mixing bowl, whisk the egg whites until foamy. Gradually add the remaining ¹⁄₄ cup of sugar while whisking until the meringue forms soft peaks. Thoroughly whisk about ¹⁄₃ of the meringue into the chocolate mixture. Then fold in the remaining meringue, using a rubber spatula.

Pour the mixture into the prepared springform pan and bake in the oven for about 1 hour, or until an inserted toothpick comes out clean.

To prepare the passion fruit chantilly: Whisk the cream and sugar together in a nonreactive bowl until slightly thickened. Whisk in the passion fruit juice until just thick. Keep refrigerated.

Remove the cake from the oven and place on a wire rack. Run a knife around the inside edge of the pan and allow to cool for 15 minutes. Release the springform and allow to cool completely before serving.

Place a wedge of cake on serving plates and add a dollop of the chantilly.

The Duval Street "Café con Leche" Cake with a Hot-Hot Honey

Yield: 6 servings.

She pictures herself out in the countryside at her momma's house back in Antigua. She and Momma are in the kitchen, talking about all the troubles and woe men does give dem. Melandra opens the cupboard and takes out the tin can Momma keeps full with hibiscus honey. She takes it out to the garden, to the pepper bush, covered with the small green cooking peppers that must be taken out of the stew before they burst and make the food too hot to eat. One cookin peppah, two cookin peppah, tree cookin peppah—into the honey. She takes the can back inside and puts it on the kerosene stove. Momma, I goin to boil dis up ahnd give it to de next mahn try to make a fool of me. Momma looks at her and shakes her head sadly. Gy-url, you does de boilin ahll your life den.

—Bob Shacochis, *Lord Shortshoe Wants the Monkey*

To keep the *café con leche* theme going with this cake, sprinkle it with a little cinnamon or chocolate.

Hot-Hot Honey (see page 8), or honey, optional

CAKE BATTER

³/₄ cup sifted flour

¹/₂ teaspoon baking powder

¹/₄ teaspoon salt

¹/₄ cup ground espresso coffee, reground in a coffee grinder or blender

¹/₃ cup blanched almonds, ground

4 eggs, at room temperature, separated

³/₄ cup sugar

4 tablespoons butter, melted and cooled

TOPPING

1 cup heavy cream

1 tablespoon Tia Maria liqueur (optional)

Prepare the honey and reserve.

Preheat the oven to 325 degrees. Butter 6 ovenproof coffee cups and lightly sprinkle with sugar. Set aside.

To prepare the cake batter: Sift the flour, baking powder, salt, and ground espresso together in a mixing bowl. Gently stir the ground almonds into the sifted ingredients and set aside.

In the bowl of an electric mixer, whisk the egg yolks on medium speed and gradually add half (6 tablespoons) of the sugar. Increase the mixer speed to medium-high and whisk until the mixture becomes thick and pale, about 4 minutes. Mix in the butter and set aside.

In a separate mixing bowl, whisk the egg whites until frothy. Gradually add the remaining sugar, 1 tablespoon at a time. Gradually increase the speed of the mixer to high and whisk until peaks form that are stiff *but not dry.* Add the sifted dry ingredients all at once to the egg yolk mixture and mix together. Stir half of the beaten egg whites into the cake mix. Then, gently fold in the remaining egg whites with a rubber spatula until thoroughly incorporated.

Pour the batter into the prepared cups, and place on a baking sheet. Bake in the oven for 30 to 35 minutes, or until a toothpick inserted comes out clean. Remove from the oven and let cool.

When ready to serve, reheat the oven to 425 degrees and warm the cakes for about 8 minutes.

To prepare the topping: Whisk the heavy cream in a large mixing bowl to stiff peaks. Remove the cakes from the oven and, if desired, drizzle with Tia Maria. Spoon the whipped cream over each cake so it looks like a *café con leche,* and drizzle with the honey.

Mandarin Orange Ice with Candied Citrus Zests and "The Wheel of Good Fortune" Cookies

Yield: 8 servings.

I worked as a carnival worker (a "carny") one summer, traveling from town to town; I came to know the games like the "wheel" and the "pool ball–silver dollar game." The snow cones that were sold at the concession stands were the first ices that I ever remember eating.

 This recipe will make about 3 dozen cookies, more than you will need to serve with the ice. Keep the others in an airtight container for another use.

MANDARIN ORANGE ICE

3 cups strained fresh mandarin orange juice

1/2 cup Simple Syrup (page 250)

Candied Citrus Zests (see recipe)

FORTUNE COOKIES

1 3/4 cups flour

1 1/4 cups superfine sugar

1 cup egg whites (about 6)

1/4 cup hot melted butter

1 teaspoon pure vanilla extract

1 1/2 tablespoons ground ginger

To prepare the orange ice: Combine the mandarin orange juice and simple syrup together in a mixing bowl. Place in an ice cream machine and freeze according to the manufacturer's instructions for preparing sorbet.

Prepare the citrus zests and set aside.

Prepare the fortune cookies in the meantime. Combine the flour and superfine sugar in the bowl of an electric mixer fitted with a paddle attachment. Add the egg whites and mix until smooth. Add the melted butter in a steady stream and mix until fully incorporated. Mix in the vanilla and ginger. Cover the bowl and place in the refrigerator for about 2 hours or overnight.

Create or choose your favorite ancient Oriental sayings or some provocative literary quotes. Type or handwrite them on small strips of paper that will fit into the fortune cookies, and set aside.

Preheat the oven to 325 degrees and warm a nonstick baking sheet in the oven for a few minutes. Place 2 dollops of the cookie batter (about 2/3 tablespoon each) on the warmed baking sheet and spread out thinly and evenly to a diameter of about 4 inches. It is important the batter is spread evenly or it will burn in spots. Place the baking sheet in the oven and bake for about 6 to 8 minutes, or until the cookies turn golden brown around the edges. Bake only 2 cookies at a time, as they harden very quickly.

Working with one cookie at a time, very quickly remove from the baking sheet and turn over so the shiny side is down. Place the fortune you have written across the center of the cookie. Fold 2 opposite edges in so that they overlap. Quickly grasp the two long ends and fold them backwards, away from the overlapped side. Pinch the edges together and hold them in place with a plastic-coated paper clip for a minute or two until the cookies harden.

Repeat for the remaining cookies and place on a wire rack to cool. Store the cooled cookies in an airtight container until ready to serve.

Arrange 2 scoops of the orange ice in a shallow soup plate or bowl and garnish with 1 teaspoon of the citrus zests and 2 or 3 of the fortune cookies. Serve immediately.

CANDIED ORANGE ZESTS

Zest of 2 oranges

Zest of 2 lemons

Zest of 2 limes

$^2/_3$ cup Simple Syrup (page 250)

$^1/_2$ tablespoon sugar, for dusting

Peel each fruit from top to bottom with a vegetable peeler, being careful to leave all of the bitter white pith behind (if necessary, simply scrape it off with a sharp knife). Place the peels in a metal strainer and blanch in boiling water for about 20 seconds. Immediately transfer to an ice bath for 20 seconds. Repeat blanching and shocking the peels in ice water, and drain.

In a saucepan, bring the simple syrup to a boil over medium heat. Drop the cooled zests into the syrup and allow them to boil for about 10 minutes, until the syrup thickens and forms large bubbles.

While this is cooking, lightly dust a baking sheet with the sugar. Remove the citrus zests from the syrup with tongs, and lay them out separately on the sugar-coated baking sheet. Let cool.

CHAPTER 12
MY TREASURE CHEST RECIPES

STOCKS AND BROTHS
Vegetable Stock
Light Chicken Stock
Dark Chicken Stock
Lamb Stock
Pork Stock
Sea Creature Stock

OILS AND VINEGARS
Annatto Oil
Chinese Chile Oil
Roasted Garlic Oil
Hot Chile Oil
Aromatic Dessert Oil

VEGETABLES
The Bean Kit
Roasted Garlic Power
Mushroom Muscle Power
Pickled Scotch Bonnet Chiles
Fire Power

RUBS AND SPICE BLENDS
My Curry Powder
The New World Spice Blend

MEATS
Norman's Chorizo

We were crawling slowly along, looking out for Virgin Gorda; the first of those numberless isles which Columbus, so goes the tale, discovered on St. Ursula's day, and named them after the saint and her eleven thousand mythical virgins. Unfortunately, English buccaneers have since given most of them less poetic names. The Dutchman's Cap, Broken Jerusalem, The Dead Man's Chest, Rum Island, and so forth, mark a time and race more prosaic.

—Charles Kingsley, *At Last*

In 1985, just days after I returned to live in Key West after a two-year absence, treasure salvor Mel Fisher culminated his decades-long search for gold with the discovery of the sunken Spanish galleon, *Nuestra Señora de Atocha,* just a few miles off the coast. The ship had been returning to Sevilla packed with booty when a storm swept up and doomed the *Atocha* and her passengers to a watery vault off the Keys. A staggering 400 million dollars' worth of gold, silver, and rare artifacts were pulled up by Mel and his colorful band, who were now suddenly rich.

Word swept the island, and then the major news stations all across the country. Until then, Mel, a former chicken farmer, had walked among us barely noticed. Another Key West story. "Today's the day" was his slogan; he said it *every* day. But that July day *was* the day, another example of all the difference in believing in, and acting on, your dreams.

Finding treasure is a fantasy everyone has at some point in their life. What I offer in this chapter are the treasured recipes I have discovered, pulled up, twisted into shape, and polished in my own way. They reflect the tastes of many traveling vessels and spirited vagabonds. These are the "coins of the realm" in my New World Cuisine.

These recipes are basics that will keep your New World pantry steered on the right course. All of them are used in the preceding recipes, and some recur several times. Many will prove useful regardless of the style of cuisine.

STOCKS AND BROTHS

Vegetable Stock

Yield: About 3 quarts.

There is a simple decision to make when starting this stock. If you want it to be darker in color as well as sweeter because of the caramelization process, allow the garlic, onions, leeks, carrots, celery, and fennel to cook for 10 to 15 minutes in the oil and butter first to bring out their color before adding the mushrooms and other ingredients. If you want a lighter stock, for example, for a cream soup or a sauce you want to keep light in color, briefly sauté the vegetables before adding the mushrooms and remaining ingredients.

 To intensify the stock, return it to a clean pan and reduce to an essence or the desired strength.

1/4 cup olive oil

2 tablespoons butter

2 heads garlic, cut in half crosswise

2 onions, roughly chopped

2 leeks, green and white parts, roughly chopped

2 large carrots, roughly chopped

6 large stalks celery, roughly chopped

1 bulb fennel, trimmed and roughly chopped

1 ounce porcini or mixed dried mushrooms, soaked in warm water

8 ounces domestic mushrooms, roughly chopped

2 tomatoes, cored and roughly chopped

6 sprigs thyme

12 sprigs Italian parsley

12 basil leaves

1 bay leaf, broken

1 tablespoon black peppercorns, toasted and crushed

1 teaspoon salt

About 3 1/2 quarts water

Heat the olive oil and butter in a large, heavy, nonreactive stockpot. Add the garlic, onions, leeks, carrots, celery, and fennel, and sauté over medium-high heat for up to 15 minutes (see note above).

Drain the rehydrated mushrooms and add to the pot together with the fresh mushrooms. Add the tomatoes, herbs, peppercorns, salt, and water. Bring to a boil, skim, and lower the heat to a simmer. Cook, uncovered, for 1 hour. Strain through a fine-mesh strainer and reserve until needed.

Light Chicken Stock

Yield: about 7 cups.

This is the most useful stock of all. It has flavor, but it won't overwhelm. Make it. Freeze it in various 1-, 2-, or 3-cup containers so you'll have it conveniently on hand. Done deal.

1 tablespoon virgin olive oil

3 tablespoons butter

3 large carrots, roughly chopped

1 large onion, roughly chopped

3 large stalks celery, roughly chopped

1 head garlic, cut in half crosswise

8 ounces mushrooms, roughly chopped

3 pounds chicken bones, wings, backs, or necks

6 sprigs thyme

6 sprigs Italian parsley

6 basil leaves

2 bay leaves

1 tablespoon black peppercorns

1 cup white wine

10 to 12 cups water, or enough to cover the chicken bones

Heat the olive oil and butter in a large nonreactive stockpot over medium heat. When the mixture begins to foam, add the carrots, onion, celery, garlic, and mushrooms, and stir together to coat. Sauté the vegetables, stirring occasionally, until shiny and glazed, about 10 minutes.

Add the chicken bones, herbs, and peppercorns. Stir in the white wine and water, and just bring to a boil. Turn the heat down to low, skim off any impurities, and simmer, uncovered, for about $2\frac{1}{2}$ hours. Remove from the heat and let the stock settle for about 30 minutes.

Strain the stock first through a colander, then through a fine-mesh strainer into a stainless steel bowl, leaving any solids behind. Chill the stock quickly over ice water until cold. Transfer to airtight containers and reserve in the refrigerator for 3 days or so; or freeze for up to 6 months.

Dark Chicken Stock

Yield: About 7 cups.

Sometimes sauces can be a little too heavy due to the darker intensity of pork or veal stock, which can mask dishes of important but less aggressive flavor nuances. When I'm looking for a bit more richness than regular chicken stock can provide I'll fire this one up.

 Many recipes for dark chicken stock call for roasting the chicken bones in the oven first. You can take this step by all means, but the caramelization of the vegetables in this recipe provides a rich flavor and color, and saves you the trouble of washing an extra pan.

1 tablespoon virgin olive oil

3 tablespoons butter

3 large carrots, roughly chopped

1 large onion, roughly chopped

3 large stalks celery, roughly chopped

1 head garlic, cut in half crosswise

8 ounces mushrooms, roughly chopped

3 pounds chicken bones, wings, backs, or necks

6 sprigs thyme

6 sprigs Italian parsley

6 basil leaves

2 bay leaves

1 tablespoon black peppercorns

1 cup white wine

10 to 12 cups water, or enough to cover the chicken bones

Heat the olive oil and butter in a large nonreactive stockpot over medium-high heat. When the mixture begins to foam, add the carrots, onion, celery, and garlic, and stir together to coat. Sauté the vegetables, stirring only occasionally, until caramelized and deeply browned, about 20 to 30 minutes.

Stir in the mushrooms and cook for 1 minute. Add the chicken bones, herbs, and peppercorns. Stir in the white wine and water, and just bring to a boil. Turn the heat down to low, skim off any impurities, and simmer, uncovered, for about 2½ hours.

Remove from the heat and let the stock settle for about 30 minutes. Strain the stock first through a colander, then through a fine-mesh strainer into a stainless steel bowl, leaving any solids behind. Chill the stock quickly over ice water until cold. Transfer to airtight containers and reserve in the refrigerator for 3 days or so; or freeze for up to 6 months.

Lamb Stock

Yield: About 6½ cups.

I use this recipe for the Rioja-Braised Lamb Shanks (page 156), but it can also serve simply as the stock for a lamb stew or a hearty soup.

6 to 7 pounds lamb neck bones

½ cup peanut oil

1 large onion, roughly chopped

1 leek, roughly chopped

3 large carrots, roughly chopped

4 large stalks celery, roughly chopped

2 heads garlic, cut in half crosswise

12 cups water

8 ounces button mushrooms, roughly chopped, or 4 dried wild mushrooms

2 tomatoes, cored and roughly chopped

2 bay leaves, broken

6 sprigs thyme

6 sprigs Italian parsley

6 sprigs rosemary

1 tablespoon crushed black peppercorns

Preheat the oven to 475 degrees. Place the lamb bones in a roasting pan and drizzle them with ¼ cup of the peanut oil. Don't crowd the bones or they won't brown properly; use 2 pans, if necessary. Roast in the oven for 30 to 40 minutes, until browned.

Meanwhile, place the onion, leek, carrots, celery, and garlic in a large bowl, and sprinkle with the remaining ¼ cup of oil. Set aside.

Remove the roasting pan from the oven, stir the bones around, and roast for 10 minutes longer. Add the reserved vegetable mixture to the pan and roast for another 45 minutes.

Remove the roasting pan from the oven and transfer the bones and vegetables to a large nonreactive stockpot (the narrower the better to avoid too much reduction); discard any excess fat in the roasting pan. Add 2 cups of water to the roasting pan and heat on the stovetop over medium-high heat. Remove any dark bits of meat and bone on the bottom of the roasting pan by scraping with a wooden spoon, and add these bits to the stockpot. Cover the contents of the stockpot with the remaining water (use more or less, as necessary).

Place the stockpot over medium heat and bring to a slow simmer, skimming as necessary to remove any impurities from the surface. Add the mushrooms, tomatoes, herbs, and peppercorns, and simmer slowly, uncovered, for 3 to 4 hours.

Remove from the heat and strain the stock first through a colander, then through a fine-mesh strainer into a stainless steel bowl, leaving any solids behind. Chill the stock quickly over ice water until cold. Transfer to airtight containers and reserve in the refrigerator for 3 days or so; or freeze for up to 6 months.

Pork Stock

Yield: 5 to 6 cups.

James Beard favored pork over any other meat. The prodigious pig has probably supplied the globe's children with more protein than any other source. The cost of pork is still reasonable and the flavors are incomparable.

 To make this a *smoked* pork hock stock, simply buy smoked pork hocks and use them instead of the unsmoked hocks called for in this recipe. Sometimes, I use half pork stock and half chicken stock for rice and bean dishes.

4 pounds meaty pork bones

4 pork hocks, or 2 pig's feet

¹/₄ cup peanut oil

¹/₃ cup olive oil

2 tablespoons butter

2 heads garlic, cut in half crosswise

2 ancho chiles, cut in half, seeds intact

2 onions, chopped

2 carrots, chopped

6 small stalks celery, chopped

2 leeks, chopped

8 ounces button mushrooms, quartered

2 tomatoes, cored and roughly chopped

1 tablespoon black peppercorns, toasted and crushed

10 to 12 cups water

Pinch of salt

6 sprigs Italian parsley

6 sage leaves

1 sprig rosemary

2 bay leaves, broken

Preheat the oven to 475 degrees. Place the pork bones and hocks or feet in a roasting pan, and drizzle them with the peanut oil. Toss to coat. Don't crowd the bones or they won't brown properly; use 2 pans, if necessary. Roast in the oven until just nicely browned, about 30 minutes.

Transfer to a bowl and pour off any excess fat. To remove any unburned bits of meat from the roasting pan, add 1 or 2 cups of water, place over medium-high heat, and scrape off with a wooden spoon. Reserve with the pork.

Heat the olive oil and butter together in a large, heavy, nonreactive saucepan or stockpot. Add the garlic, anchos, onions, carrots, celery, and leeks; stir together and sauté over medium-high heat until the vegetables are well glazed and begin to caramelize, about 15 to 20 minutes. Add the mushrooms, tomatoes, peppercorns, reserved pork, water, and salt. Bring to a boil; skim as necessary but don't stir. Add the herbs, lower the heat to a low simmer, and cook, uncovered, for about 3 hours.

Strain the stock first through a colander, then through a fine-mesh strainer into a stainless steel bowl, leaving any solids behind. Chill the stock quickly over ice water until cold. Transfer to airtight containers and reserve in the refrigerator for 3 days or so; or freeze for up to 6 months.

Sea Creature Stock

Yield: 8 cups.

This stock can be used as an intense glaze to strengthen seafood sauces or soups. Take 2 cups of the stock, reduce to $1/2$ cup or less, and add to the sauce or soup.

 This is a great stock to use when you need the sweetness of the crustacean flavor. I use it in my Criolla Tomato Mama recipe (page 52).

$1/4$ cup olive oil

2 tablespoons butter

1 large white onion, roughly chopped

3 stalks celery, roughly chopped

1 large carrot, roughly chopped

1 leek, white and light green parts only, roughly chopped

1 small bulb fennel, trimmed and roughly chopped

1 head garlic, cut in half crosswise

2 tomatoes, roughly chopped

6 basil leaves

6 sprigs Italian parsley

6 sprigs thyme

2 bay leaves, broken

1 tablespoon black peppercorns, crushed

2 pounds shellfish shells (shrimp, lobster, and/or crab)

2 cups Chardonnay wine

10 cups cold water

Heat the olive oil and butter over medium heat in a large nonreactive stockpot. When the butter begins to foam, add the onion, celery, carrot, leek, fennel, and garlic. Stir the vegetables together to coat in the butter and sauté until translucent, about 15 to 20 minutes.

Add the tomatoes, herbs, peppercorns, and shells, and cook for 2 minutes. Add the wine and water and increase the heat. When the liquid begins to boil, skim off the impurities that rise to the surface. Lower the heat to a simmer and cook for about 1 hour.

Turn off the heat and let the stock settle for 20 minutes. Strain the stock first through a colander or large-mesh strainer, then through a fine-mesh strainer with a cheesecloth lining into a stainless steel bowl, discarding any solids left behind. Chill the stock quickly over ice water until cold. Transfer to airtight containers and reserve in the refrigerator for 3 days or so; or freeze for up to 6 months.

OILS AND VINEGARS

Flavored oils and vinegars are an excellent way of packing extra punch to recipes. They are becoming increasingly popular substitutes for butter, cream, and other high-calorie ingredients.

When buying oils to prepare some of the recipes that follow, bear in mind some of these useful tips:

· Buy oils in stores with high turnover. Oils are at their best at the time they are pressed, and inevitably decline in quality over time. The fresher they are at the time of purchase, the better.

· Keep oils stored in a dry, dark place.

· Keep in well-sealed, airtight bottles or containers.

· Try to use them up quickly; the oils made with these recipes will keep at least a month before the flavors begin to fade.

Annatto Oil

Yield: About 1 (generous) cup.

I discovered annatto seeds while roaming in a little grocery store in Key West one day, a long time ago. In those days, there wasn't much I was able to find out about such ingredients, and there was no one I knew who could tell me about them. Fortunately, reading material about this small, beautiful tropical tree has since become available.

 Beware! Few things stain as well as annatto. Rub annatto paste on chicken, game birds, or meat before grilling for its delicate flavor as well as color. Pre-Columbian Indians used annatto seeds (also called "achiote") to paint their bodies. The oil we make here would make a good body paint, I'm sure, but I'm suggesting only that you cook with it. After that, you're on your own.

1 cup olive or canola oil

¹/₄ cup annatto seeds

Place a small, heavy saucepan over medium heat. Add the annatto seeds. When they begin to get warm and release puffs of smoke, add the oil. Bring the oil almost to a simmer and then turn off the heat; let stand for at least 30 minutes before straining into a glass bottle or container. Reserve.

Chinese Chile Oil

Yield: About 1¹/₂ cups.

This makes a great alternative to unflavored oil whenever you want to have the more exotic and complex flavors of the Orient in one of your dishes. Try it instead of olive oil with some hot or cold steamed asparagus and a spritz of soy sauce.

2¹/₂ tablespoons Sichuan peppercorns

2 tablespoons black peppercorns

1 cup olive oil

¹/₂ cup peanut oil

2 tablespoons dark roasted sesame oil

¹/₄ cup dried hot red chiles, broken up, with seeds

³/₄ teaspoon cayenne

2 star anise

In a dry saucepan or skillet over medium heat, toast the Sichuan and black peppercorns for 1 minute, or until fragrant. Add the oils, dried chiles, cayenne, and anise, and bring to a simmer. Remove from the heat, cover, and let stand for 6 hours. Strain the oil into a bottle or container and reserve.

Roasted Garlic Oil

Yield: About 1 1/2 cups.

This is an invaluable byproduct of the Roasted Garlic Power, so you can kill two birds with one stone. Use it whenever you want the flavor of olive oil scented with a garlicky perfume. Enjoy!

 The yield may depend on the size of the pan used for the Roasted Garlic Power recipe.

1 recipe Roasted Garlic Power (page 281)

Make the garlic power. Strain off the oil into a bottle or container, using a fine-mesh strainer. Reserve in a cool, dark place.

Hot Chile Oil

Yield: About 2 cups.

I use this oil often! It doubles as a cooking oil and as a quick and tasty drizzle for pizzas, a bowl of steamed clams, or warm rolls. Chiles—offered here in the form of crushed red pepper—are good for you, so be good to yourself.

 For a more potent flavor and a pretty darn sexy appearance, leave the crushed red pepper in the oil instead of straining it out after they have infused. If you use a whole bottle of olive oil for this recipe, you can strain the oil back into the container.

2 cups olive oil

3 tablespoons crushed red pepper

In a heavy saucepan over medium heat, bring the oil and crushed red pepper to a simmer. Simmer for 3 minutes and then remove from the heat. Allow the mixture to infuse for at least 30 minutes.

Using a fine-mesh strainer and funnel, strain the oil into a bottle or glass container. Label and date the bottle, and reserve until needed.

Aromatic Dessert Oil

Yield: About (a generous) ³/₄ cup.

Infused and flavored oils have become quite the rage. This recipe proves that we don't have to confine our thinking to savory dishes.

 This oil will keep its flavor for at least a month in an airtight container. I use it in the Stir-fry of Tropical Fruits (page 253).

³/₄ teaspoon cloves

³/₄ teaspoon coriander seeds

1 vanilla bean, split in half lengthwise

1 cup grapeseed oil

2 cinnamon sticks

1 orange, thinly sliced (peel left on)

Heat the cloves and coriander in a saucepan, and toast over medium heat until fragrant. Scrape the seeds out of the vanilla bean and add the seeds and bean to the pan. Add the oil and cinnamon sticks, and heat until almost boiling. Turn off the heat. Place the orange slices in a nonreactive bowl and pour the oil over. Cover and let infuse overnight. Strain before using.

VEGETABLES

The Bean Kit

Yield: About 2$\frac{1}{2}$ cups (at the "ready stage").

The first thing you may ask yourself about this recipe is "Why are there no beans in something called The Bean Kit?" Well, back in the old days when I was first a cook, it was my job to "prep" food and do the more simple tasks *over* and *over* and *over* again. It gives you a certain perspective, this repetition. In those "prep cook" days in Key West, I often made the classic French "mirepoix" vegetable preparation for soups, sauces, and stocks. Nearly as often, I made another "kit" of vegetables for black bean soup, which the restaurant sold by the tubful. These vegetables for the soup base were more potent, as my running eyes and stinging fingers attested. One day I asked my kitchen colleague Black Betty about this: "Why can't we just use the same vegetables we do for the mirepoix?" Betty screwed up her face in a menacing scowl, leaned way into me, and hissed, "Dose beans'd kick ta *hell* out o' dose damn wimpy white-boy begetables you so fond of. Yah gotta have some *shtrong* red onions, *hot-ass-hell* peppers, a lotta garlic an' stuff to make them beans black and gumptious, like me, baby."

Years later, I realized that Betty's "Bean Kit" was a type of *sofregit*—one of the fundamental flavors of Caribbean and Spanish cooking much like the French *mirepoix* or Italian *battuto*. But it's always been the "Bean Kit" to me; here, then, is the recipe for gumptious beans and soups.

 In other recipes that refer back to this one as a building block, I call for bringing the bean kit "to the ready stage." Just make up this recipe, and you're all set. Adding the garlic and jalapeños together at the beginning, once the cooking fat is ready, sets the stage for the best way to capture all the flavors.

2 ounces smoked bacon, rind removed if necessary, and finely diced (about $\frac{1}{2}$ cup)

2 tablespoons olive oil

2 tablespoons butter

5 cloves garlic, minced

3 jalapeño chiles, seeded and minced

1 red bell pepper, diced small

1 poblano chile, diced small

1 red onion, diced small

2 large stalks celery, cleaned and diced small

1 large carrot, peeled and diced small

1 small bulb fennel, trimmed and diced small

1 tablespoon toasted and ground cumin

1 tablespoon toasted and ground black peppercorns

2 bay leaves, broken up

Heat a saucepan over medium heat; add the bacon and the olive oil. Cook the bacon until it's almost cooked through. Then add the butter. When the butter begins to foam, add the garlic and jalapeños, and stir in, allowing them to flavor the oil mixture for about 1 minute.

Turn up the heat to medium-high and add the bell pepper, poblano, onion, celery, carrot, and fennel; stir to coat with the oil. Cook for about 20 minutes, stirring occasionally, until the vegetables are caramelized.

Stir in the cumin, black pepper, and bay leaves. The bean kit is now at the "ready stage," for use in other recipes.

Roasted Garlic Power

Yield: About ⅔ cup.

I hope the day is not far off when we can drop by the grocery store and pick up an invaluable product like this. It wasn't so long ago that the culinary world was vastly improved by the availability of prepeeled garlic in our stores. As long as the product is fresh, with no harmful additives or chemicals, I'm all for the convenience it offers. Until this recipe hits the market, then, here is a wonderfully addictive and adaptable recipe.

 If the garlic seems a little undercooked after the allotted cooking time, let it sit in the oil while cooling. On the other hand, if it is cooked completely, remove the garlic from the oil to cool separately. For best yield, squeeze the garlic out of the husks as soon as they are cool enough to handle. Place the husks back into the roasted garlic oil to get every last bit of flavor out of them. This recipe will keep for several weeks stored in an airtight container in the refrigerator.

4 large heads garlic

Olive oil, to cover the garlic (about 2 cups)

2 sprigs fresh thyme

1 sprig fresh rosemary

1 bay leaf

12 black peppercorns, slightly crushed

Preheat the oven to 300 degrees. Cut off the tips of the garlic heads and peel off some of the papery outer skin. Arrange the garlic heads snugly, side by side, in a casserole dish or roasting pan. Pour enough olive oil over them to cover them completely. Scatter the herbs and peppercorns over the garlic, and submerge in the oil. Cover the dish with aluminum foil and bake in the preheated oven for 1 to 1¹/₄ hours.

Remove the pan from the oven and allow to cool. Squeeze the garlic out of the husks and into a bowl. If you want chopped roasted garlic for another recipe, chop the firmer cloves and use. Otherwise, mash the garlic with the back of a fork, place into a nonreactive airtight container, and reserve for another use.

Strain the garlic-infused olive oil through a fine-mesh strainer into a clean bottle or container and store this Roasted Garlic Oil (see page 277) until needed.

Mushroom Muscle Power

Yield: About 1³/₄ cups.

Mushrooms rot. Now that we have come to grips with *that* fact of nature, I think we can go on to say that you can also do something about it! Because mushrooms have a lot of watery weight, cooking them offers us a chance to concentrate that water into a much deeper flavor. So if it seems your investment in mushrooms is going to go to waste, make this recipe out of them instead.

 This recipe can be used as an addition to the Mer Noir sauce (page 136). It can also be added to the pan juices of roast chicken, served with grilled salmon or grilled steaks, or used as an elegant pizza topping. It'll also add a woodsy depth of flavors to a side dish of sautéed julienned green beans, almonds, and shallots. Substitute whatever mushrooms you have in the refrigerator for this recipe.

¹/₄ cup mixed dried wild mushrooms	*1 teaspoon rosemary sprigs, finely chopped*
6 tablespoons butter	*1 teaspoon sage leaves, finely chopped*
2 tablespoons olive oil	*1 teaspoon thyme leaves, finely chopped*
3 shallots, thinly sliced	*Salt to taste*
4 large garlic cloves, thinly sliced	*1 teaspoon black pepper*
2 generous cups sliced, mixed fresh mushrooms	

Put the dried mushrooms in a bowl and just cover with water. Let them soak for 1 hour. Add the butter to a saucepan over medium-high heat and add the olive oil. When the mixture begins to foam, add the shallots and garlic, and cook for about 2 minutes, until cooked through.

Add the fresh mushrooms and cook for 2 minutes, stirring. Drain the liquid from the re-hydrated dried mushrooms and add the liquid to the pan. Finely chop the rehydrated mushrooms and add together with the herbs, salt, and pepper. Reduce the heat to medium-low and cook until just a little of the mushroom liquid remains, about 7 to 9 minutes.

Transfer the mixture to a bowl and cover with plastic wrap to seal in the wonderful woodsy aroma of the mushrooms. Let cool and store in the refrigerator until needed.

Pickled Scotch Bonnet Chiles

Yield: About 1 quart.

This condiment adds a hot, piquant note to a variety of dishes. It can be used as a substitute for unpickled, fresh Scotch bonnets when you think it's the right thing to do. I also like to make a tartare sauce with them for a truly "flying fish" sandwich.

 Get out your rubber gloves before handling the chiles, pardners. And never touch your face or eyes while working with them.

8 ounces whole Scotch bonnet chiles, stems and seeds intact

6 cloves garlic, thinly sliced

1 tablespoon mustard seeds

1 tablespoon dill seeds

6 small bay leaves

1 cup apple cider vinegar

1 cup champagne vinegar

1 cup water

Make a small, thin slit along the side of each chile to aid the pickling process. Place the chiles and garlic in a bowl, and set aside.

Place the remaining ingredients in a nonreactive saucepan and bring to a boil over medium heat. Pour the boiling mixture over the chiles and garlic, and weigh them down with a plate so they are completely submerged. Let cool.

Transfer the chiles and the liquid to an airtight jar or container, and keep refrigerated for up to a month.

Fire Power

Yield: $^1/_2$ to $^3/_4$ cup.

Canned chipotle chiles en adobo (smoked jalapeños in a vinegary stew), available at Mexican and Southwestern stores, are familiar to many home cooks. One day, when scouring stores in Miami and failing to find them, I figured out a way of creating a very similar flavor. This experience brought two truths to mind: First, not everyone has the resources of a professional restaurant; and second, necessity is the mother of invention.

 I like to have fire power on hand in the refrigerator or freezer whenever I want to add some complex heat to a dish, and when simply sprinkling on some pepper or cayenne won't do. Add it to barbecue sauces, cream sauces, or use it as a dipping condiment.

4 teaspoons Dried Chiles Mezcla (page 143)

$^1/_4$ cup Spanish sherry vinegar

4 poblano chiles, roasted, peeled, and seeded

In a heavy saucepan, reduce the chiles mezcla and vinegar over low heat until almost no liquid remains. Transfer the mixture to a blender and add the poblanos. Purée together, stopping the blender to scrape down the sides 2 or 3 times, as necessary. Transfer to an airtight container and keep refrigerated until needed.

RUBS AND SPICE BLENDS

My Curry Powder

Yield: About (a generous) $^1/_2$ cup.

There's a world of difference between freshly ground, homemade curry powder and the store-bought bottled stuff. Curry is traditionally made up of a mixture of 20 to 25 spices and seeds, including all of those used here. Others sometimes used are cloves, fennel seeds, mace, and tamarind, all of which are optional here. The word *curry* is derived from the South Indian *kari,* which means "sauce."

The island term for curry dishes is *colombo,* named for the Sri Lankan capital, probably because many Hindus settled in Martinique and brought curries with them that still figure in many dishes.

 You can buy the curry leaves and cardamom in Indian stores. If the cardamom seeds are still in their pods, remove the seeds and discard the pods.

$^1/_4$ teaspoon mustard seeds

$^1/_4$ teaspoon cardamom

$^1/_4$ teaspoon black peppercorns

2 tablespoons cumin seeds

2 tablespoons coriander seeds

20 to 25 fresh curry leaves, or dried, optional

1-inch cinnamon stick

2$^1/_2$ tablespoons hot chile molido powder, or pure red chile powder

$^1/_4$ teaspoon dried ground ginger

2 tablespoons turmeric

1 tablespoon fenugreek

Put the mustard seeds, cardamom, peppercorns, and cumin and coriander seeds in a dry skillet, and toast over medium heat until fragrant and slightly smoking, about 1 to 2 minutes. Transfer the toasted spices to a spice grinder.

Toast the curry leaves separately in the same skillet over medium heat until fragrant, about 30 seconds. Add to the spice grinder together with the cinnamon stick. Grind all the spices together and transfer to a bowl. Add the chile powder, ginger, turmeric, and fenugreek, and mix thoroughly. Store in an airtight container until needed.

The New World Spice Blend

Yield: About ¼ cup.

The axis of my New World and its cuisine usually spins around the pairing of Latin American and Asian ingredients. So naturally, the spice blend I love to use most features the spices that are also the favorites of cooks in both of these cuisines. I use this blend for my New World Chips (page 15), but the mix is very versatile, and you can enjoy it with chicken, veal chops, shrimp, and scallops.

 The aroma from toasting your own spices is wonderful, but bear in mind the process can lead to filling up your kitchen with their powerful (and sometimes overwhelming) fragrance—so ventilate the room properly. Mind you, I've found that toasting spices is a good way of removing overly fastidious food writers and reporters from your kitchen!

10 small red dried chiles

2 teaspoons cumin seeds

1 teaspoon coriander seeds

1 teaspoon black peppercorns

½ teaspoon mustard seeds

3-inch cinnamon stick, broken into small pieces

1 teaspoon sugar

1 teaspoon dried ground ginger

1 teaspoon dried lemongrass flakes

½ teaspoon cayenne

½ teaspoon mace, or nutmeg

½ teaspoon achiote powder, optional

½ teaspoon salt

Put the chiles, cumin, coriander, peppercorns, mustard seeds, and cinnamon stick in a dry skillet, and toast over medium heat until fragrant and slightly smoking, about 2 to 3 minutes.

Transfer the toasted spices to a spice grinder. Add the sugar, ginger, lemongrass, cayenne, mace, achiote, and salt, and pulverize to a powder. Sieve the mixture through a medium-fine strainer and store in an airtight container, if not using immediately.

MEATS

Norman's Chorizo

Yield: 3 pounds (about 12 sausages, 4 ounces each).

This is my version of chorizo, the traditional, highly seasoned sausage used widely in both Mexico and Spain. (In Mexico, and in this recipe, the sausage is used in its fresh, soft form; in Spain, it's a hard, preserved sausage.) There are many recipes for chorizo that vary little, but the big difference here is the addition of my moist Mexican adobo paste, which gives the sausage a complexity of flavor and a richer, darker color.

This recipe calls for a meat grinder to process the meat and fat. If you don't have one, ask your butcher to do it for you. Likewise, if you don't have a sausage stuffer, you can make patties instead of sausages. You can gussy up the chorizo in all kinds of ways if you like. For example, add a cup of currants macerated in Spanish brandy; or rehydrated, chopped ancho chiles; dried tropical fruits; pine nuts; or more chiles if you like your chorizo really spicy. Have fun . . . it's your kitchen!

 This recipe calls for preparation to begin 4 days in advance of using the sausages. The 3-day period of refrigeration firms up the sausages and improves the texture as well as flavor. Put the meat, fat, and even the grinding blade and knife into the freezer for 30 minutes before grinding. This helps the meat cut cleanly rather than getting squished during the grind, which contributes to a better texture.

2 pounds boneless pork butt (or 4 pounds, bone-in)

8 ounces pork fat back

1/2 cup Mexican Adobo Paste (page 155)

1/4 cup Spanish sherry vinegar

3 jalapeño chiles, seeded and minced

3 serrano chiles or Scotch bonnets, seeded and minced

1 teaspoon coarsely cracked black pepper

1/2 teaspoon cayenne

1/2 teaspoon crushed red pepper

1/2 teaspoon chile molido, or pure red chile powder

1 tablespoon toasted cumin seeds

1/2 teaspoon ground cumin

2 teaspoons salt

1/4 cup chopped cilantro leaves

Grind the pork meat and fat with a meat grinder, using a 1/4-inch plate, into a large mixing bowl. Mix together all the remaining ingredients, add to the bowl, and combine thoroughly with your hands. Cover and refrigerate overnight.

Remove the mixture from the refrigerator and form into patties or stuff into sausage casings. Return to the refrigerator for at least 3 days, resting directly on the wire racks with a pan or plate directly underneath. Cook according to individual recipe needs.

A DAY OFF IN THE LIFE

How beautiful it is to do nothing and then to rest afterward.

—Spanish proverb

ACKNOWLEDGMENTS

Our entire staff at Norman's

My counsel and friend, Russell Alba

Maida Heatter, my guardian angel

The James Beard Foundation

The American Institute of Wine and Food

The International Association of Culinary Professionals

John Harrisson, my co-conspirator and tireless tracker on our voyage

Tim Turner

Georgiana Goodwin

Jason Epstein, my editor at Random House and poetry mentor

Marsha Sayet, partner, friend, and true believer

My brothers in "The Triangle": Charlie Trotter and Emeril Lagasse

Steven Greystone

Jimmy Breen, in memoriam

RECOMMENDED READING LIST

I read all kinds of cookbooks that teach me and help me celebrate my love of cooking in the styles of many different cuisines. The following books, however, are a short list of some of my personal favorites that have been touchstones to my vision of this New World Cuisine. In my first book, *Norman Van Aken's Feast of Sunlight,* I listed more French and Italian books that influenced me tremendously, especially early in my career. The reverberations of those early teachers are not diminished, nor are they forgotten. But as I determined to hone the cooking style that most perfectly suits me now, I have made the following selection of works.

Colman Andrews, *Catalan Cuisine* (New York: Atheneum, 1988).

Jean Andrews, *Red Hot Peppers* (New York: Macmillan, 1993).

Pepita Arias, *Recipes from a Spanish Village* (New York: Simon & Schuster, 1990).

Rick and Deann Bayless, *Authentic Mexican* (New York: Morrow, 1987).

Penelope Casas, *The Foods and Wines of Spain* (New York: Knopf, 1984).

Dave DeWitt and Nancy Gerlach, *The Whole Chile Pepper* (Boston: Little, Brown, 1990).

Linnette Green, *A Taste of Cuba* (New York: Dutton, 1991).

Jessica B. Harris, *Sky Juice and Flying Fish* (New York: Simon & Schuster, 1991).

Barbara Karoff, *South American Cooking* (Berkeley: Aris Books, 1989).

Christine Mackie, *Food and Life in the Caribbean* (New York: New Amsterdam Books, 1991).

Maite Manjon, *The Gastronomy of Spain and Portugal* (New York: Prentice Hall, 1990).

Copeland Marks, *False Tongues and Sunday Bread* (New York: Primus, 1985).

Mark Miller, *The Great Chile Book* (Berkeley: Ten Speed Press, 1991).

Jill Norman, *The Complete Book of Spices* (London: Viking Studio Books, 1990).

Elizabeth Lambert Ortiz, *The Book of Latin American Cooking* (New York: Knopf, 1979).

———, *The Complete Book of Caribbean Cooking* (New York: Ballantine, 1973).

Mary Urrutia Randelman, *Memories of a Cuban Kitchen* (New York: Macmillan, 1992).

Jean-Francois Revel, *Culture and Cuisine* (New York: Doubleday, 1982).

Elizabeth Rozin, *Blue Corn and Chocolate* (New York: Knopf, 1992).

Elizabeth Schneider, *Uncommon Fruits and Vegetables* (New York: Perennial Books, 1986).

Raymond Sokolov, *Why We Eat What We Eat* (New York: Summit Books, 1991).

Reay Tannahill, *Food in History* (New York: Crown, 1988).

Herman Viola and Carolyn Margolis, *Seeds of Change* (Washington D.C.: Smithsonian Institution Press, 1991).

Jean Voltz and Caroline Stuart, *The Florida Cookbook* (New York: Knopf, 1993)

INDEX

ABOUT THE AUTHORS

NORMAN VAN AKEN was born and raised in rural Diamond Lake, Illinois. After a few years of college, he rambled around the country working at odd jobs—from short order cook to carny. He moved to Hawaii in 1970 and to Key West in 1973 where he developed a passion for vibrant Asian and Caribbean flavors. A self-taught culinary genius, he now lectures internationally on New World Cuisine.

Van Aken was the first chef to use the term "fusion cooking" in describing the principles of New World Cuisine. After close to two decades in Key West, Van Aken moved to Miami and opened Norman's, a highly acclaimed, award-winning restaurant in the historic section of Coral Gables.

JOHN HARRISSON was raised and educated in England and became a food writer by way of an earlier career as an academic economist. He has co-authored cookbooks with many of America's leading chefs, including Mark Miller (*Coyote Cafe*), Roy Yamaguchi (*Feasts from Hawaii*), Stephan Pyles, and John Sedlar. The cookbooks to which he has contributed have sold over three quarters of a million copies.

ABOUT THE PHOTOGRAPHER

TIM TURNER was nominated for a James Beard Award for Best Food Photography for *The Inn at Little Washington Cookbook*. His other books include *Charlie Trotter's, Charlie Trotter's Vegetables,* and *Charlie Trotter's Seafood*, and his photographs have appeared in *Food & Wine, Bon Appétit,* and *Ladies' Home Journal,* among other publications, as well as in numerous advertisements.

ABOUT THE TYPE

This book was set in Optima—a sans serif typeface with a neoclassical flavor. It was designed by Hermann Zapf in 1952–55. It was issued by both Stempel and Linotype in 1958.